Gender and Disorder in Early Modern Seville

FIGURE 1.   *Women at the Window*, by Bartolomé Murillo (National Gallery of Art, Washington; Widener Collection).

Gender and Disorder
in Early Modern Seville

Mary Elizabeth Perry

PRINCETON UNIVERSITY PRESS

PRINCETON, NEW JERSEY

Copyright © 1990 by Princeton University Press
Published by Princeton University Press, 41 William Street,
Princeton, New Jersey 08540
In the United Kingdom: Princeton University Press,
Chichester, West Sussex

Library of Congress Cataloging-in-Publication Data

Perry, Mary Elizabeth, 1937–
Gender and disorder in early modern Seville /
Mary Elizabeth Perry.
p.   cm.
Includes bibliographical references.
1. Women—Spain—Seville—Social conditions.
2. Sex role—Spain—Seville—History.
3. Women—Spain—Seville—History.
4. Marginality, Social—Spain—Seville—History.
5. Seville (Spain)—Social conditions. I. Title.
HQ1695.S48P47   1990   90-32784

ISBN 0-691-03143-6 (alk. paper)
ISBN 0-691-00854-X (alk. paper)

Publication of this book has been aided by the Whitney Darrow
Fund of Princeton University Press

This book has been composed in Linotron Galliard

Princeton University Press books are printed on acid-free paper,
and meet the guidelines for permanence and durability of the
Committee on Production Guidelines for Book Longevity of the
Council on Library Resources

Printed in the United States of America

1   3   5   7   9   10   8   6   4   2

3   5   7   9   10   8   6   4   2

(Pbk.)

For Antonio Domínguez Ortiz

———————————

CONTENTS

ILLUSTRATIONS

TABLES

ACKNOWLEDGMENTS

I AM GRATEFUL for the funding that has made possible many research trips to Spain: a Fulbright-Hays Fellowship, research grants from the Del Amo Foundation, and a travel grant from the American Council of Learned Societies.

Special thanks to those individuals who read earlier versions of this book and gave me helpful comments: Olwen Hufton, Richard Kagan, Miriam Lee Kaprow, and Karen Offen. Their suggestions helped me to improve the book, but I did not always agree with them and must be held responsible for the final version. Joanna Hitchcock and Ralph Perry provided the wise counsel that enabled me to work with these suggestions.

Countless people have assisted me in the archives and libraries of Spain. I want to acknowledge the courtesy and kindness of staff members of the Archivo Histórico Nacional, Biblioteca Nacional, Archivo Municipal de Sevilla, Archivo General de las Indias, Archivo de Protocolos de Sevilla, Archivo de la Diputación de la Provincia de Sevilla, and the Biblioteca Capitular. In particular, I wish to thank these individuals: doña Eulalia de la Cruz Bugallal, doña Hermine Meós González, don Francisco Alvarez Leisdedos, don José Jaén Santiago, and the Count of Peñaflor de Argamasilla.

Finally, I want to thank Antonio Domínguez Ortiz for the inspiration that has prompted me to ask more questions and seek more answers. Although I was never able to study with him, I know from reading his many publications that his work stands as a shining example, and I respectfully dedicate this book to him.

ABBREVIATIONS

ADPS	Archivo de la Diputación de la Provincia de Sevilla
AGI	Archivo General de las Indias
AHN	Archivo Histórico Nacional
AMS	Archivo Municipal de Sevilla
APS	Archivo de Protocolos de Sevilla
BC	Biblioteca Capitular de Sevilla
BM	British Museum
BN	Biblioteca Nacional
HSC	Hospital de la Santa Caridad de Sevilla

Gender and Disorder in Early Modern Seville

NEITHER BROKEN SWORD NOR
WANDERING WOMAN

SEVILLE entered the sixteenth century as a city of contrasts where sharpening conflicts and astonishing excesses clearly revealed in magnified detail the significance of gender for social order. Spanning the Guadalquivir River in southwestern Spain, this inland seaport harbored both saints and sinners, highly visible in unusual numbers and strange intensity. A huge Gothic cathedral, the third largest in all Christendom, dominated the center of the city. Above its flying buttresses soared the Giralda, the bell tower that had once been a minaret when Muslims ruled the land, from which a *muezzin* had called the faithful to prayer and astronomers gazed at the heavens. Now, crowned with a Renaissance tower and a female figure of Faith, it symbolized Christian Seville, seat of an archbishop and site of a permanent tribunal of the Inquisition. Near the cathedral, a Franciscan monastery stood sentinel over a large plaza where workers often erected the scaffolding and gallows for public executions. Closer to the river huddled ramshackle houses, their rents deeded to religious foundations and their use regulated as the city brothel.

In 1480 Ferdinand and Isabel had sent two Dominicans to Seville to establish the first tribunal of the Spanish Inquisition. Here, where so many *conversos*, or Christianized Jews, had thrived, inquisitors found evidence of a network of conversos whom they accused of secretly practicing Jewish rites. According to legend, the group was betrayed by Susana, the daughter of a wealthy rabbi in Seville.[1] In love with a Christian named Guzmán, she let him know that a group of conversos was to meet in her house with her father to discuss resistance to the Inquisition. The Holy Office moved quickly and sentenced her father and six other conversos to be "relaxed," or given over to secular authorities to be burned at the stake as apostates. Susana, it was said, entered a convent in remorse for her betrayal and then left it to end her life in poverty and shame.

The long coexistence of Christians, Jews, and Muslims that had been mostly peaceful in Seville now crumbled, assaulted again in 1492, when

---

[1] Amantina Cobos de Villalobos, *Mujeres célebres sevillanas* (Seville: F. Díaz, 1917), pp. 106–12; Henry Kamen, *Inquisition and Society in Spain* (Bloomington: Indiana University Press, 1985), pp. 31–32. Please note that names and titles throughout this book will appear as they were spelled and accented in historical sources.

Ferdinand and Isabel decreed the expulsion of all Jews from their kingdoms, and ten years later when they ordered the forcible conversion of all Muslims. Neighbor denounced neighbor in this climate of growing suspicion, and divisions widened between Old Christians and those whose family members had once converted to Christianity from Judaism or Islam. As inquisitors called on the faithful to identify anyone suspected of heresy or apostasy, even the strongest family bonds eroded.

Seville played a major role in the discovery of the New World in this same period, for it was this port that Isabel ordered to outfit the small ships that Christopher Columbus would use to seek a western route to the Indies.[2] After the royal government decreed in 1503 that all ships sailing between Europe and the lands claimed for Spain in the New World should pass through the port of Seville, this city grew rapidly from a provincial market center into the commercial capital of the Spanish Habsburg empire. The Lonja, a beautiful Renaissance building, was erected near the cathedral as site for the Casa de Contratación, the royal agency to regulate trade and colonization of the New World. At the same time, a new customs house began operations closer to the port. Stevedores, outfitters, sailors, and inspectors thronged the spaces along the riverfront. Protected from English and Dutch marauders, this inland seaport launched hundreds of ships and thousands of human lives. Through it passed earnest missionaries and venturesome soldiers of fortune. An official bureaucracy of clerics and laymen mushroomed, and so did a large population of transients.

By 1530, Seville had a population of some sixty thousand that included 6,634 taxable residents (*vecinos pecheros*) and 2,229 widows.[3] Census figures for this period did not include nobles and secular or religious clergy, who were exempt from paying most taxes. Nor did they account for the servants, slaves, illegitimate children, clients, and other "protected" people who might live within a taxable household. A 1565 census reported that the number of taxable citizens had grown to 21,803 and added that Seville now had 66,244 *personas de confesión*, or baptized people of fifteen years or older, and 12,967 minors, as well as 6,327 slaves.

Clearly, Seville's thriving commerce attracted growing numbers of im-

[2] Diego Ortiz de Zuñiga, *Anales eclesiásticos y seculares de la muy noble y muy leal ciudad de Sevilla* (1677), 5 vols. (Madrid: Imprenta Real, 1796), 3: 163.

[3] For this and subsequent information on population, see Antonio Domínguez Ortiz, *Orto y ocaso de Sevilla: Estudio sobre la prosperidad y decadencia de la ciudad durante los siglos XVI y XVII* (Seville: Diputación Provincial de Sevilla, 1946), pp. 42–45. Also, see idem, *The Golden Age of Spain 1516–1659*, trans. James Casey (London: Weidenfeld and Nicholson, 1971), p. 134, esp.; and Tomás González, ed., *Censo de población de las provincias y partidos de la corona de Castilla en el siglo XVI, con varios apéndices para completar la del resto de la peninsula en el mismo siglo, y formar juicio comparativo con la del anterior y siguiente, según resulta de los libros y registros que se custodian en el Real Archivo de Simancas* (Madrid: Imprenta Real, 1829), pp. 83–84.

migrants who hoped to find better opportunities here than in the increasingly depressed countryside, but some of the population increase resulted from growing numbers of births. Parish records for San Vicente, for example, show that births nearly doubled between 1530 and 1570. In the parish of Sagrario, births increased from 187 in 1534, to 540 in 1562, and 685 in 1594. Seville had become the fourth largest city in Europe by the end of the sixteenth century, with a population of more than 100,000, not counting the indeterminate number of vagrants and transients. As available living space filled in the center of the city, new buildings appeared along and beneath the city walls. Large old structures that had housed proud families in former times crumbled into collective housing for the poor, and areas to the south and east of the city walls that had once harbored criminals and vagrants grew into the new parishes of San Roque and San Bernardo.

Hustling women cluttered this landscape of piety and profanity. Along the waterfront and beneath the Torre de Oro, the famous tower familiar to so many sailors in this period, prostitutes and procuresses, potion makers and fortune-tellers solicited business from the mariners and merchants who moved in and out of the city. Some also worked as street hawkers, calling out prices and names of produce, fish, tripe, and dairy products. Their voices contributed to the cacophony of the city, and their physical presence could not be ignored in the crowded streets and the jostling throngs.

Less visible, but even more troubling to churchmen, women who had dedicated their lives to God described ecstatic visions and used strange powers to heal and prophesy. Women accused of heretical teachings and false miracles bobbed in and out of view, imprisoned in buildings of the Inquisition and later released to appear in an *auto de fe*, the ceremony of penitence and affirmation of faith for those found guilty by the Holy Office. Often gagged, these women paid with silence the penance demanded of audacious females.

Whether deviant or obedient, women became increasingly significant in this city of intensified change. As husbands or fathers left for the New World, women made decisions, raised children, and handled business at home. Many women dedicated their lives to God, but some neither married nor entered a convent, finding ways to survive and serve the practical needs of the community. Symbolically, women performed roles of critical importance to a patriarchal order, signifying virtue and evil, providing a negative foil against which men could define themselves, and permitting a justification for male authority.[4] On the basis of gender, "symbolic lines

---

[4] For a stimulating discussion of gender symbols, see Joan Scott, "Gender: A Useful Cate-

and boundaries" could be drawn, which anthropologist Mary Douglas has described as "a way of bringing order into experience."[5]

In Seville, where great changes occurred so quickly, order seemed especially elusive. The Inquisition called on citizens to denounce themselves and one another for heresies that appeared even among the wealthiest and most powerful. Commercial expansion attracted thousands but also pushed others onto the ships setting out for the New World. As Seville's population more than doubled between 1520 and 1580, the city metamorphosed from a mere appendix of Europe into "the center of the world, a New Rome," in the words of fray Tomás de Mercado.[6] Bureaucracies grew for royal agencies, local government, Church, and Inquisition. Lengthening lines of authority complicated the task of preserving order.

In this period of the Counter-Reformation, religious beliefs permeated gender ideology. Enclosure and purity developed as strategies for defending the faith at this time, for separating the sacred from the profane, and also for protecting the social order. Women, warned theologians, were especially vulnerable to temptations of the devil, and they required the special protection of enclosure.[7] *Limpieza de sangre*, or genetic purity free from intermarriage with other religious groups, determined who could hold office or enjoy privilege, and it depended directly on female chastity.

Religion played a very political role in this period as it justified a gender system that supported the existing social order. Religious symbols of female martyrs promoted the belief that women should be self-sacrificing, giving themselves up to pain and humility for a higher cause. The Holy Virgin represented a standard of female perfection that no mortal could hope to attain, and Mary Magdalen demonstrated that weak, sinful woman must assume the kneeling position of the penitent, which justified female submission and male domination. One of the reasons for the persistence of gender beliefs is that they were sanctified, first by the Church, and then later, in the years following the Counter-Reformation, by an increasingly secularized faith in rational nature.

Nothing better demonstrates the heightened anxiety about order and gender than the great number of publications in this period that prescribed

---

gory of Historical Analysis," *American Historical Review* 91, no. 5 (December 1986): 1067–68, esp.

[5] Mary Douglas, *Natural Symbols: Explorations in Cosmology* (London: Cresset Press, 1970), p. 50. Note that I am using the term *patriarchal* to refer to a system in which a group of men have the institutionalized privilege to exploit women, children, and other men; see Gerda Lerner, *The Creation of Patriarchy* (New York: Oxford University Press, 1986), pp. 238–39.

[6] Quoted in Vicente Lleó Cañal, *Nueva Roma: Mitología y humanismo en el renacimiento sevillano* (Seville: Diputación Provincial de Sevilla, 1979), p. 9. For population growth, see Domínguez Ortiz, *Orto y ocaso*, pp. 41–42.

[7] Fray Luis de León, *La perfecta casada* (1583), in *Biblioteca de Autores Españoles* (Madrid: M. Rivadeneyra, 1855), 37: 240–41, esp.

the "natural order" in which women and men ought to live. Basing their ideals on what they presumed were God's intentions for his creation, Spanish writers described doctrine, defined dogma, and discussed the nature of man. And as they did so, they raised again the age-old question: what is woman?

The dialogue served as a literary form for the discussion of this question in many sixteenth-century writings, such as Juan de Espinosa's treatise, *Diálogo en laude de las mujeres*. Women, declares one young man in this treatise, are not all sweetness and love; in fact, the real question is how to distinguish a good woman from a bad one. That is not difficult at all, his friend replies; as the proverbs say, simply look at how a woman presents herself. He then quotes a stream of proverbs that caution the prudent about masked women, running women, wandering women, acquisitive women, and good-looking older women. Such long-held wisdom proves, the confident young man asserts, "the little modesty of some women, and of others their insanity and vanity."[8]

This dialogue, obviously more critical than laudatory, reflects far more than male distrust and female perfidy. It presents a concept of social order posited on sex relations that are at once parallel and asymmetrical. One of the proverbs discussed in the dialogue cautions, "Neither broken sword nor wandering woman," emphasizing the complexity of these sex relations in a juxtaposition of two symbols of disorder: the broken sword, representing dishonored man, and the wandering woman, representing female shame. The social order derived from this juxtaposition is doubly dependent, first on male honor, which, in turn, depends on control imposed upon women. Society thus develops an ethos of gendered honor as well as a sexual economy.

With few exceptions, Spanish writers in this period believed that women by nature were less suited to exercise power than men. They associated men with reason and women with emotion, men with culture and women with nature.[9] This was not a symmetrical comparison, however, for clerics used the Bible to justify male predominance. Citing Exodus 13, for example, Juan de la Cerda wrote that God demonstrated the superiority of male to female when he ordered sacrifices of male animals.[10] He also declared

---

[8] Juan de Espinosa, *Diálogo en laude de las mujeres* (1580), ed. Angela González Simón (Madrid: Consejo Superior de Investigaciones Científicas, 1946), p. 258.

[9] Sherry Ortner, "Is Female to Male as Nature Is to Culture?" in *Woman, Culture and Society*, ed. Michelle Zimbalist Rosaldo and Louise Lamphere (Stanford: Stanford University Press, 1974), pp. 67–87.

[10] Juan de la Cerda, *Vida política de todos los estados de mugeres: en el qual se dan muy provechosos y Christianos documentos y avisos, para criarse y conservarse devidamente las mugeres en sus estados* (Alcalá de Henares: Juan Gracian, 1599), p. 323ʳ. Note that ʳ here and hereafter refers to the reverse side of the page.

that men have greater perfection because Adam was the cause and Eve, who proceeded from him, the effect. Another cleric quoted philosophers from classical Greece and Rome who asserted that nature divides the work of men and women so that he is suited for speaking out in public, while she is meant to be silent in the home.[11]

Such writings asserted that power was not appropriate for women, but they did not deny that women actually had power. In fact, many believed that women had a special power to heal, divine, and foresee the future. Those who appreciated this power said it demonstrated female proximity to God; those who feared it said that it came from the devil. It is no accident that almost all of the people denounced for love magic were women, nor that female mystics were most effectively discredited by reinterpreting their inner experiences as visitations from the devil. Women who succumbed to their weak and sinful natures held the power of evil, it was believed; and when they lost their fear and timidity, there was no one stronger or less afraid, or more infused with power to seduce, ensnare, and infect.

Biblical passages and proverbs, such as those considered by the friends in Espinosa's dialogue, speak through a rhetoric that presumes to present fixed and immutable truth; but expressions of sexuality and relations between the sexes are neither timeless nor universal. Recent scholarship has revealed that intimate relations between women and men have varied over time, that class affects norms for sexual behavior, and that sex relations express both power positions and *mentalités* in the larger social order.[12] During the sixteenth and seventeenth centuries, however, most people did not distinguish between sex, a biological condition, and gender, which is a socially constructed set of beliefs about sex.[13] They assumed that their be-

[11] Fray Martín de Córdoba, *Jardín de nobles donzellas*, ed. Harriet Goldberg, University of North Carolina (Chapel Hill Campus) Studies in the Romance Languages and Literatures, no. 137 (Chapel Hill: University of North Carolina Department of Romance Languages, 1974), p. 206.

[12] Lawrence Stone, *The Family, Sex and Marriage in England 1500–1800* (New York: Harper, 1979), pp. 21–24, 340–404, esp. See also Cissie Fairchilds, "Masters and Servants in Eighteenth-Century Toulouse," *Journal of Social History* 12 (Spring 1979): 368–93; Jean-Louis Flandrin, *Families in Former Times: Kinship, Household and Sexuality*, trans. Richard Southern (Cambridge: Cambridge University Press, 1985); and Michel Foucault, *The History of Sexuality*, vol. 1, trans. Robert Hurley (New York: Pantheon, 1978).

[13] Sherry B. Ortner and Harriet Whitehead, eds., *Sexual Meanings: The Cultural Construction of Gender and Sexuality* (Cambridge: Cambridge University Press, 1981), pp. 1–13, esp. Note that I am using the term *Counter-Reformation* to refer to a period of time and a set of mentalités; A. G. Dickens, *The Counter-Reformation* (London: Thames and Hudson, 1968), p. 81, refers to this as an "order-seeking" period; also, see John Bossy, "The Counter-Reformation and the People of Catholic Europe," *Past and Present* 47 (1970): 51–70; and Steven Ozment, *The Age of Reform, 1250–1550: An Intellectual and Religious History of Late Medieval and Reformation Europe* (New Haven: Yale University Press, 1980).

liefs about the sexes reflected nothing more nor less than God-given "natural qualities."

The fact that women and men did not always behave according to gender beliefs did not prevent lay and secular officials from repeatedly invoking these beliefs.[14] Nor did they hesitate even when their gender ideals seemed completely incongruous with actual living conditions. In fact, gender beliefs that women required special protective enclosure seemed to be even more strongly invoked as men's preoccupation with wars and colonizing required women to participate more actively in the life of the city. The emphasis on gender prescriptions reveals deep social ruptures in this period, and the tension between real and ideal infused everyday immediacy into larger concerns about disorder.

Focusing on women in a male-dominated city, this study proposes that answers to questions central to social order may best be sought on the "outskirts of life," in the words of historian Lucien Febvre.[15] Those disreputable women encapsulated in the proverbs pervading Espinosa's treatise represent marginality both in standing outside the pale of respectability and in presenting the voice of folk wisdom rather than official knowledge. In both senses, they occupy the liminal space that anthropologists have described for those who temporarily drop out of the social structure.[16] Deviant from the male norm, all women floated along the margins of respectability, bobbing between ostracism and integration, in an ambiguous area where social rules can be played with, questioned, or waived. It is here that cultural attitudes appear very clearly, but they should not be reduced to mere polarities. In constantly changing patterns, these attitudes overlap with one another, sometimes in opposition, sometimes in agreement, often contrasting with actual conditions in the lives of women and men.

The problem, of course, is that very few sources present information about these marginal people that is not filtered through the reporting of those at the center of power. Seville offers a rich variety of sources, including art and literature from the period, Inquisition records, laws and regulations, city government papers, chronicles, legal documents, parish records, and a census of the poor. However, the voices of women that appear in these records most often represent what they believed officials wanted

[14] Yolanda Murphy and Robert F. Murphy, *Women of the Forest* (New York: Columbia University Press, 1974), describe the Mundurucú culture in Brazil in which an ideology of male dominance that is clear in rite and myth seems to be contradicted in daily life.

[15] Lucien Febvre, *A New Kind of History and Other Essays*, ed. Peter Burke, trans. K. Folca (New York: Harper and Row, 1973), p. 25. Note that he used this term to urge historians to consider thoughts and feelings as well as official records, not to focus specifically on women.

[16] Victor Turner discusses liminality in many of his studies, but see especially *From Ritual to Theatre: The Human Seriousness of Play* (New York: Performing Arts Journal Publications, 1982), pp. 44–45.

to hear and how officials wanted to report it. With a few remarkable exceptions, the writings of women usually conformed to the demands of a male canon. Artists such as Bartolomé Murillo, who lived and worked in Seville during the seventeenth century, portrayed women either as symbols of religious purity or as happy, well-fed, and nonthreatening flirts who peeked out of windows or from behind a concealing veil. In his painting of a flower girl (fig. 2), Murillo uses a smile and a graceful figure to mask the difficulties and vulnerability of any young woman who tried to earn a livelihood by selling flowers on the streets.

For the most part, males dominate the discourse of available evidence, filling it with formulaic rhetoric that disguises considerable female silence. Feminist literary criticism suggests one way to remedy this problem of gender bias in historical sources.[17] Reading a subtext, we can ask what was not said and why. We can look at the power context in which statements were made and recorded, and we can look for the ways that women spoke with their feet and hands, doing things that belied or refined testimony about them.

Historians sometimes criticize feminist scholarship for attempting to impose on the past attitudes of the present time. One way to avoid this problem is to let the people of the past speak for themselves through their documents. It is true, of course, that the historian selects the documents to be studied and decides what to ask of them. It is also true that historians must interpret from their own experience the information that they have found in documents. Nevertheless, it is possible to respect the past and accept its differences from the present, even as the historical record is used to increase understanding of our own times. Here I attempt to do this by carefully choosing the words I use to interpret the past, and by consciously seeking to employ feminist analysis as the basis for a critique rather than a polemic.

Historians must also be conscious of the devices they use to try to render the past more meaningful. This study of the significance of gender in early modern Seville has found especially useful certain theoretical approaches of cultural anthropology and the sociology of deviance. In addition, I have chosen to use specific examples wherever possible as a way to render this city and this period of time less abstract. To ensure that these examples from the past do not become mere anecdotal history, I have consciously selected them to make particular points and placed them within the larger historical context. Literature and art have been considered in addition to more traditional forms of historical evidence; in all cases, I have attempted

---

[17] Annette Kuhn, "Passionate Detachment," in *Women's Pictures: Feminism and Cinema* (Boston: Routledge and Kegan Paul, 1982), p. 15; but also see the anthology edited by Elaine Showalter, *The New Feminist Criticism: Women, Literature and Theory* (New York: Pantheon, 1985); and Natalie Zemon Davis, *Fiction in the Archives: Pardon Tales and Their Tellers in Sixteenth-Century France* (Stanford: Stanford University Press, 1987), p. viii.

FIGURE 2. *Girl with Flowers*, by Bartolomé Murillo (By Permission of the Governors of Dulwich Picture Gallery, London).

to look at them critically, distinguishing beliefs from facts, in order to avoid a monocausal explanation of women's lives.

Although feminist critiques of historical practice have argued for shifting the focus from center to the margins of society, they have also insisted upon the significance and complexity of the relationship between center and margins. In addition, feminist critiques have pointed out the problems of relying exclusively on structural analysis.[18] The major methodological assumption of this study is that society may be better studied through a model of multiplicities, such as the tapestry, rather than the traditional model of dichotomized center and margins. Society is analyzed as a complex of many diverse threads that have been woven together in patterns that both change and continue. Rather than a strictly linear chronological development, this model shows that history unfolds unevenly, sometimes harking back to the past, occasionally anticipating what is ahead.

This inquiry into gender and disorder begins with an examination of the practical and symbolic roles of women in sixteenth- and seventeenth-century Seville. Chapter 1 analyzes the work of women as husbands and fathers left to colonize and subdue distant peoples in Spain's changing empire. As Seville's population grew, however, and as traditional occupations suffered reverses, women's work became discredited. In addition, guild regulations and laws for developing professions made most work increasingly gender specific. The second chapter describes the religious symbols of virgins and martyrs and shows how they served to fortify the traditional gender system, including legalized prostitution. It argues that these religious symbols preserved a gender ideology that emphasized the weakness and passivity of women, even as women's active participation became more essential in the city.

Religion or marriage provided the most respectable status for women, but neither offered an entirely safe enclosure for them. Marriage, the subject of chapter 3, was believed to serve as an antidote for the problem of disorderly women, but bigamists, single mothers, widows, and abandoned wives appeared in growing numbers as epidemics and famines struck Seville, especially in 1580–1582 and 1599–1600. Providing a context for unpaid and low-wage female labor, marriage was also believed essential to preserve a system of domestic production increasingly challenged by developing capitalism. The convent as an option for women is presented in chapter 4, which argues that religious cloisters could be liberating as well as oppressive, a place where women's inner worlds could flourish despite surveillance by male confessors. Chapter 5 discusses women who dedicated their lives to God but lived outside convents and the rules of religious orders. Some of these *beatas* became revered for their holiness, but others

---

[18] Susan Mosher Stuard, "The *Annales* School and Feminist History: Opening Dialogue with the American Stepchild," *Signs* 7, no. 1 (1981): 135–43.

were penanced by the Inquisition for heresies, "spiritual arrogan
visions, and miracles.

Women who lived outside respectability attracted ever more attention as
Seville's population and fortunes began to decline in the seventeenth century. "Manly women" who behaved more as men than women sometimes
won praise as heroes, as chapter 6 demonstrates, but most women and men
who broke sexual codes of conduct were prosecuted as adulterers, fornicators, and sodomites. Intensifying attacks on the city's system of legal
prostitution in the seventeenth century are the subject of chapter 7. Here
it is argued that the patriarchal order changed and secular male officials
became stronger as they attempted to convert the legal brothels into effective enclosures for women. Ships were growing larger at the same time that
silt began to fill Seville's river, so that Cadiz gradually replaced this city as
site for the royal agency regulating trade and colonization. Chapter 8 describes the poverty that grew in Seville as fewer fleets from the New World
came into its port. Poverty became largely the problem of women and children, while charity became the province of Church and local government.
Strategies for giving charity or receiving it reflected a deeply rooted gender
ideology even as material conditions changed. According to the book's
concluding argument, attempts to restore order in early modern Seville
increasingly invoked a gender ideology that viewed all women as Susana's
daughters. They required special enclosure, in this view, for they had to be
protected from their own weakness, and society had to be protected from
their propensity for disorder.

Counter-Reformation Seville offers an example of patriarchy in crisis,
when officials had to respond to a growing central government, an expand-
ing empire, developing capitalism, increasing population, external attacks
on the Church, an intensification of ecclesiastical attempts to impose orthodoxy, and a changing local economy tied ever more strongly to imperial
interests. Their response was to strengthen their authority through a political system that was closed to women, through guild regulations that multiplied to restrict the economic activities of women, and through more
careful enclosure of women in convent, home, or brothel. For officials of
this period, restoration of the social order required the sword of authority
repaired and the wandering woman restrained.

The case of Seville presents more than one atypical city in disorder, and
it cannot be dismissed as merely a male conspiracy to control women. Efforts to preserve and restore order here reveal the primary role that gender
has played in human history. Many women participated in these efforts,
internalizing gender beliefs that they had been taught from their earliest
years, accepting a more subtle psychic enclosure in idealized expectations.
Yet other women resisted with quiet subversion and noted the gap between gender ideals and the actual conditions of their rapidly changing
city.

Chapter 1

IN THE HANDS OF WOMEN

In 1525 Andres Navagero, the Venetian ambassador to Spain, wrote a description of Seville that included among its noteworthy marvels the fact that so many men had left for the New World that Seville had become a city "in the hands of women."[1] Fortunately, as the prevailing sense of public order would have it, enough men remained to fill the offices of local government as well as those of the Church and Inquisition. But Navagero's remark cannot be dismissed as the sort of unfounded exaggeration conventional to travel literature, for men did leave their wives and children when they embarked for other parts of the world as soldiers, sailors, merchants, and royal officials. As men took on the important Counter-Reformation work of proselytizing non-Christians and subduing colonial territories, women assumed more responsibility at home. In fact, much of the life of this city was carried out by women without the help of men. Despite a legacy of gender symbols prescribing female deference and self-sacrifice, which will be discussed in chapter 2, Seville's women participated actively in the life of the city. Periodically, however, male officials who remained in Seville took action to check the developing female confidence and to reinforce a male-dominated gender order.

Notarized documents from the sixteenth century indicate that women bought and sold property, rented it, arranged marriages for their children, made wills, and arranged for the care of children in the absence of their husbands. On May 20, 1550, for example, Mariana de los Ríos, the wife of Damian de los Ríos, a surgeon who was in the Indies, signed and notarized a letter that gave power to a local merchant to represent her in the Casa de Contratación and receive in her name whatever her husband had sent from the Indies. A few months later Francisca de Carvajal, "wife of Pedro Alvarez, who is in the Indies," signed a rental agreement with Bartolomé Pérez for some houses; and Gregorio Rodríguez, in the name of Agueda Rodríguez, his aunt, signed an agreement to rent some houses to Isabel de Medina, widow of Cristóbal de Carvajal and Francisca Nuñez, wife of Gregorio Hernández, "who is in the Indies." While her husband was in the Indies, Costanza López signed a statement that she would pay a dowry for her daughter, Luisa López, in installments following an initial

---

[1] Andres Navagero, *Viaje a España*, trans. José María Alonso Gamo (Valencia: Editorial Castalia, 1951), p. 57.

payment of ten thousand maravedís. Catalina Rodríguez, "wife of Luis Valera, carpenter, who is in the Indies," signed a formal recognition that she owed twenty ducats to Pablo de Basynana.[2]

In some of the most poignant documents of this period, women in Seville had to deal with the deaths of their husbands and sons in the New World. Juana de Ortega, widow of Piero Rondinelli, claimed her rights as the heir of her legitimate son, Piero Rondinelli, who died "coming by sea to this city" from the Indies. María de Silva, widow of Luis Cuello, gave power to a resident of Mexico City to represent her as heir of her son, Gaspar Cuello, who had died in Mexico. Beatriz Martínez, widow of a merchant who had died in Mexico, filed two letters of power to claim her inheritance—one for her brother-in-law to represent her in New Spain, and another for a nephew to collect from officials of the Casa de Contratación and from ships' masters anything that had been sent to her from her husband's estate in the New World.

Other notarized documents indicate that women participated in many legal transactions regardless of whether their husbands were in the Indies. Widows, of course, not only had to protect property they inherited; they could also act as legal guardians of their minor children. They provided dowries for their daughters, signed rental agreements, bought and sold property, and wrote their own wills. Some women whose husbands were still alive carried on their own legal and commercial transactions, although they usually acknowledged that they did so "with license of my husband." Much less often a woman signed a legal document on her own behalf with no mention of her status as wife, widow, or daughter. Beatriz Ponce de León, for example, gave power to Andrés de Herrera to demand and receive in her name all that was owed to her, "whether in wheat, barley, hens, or anything else."

Women invested in commerce and formed their own commercial companies in early modern Seville. Sometimes their companies included only women, but they usually had to have the aid of a male merchant to carry out their business in the Indies.[3] Female-owned shops in the silver quarter of the city sold silks, buttons, and linens.[4] Widows of wealthy businessmen

[2] APS, 1550, Oficio 1, Libro 1, contains all of these cases and the other examples described in the ensuing three paragraphs about women in notarized documents. The maravedí was a vellón coin of little value, but it was the most commonly used coin, along with the escudo or ducat. Their value fluctuated widely, but usually it required between 400 and 612 maravedís to equal one escudo or ducat. In 1650 a kilo of bread cost 16 maravedís, a liter of wine cost about 34 maravedís, and a liter of oil cost about 68 maravedís.

[3] Blanca Morell Peguero, *Mercaderes y artesanos en la Sevilla del descubrimiento* (Seville: Diputación Provincial de Sevilla, 1986), pp. 77–78. Note that this historical ethnography is based on documents in the Archivo de Protocolos de Sevilla.

[4] Antonio Domínguez Ortiz, *Sociedad y mentalidad en la Sevilla del Antiguo Régimen* (Seville: Ayuntamiento, 1979), p. 44.

continued their husbands' businesses and investments, but women from this social level never invested by themselves; instead, they empowered their sons or male servants or agents to represent them in the commercial world.[5] Class consciousness and gender beliefs directly affected women's participation in the economic life of the city because a woman of means was expected to work only in her own home.

Most occupations of women in this period conformed to beliefs about the work "most suited" for women. Juan Luis Vives, for example, proposed that girls learn "to spin, sew, weave, embroider, cook, and the rest of the things of the house."[6] When they married, they would be able to use these skills to preserve and increase their husbands' estates, or, if a man was unable to completely support the family, his wife could use them "to work with her own hands" to earn money.[7] Silk weaving, sewing, embroidering, selling food, and nursing the ill became common female occupations in the later sixteenth and seventeenth centuries, providing work believed appropriate for women, not only suitable to female nature, but also readily undertaken in the home.

Women of little wealth had worked outside their homes for centuries. Before the great population growth of the sixteenth century, many people had worked outside the city walls where certain agricultural occupations were exclusively female, such as goatherding, dairy production, esparto grass gathering, and fruit and vegetable production.[8] Inside the city, certain retail occupations were filled only by women, who sold fruits, vegetables, fish, tripe, and dairy products. Both women and men sold meat and bread and worked as bakers, innkeepers, tavernkeepers, and shopkeepers.

Female participation in the city's labor force may have increased during the sixteenth century when so many men left Seville, but reliable figures are not available. Declining marriage rates disturbed those who saw that the lower wages offered to women meant that those without husbands

[5] Morell Peguero, *Mercaderes*, p. 78. See also Antonio Domínguez Ortiz, "La mujer en el tránsito de la edad media a la moderna," in *Las mujeres en las ciudades medievales*, Actas de las Terceras Jornadas de Investigación Interdisciplinaria, ed. Cristina Segura Graíño (Madrid: Universidad Autónoma de Madrid, 1984), pp. 173–76.

[6] Juan Luis Vives, *Del socorro de los pobres, o de las necesidades humanes*, (1526) (Madrid: Sucesores de Hernando, 1922), pp. 283–84.

[7] Juan de Soto, *Obligaciones de todos los estados, y oficios, con los remedios, y consejos mas eficaces para la salud espiritual, y general reformación de las costumbres* (Alcalá: Andres Sánchez de Ezpleta, 1619), p. 106.

[8] Cristina Segura Graíño, "Las mujeres andaluzas en la baja edad media," in *Las mujeres*, p. 150. See also Mercedes Borrero Fernández, "El trabajo de la mujer en el mundo rural sevillano durante la baja edad media," in *Las mujeres medievales y su ámbito jurídico*, ed. María Angeles Durán, Actas de las Segundas Jornadas de Investigación Interdisciplinaria (Madrid: Universidad Autónoma, 1983), pp. 191–99; and José Manuel Escobar Camacho, Manuel Nieto Cumplido, and Jesús Padilla González, "La mujer cordobesa en el trabajo a fines del siglo xv," in *Las mujeres*, pp. 153–60.

could not support themselves with their own labor.[9] While Juan Luis Vives and other sixteenth-century writers idealized a wife of virtue and industry, actual economic conditions ensured that most women would work regardless of their marital status. Whether a woman married, took a vow of religion, remained single, or became a widow, those with little wealth worked. Even though the dowry was to revert to a woman when her husband died, a widow with a very small inheritance worked in order to survive, frequently continuing the trade or business of her husband.

The economic activities of widows tended to break gender restrictions and defined a group of women who seemed particularly threatening to clergymen such as the Augustinian Juan de Soto. He prescribed strict enclosure for them in the early seventeenth century and advised widows to leave their houses only to attend church, citing the admonition of Saint Paul to flee from young widows who go from house to house chatting and visiting.[10] True widows, the cleric wrote, deserve honor, but there are those who "are full of garbage" beneath the white veil of the widow. More concerned with the woman's body than with her economic need, Soto asserted that the honorable widow wears a veil that reaches midway between her head and feet to show that half her body had died along with her husband.[11]

Evidently, widows did not actually act as though half their bodies had died, for guild regulations specifically provided that widows of guild members should be permitted to inherit husbands' shops, tools, and guild membership, even when they prohibited membership for individual women. Widows of carpenters, wood-carvers, or stringed-instrument makers could keep their husbands' shops as long as they remained single, but they would forfeit them if they married a man outside the profession.[12] The silk-weavers' guild, which admitted both women and men as members, provided that the wife of a member who was dead or absent could have his looms and cloths for one year without incurring any penalty. After that time, she could submit her work for guild examination, if she knew how to weave, and the guild could then permit her to keep one loom to sustain herself. She could not have more than one loom, however, nor could she have apprentices unless they were her own children.[13]

---

[9] See, for example, the complaints in Joaquin Guichot y Parody, *Historia del Exmo. Ayuntamiento de la muy noble, muy leal, muy heróica é invicta ciudad de Sevilla* (Seville: Tipografía de la Región, 1896), 2: 299; and in *Memoriales y discursos de Francisco Martínez de Mata*, ed. Gonzalo Anes Alvarez (Madrid: Moneda y Crédito, 1971), p. 129.

[10] Soto, *Obligaciones*, p. 132.

[11] Ibid., p. 134ʳ.

[12] AMS, *Ordenanzas de Sevilla* (Seville: Diego Hurtado de Mondoca, 1631), "Carpenters," fol. 148. Dating from the fourteenth-century reign of Alfonso XI, these ordinances were subsequently amended and republished.

[13] AMS, Sección Especial, Papeles del Señor Conde de Aguila, Libros en folio, Tomo 25, Número 2, "Ancient Ordinances of Master Silk-Workers," dated December 16, 1605.

Silk weaving in Seville became associated with women in particular. A proposal to the monarchy to revitalize the silk industry asserted that "the kingdom of Seville is kept rich by the women, for its greatest wealth comes from this occupation."[14] By the middle of the seventeenth century, the city was believed to have some three thousand looms, mostly concentrated in six parishes. Reports referred to thirty thousand workers in the silk industry, a large proportion of them women, who could perform this work in small workshops or in their own homes, where they could also watch their children.[15]

Foreign competition, particularly from France, undersold silk weavers in Castile, and the silk industry became increasingly depressed. A memorial to Philip IV in 1655 from two officials of the silk-weavers' guild complained that only sixty of the city's looms were still in production, with the result that a third of the city no longer had residents.[16] Vulnerable to a widely fluctuating market tied so closely to the Indies, silk masters became increasingly dependent on merchants who furnished the raw material and then distributed and sold the finished products.[17] The guild continued to license female silk weavers, but many worked for masters in an exploitative piecework system. The guild also permitted female weavers to teach other women to weave, but regulations prohibited them from teaching men other than husbands or sons.[18] At the same time that silk weaving became increasingly an industry of female sweated labor, guild efforts redoubled to prevent women from becoming master silk weavers.

To support themselves and their families, women turned to selling food, which could be far more difficult than paintings of the period suggest. Bartolomé Murillo idealized female food sellers in seventeenth-century Seville as cheerful and well-fed, lovely and healthy as the girl in figure 3.[19] Women fortunate enough to have access to an oven baked bread and pastries, and others sold fruits and vegetables in the streets. Some women tried to sell food out of their homes, but the city prohibited this in 1629, calling for a fine of four hundred maravedís for the first offense and two years exile for the second.[20] At this same time, the city government prohibited the sale of food in houses where boarders stayed, and it forbade unmarried women to keep a tavern or to work in one. Periodically, the city also enforced regu-

[14] Quoted in Domínguez Ortiz, *Orto y ocaso*, p. 25.

[15] Domínguez Ortiz, *Orto y ocaso*, pp. 22–25. Parishes include Feria, Santa Marina, San Gil, San Julian, Santa Lucia, San Juan de Acre.

[16] *Memoriales de Martínez de Mata*, pp. 194–95.

[17] Domínguez Ortiz, *Orto y ocaso*, pp. 25–26.

[18] AMS, *Ordenanzas*, Número 59.

[19] For more on Murillo and painting in his period, see Juan Miguel Serrera and Enrique Valdivieso González, *La época de Murillo: Antecedentes y consecuentes de su pintura* (Seville: Diputaciones, 1982).

[20] This decree of the asistente in 1629 is in Guichot y Parody, *Historia*, 2: 210–11.

FIGURE 3. *Girl with Fruit and Flowers*, by Bartolomé Murillo (Pushkin Museum of Fine Arts, Moscow).

lations against female street hawkers. Complaining that "many women, especially *moriscas* and even *moras*," were selling baked goods that they made, pastry makers appealed to the prejudices of city officials and got from them a prohibition that forbade guild nonmembers to bake and sell pastries and bread.[21]

The economic distress that developed throughout Spain in the seventeenth century hit female artisans in particular in Seville. Sumptuary laws that prohibited clothing of silk and brocade, limited gold and silver embroidery, and fixed a permissible number of domestic servants compounded the problems of inflation and foreign competition that resulted in unemployment and reduced earnings. A royal minister reported from Seville in 1685, describing "the most miserable state" of the area where people were dying from hunger. Women, he wrote, begged from door to door "because the work of their hands could not sustain them, and other women retired into their houses without having clothing to even attend mass."[22]

Nursing, an occupation traditionally believed suitable for women, provided a livelihood for fewer women after the late sixteenth century. One problem was that it often required women to leave their homes, although they commonly remained in their neighborhoods; an even more serious problem was that female healers became suspect in the view of both the Inquisition and a developing male medical profession. During the seventeenth century official culture increasingly insisted on a medicine of books and learned men, while women practiced a medicine based on experience and supernatural powers. Oliva Sabuco de Nantes Barrera provided the one major exception to this gender pattern: her late sixteenth-century medical treatise emphasized the significance of the lymph system and argued that emotions govern the health of the body.[23]

The women of Seville performed a great part of the work of healing in the sixteenth and seventeenth centuries, despite the clash between popular and official cultures and the growing determination of men who dominated official culture to control the women working within a popular tra-

---

[21] AMS, Sección Especial, Papeles del Señor Conde de Aguila, Libros en folio, Tomo 27, Número 3.

[22] Quoted in Guichot y Parody, *Historia*, 2: 299.

[23] See Oliva Sabuco de Nantes Barrera, "Coloquio del conocimiento de sí mismo" (1587) in *Biblioteca de Autores Españoles*, 65: 332–72 (Madrid: Librería de los Sucesores de Hernando, 1922). This is a portion of her book *Nueva filosofía de la naturaleza del hombre no conocida ni alcanzada de los grandes filósofos antiguos, la cual mejora la vida y salud humana*, which was published in Madrid in 1587. Also see Mary Elizabeth Perry, "Las mujeres y su trabajo curativo en Sevilla, siglos XVI y XVII," in *El trabajo de las mujeres: Siglos XVI–XX*, ed. María Jesús Matilla and Margarita Ortega, Actas de las Sextas Jornadas de Investigación Interdisciplinaria Sobre la Mujer (Madrid: Universidad Autónoma, 1987), pp. 40–50; and chapter 6, below, on sexual rebels.

dition. In their homes they prepared remedies for ailing members of the family. In the city's hospitals and prisons they cared for the sick, giving them food and drink, washing their sores and wounds. As Seville's population more than doubled in the sixteenth century, the healing work of women increased also; and their power developed out of "woman's work" traditionally performed in domestic arenas, far from the places that are usually recognized as centers of power.[24]

However, not much is known of the work of these women. In most historical documents, the female healer is not visible, except as a discredited person who must be punished by authorities. Her work is not seen, nor official, nor noted, nor remunerated. Medicine in historical records appears only in the male world, a science to be regulated and studied in books, protected in particular from "female superstitions."

It is possible, nevertheless, to learn of women's healing work through some sources: Inquisition cases, salaries paid by the city government, local and royal regulations of medicine, hagiographies of female saints, and the literature of the time. These sources have limitations, which should be noted. Because the voices of women can be heard in these writings only in discourse with male officials, this evidence reveals more of what official males thought of female healers than of the actual work of these women. It also tells more of what male officials wanted to hear than of what the women wanted to say. But these sources can be read for a subtext, that is, women's experiences can be found within and beneath the words that men used to describe a male-dominated world.[25]

Much of the traditional medicine practiced in Seville derived from recipes of herbs and other materials, often cooked or combined in the kitchen. Juan de Aviñon, for example, included many such recipes in his book, *Sevillana medicina: que trata el modo conservativo y curativo de los que habitan en la muy insigne ciudad de Sevilla, la cual sirve y aprovecha para cualquier otro*

[24] Mary Nash, "Desde la invisibilidad a la presencia de la mujer en la historia: Corrientes historiográficas y marcos conceptuales de la nueva historia de la mujer," in *Nuevas perspectivas sobre la mujer*, ed. María Angeles Durán, Actas de las Primeras Jornadas de Investigación Interdisciplinaria, 2 vols. (Madrid: Universidad Autónoma, 1982–83), 1: 21–22. Also, see María Luisa Remón Pérez, "Trabajo doméstico e ideología patriarcal: Una constante histórica," in *Nuevas perspectivas*, 2: 201–12, for a discussion of the invisibility of women's work. See Cristina Segura Graiño, "Las mujeres en el medievo hispano," *Cuadernos de Investigación Medieval: Guía crítica de temas históricos* 1, no. 2 (1984): 46, for the invisibility of women in medicine; and also Natalie Zemon Davis, "Women's History in Transition: The European Case," *Feminist Studies* 3, nos. 3–4 (1976): p. 90.

[25] For a more extensive discussion of discourse dominated by men and the importance of subtext in the study of women, see the Introduction, above, and also my essay, "Male Discourse and Female Offenders in the Spanish Inquisition," in *Social Bodies, Spiritual Selves: Women and Religion in Early Modern Spain*, ed. Darcy Donahue (forthcoming).

lugar de estos reinos.[26] Although some of the ingredients represented a luxury that many could not afford, these medical recipes signified a practical and unmystified tradition that flourished not in rare books written by learned men, but at the family hearth where women could prepare medical remedies as well as food and drink.

Juan de Aviñon's book was not published until 1545, sometime after his death, when Seville had experienced population growth and its attendant problems. Dr. Nicolás Monardes wrote a prologue in which he noted the importance of health for the social order. "Without health," he wrote, "the wise person does not extend knowledge, nor does the good person work, nor the captain govern, nor the official carry out his office." The subtext of Monardes should be noted here because while he and Juan de Aviñon wrote of the importance of diet and healing recipes for health, neither one says that much of the work of preserving health is in the hands of women, who feed and care for their husbands, children, and neighbors.

Other books of this period also describe a domestic medicine. *Thesoro de los pobres* by Pedro Hispano, which was reprinted in many editions, describes the use of medical auxiliaries and medicine in the home.[27] A short time later the text of domestic medicine by Girolamo de Manfredi was translated into Castilian, and Gregorio López published his book, *Tesoro de medicinas*, which had the subtitle *Cuatro libros de la naturaleza y virtudes de las plantas y animales . . . muy útil para todo género de gente que vive en estancias y pueblos do no hay médico, ni botica.*[28] Although these books were not available to many people, their assumption that the practice of medicine was a domestic task reflects a common belief. Men wrote about a medical tradition that had been carried out for centuries especially by women.

Popular proverbs, in fact, contained much folklore about domestic medicine. According to the doctor Juan Sorapan de Rieros, in his collection *Medicina española contenida en proverbios vulgares de nuestra lengua*, food "not only serves as fuel, but also as medicine."[29] He adds that hens, their manure, their bile, and especially their eggs are excellent remedies to cure snakebites, cataracts, cloudiness and pustules in the eyes, open wounds, and dysentery. Describing the verse, "Carne de pluma quita del rostro el arruga," he says that the best remedy for wrinkles is to eat hens. In affirm-

---

[26] (Seville: Enrique Rasco, 1885, orig. 1545). For the subsequent quotation, see the prologue by Nicolas Monardes, p. 1.

[27] See Luis S. Granjel, *La medicina española renacentista* (Salamanca: Ediciones Universidad de Salamanca, 1980), p. 136.

[28] Ibid., p. 136; and also Gregorio López, *Tesoro de medicinas para diversas enfermedades* (Madrid: Imprenta de Música, 1708).

[29] Dr. Juan Sorapan de Rieros, *Medicina española contenida en proverbios vulgares de nuestra lengua*, in *Biblioteca clásica de la medicina española*, vol. 16 (Madrid: Real Academia Nacional de Medicina, 1949), p. 136.

ing the relationship between diet and beauty, he also reveals the combination of medicine with cosmetology that was so common in attitudes about the body in this period.[30] However, the description can be read for a subtext, or what Sorapan does not say: that is, that medicine and cosmetology came together in a female world. Sorapan invokes the ancient authorities such as Galen and Dioscorides, who recognized the excellence of garlic as a "peasant remedy."[31] This humble plant was used commonly to relieve gas, stimulate the bowels, to dry the stomach, heal snakebites and the bites of rabid dogs, to clarify the voice of musicians, and provide protection from the plague.

Prescriptive literature of the sixteenth century promoted the concept of domestic medicine. Although these prescriptions do not tell us anything of the actual practices of women, they indicate the manner of thinking about women's obligations and also the anxieties that those obligations raised.[32] Emphasizing the duties of married women, books such as *Instrucción de la mujer cristiana* by Juan Luis Vives noted that women were expected to care for the ill in their homes.[33] When her husband is sick, Vives writes, the wife must attend him in person. "You touch his wounds, his sores, you with your hands treat his pitiful and ulcerated body, you cover him, you uncover him, you give him medicine, you empty the basin if it is necessary. Do not flee nor refuse, queen, to do kindness for your husband, nor to serve him as much as you can. Do not leave his care to maidservants," he advises, "who do not care what comes or goes, because they do not all have true love, and as the sick one feels he is not loved, his illness grows and he suddenly takes a turn for the worse." Again, the subtext should be noted, what Vives does not say: he recognizes the importance of love in healing, and he requires it of the woman as a solemn obligation; but he does not acknowledge the power that love grants to women, a power of life and death not only for an individual, but for the entire social order. Such power, uncontrolled, could be frightening: officials may have seen this as all the more reason to take it from women who rarely received the formal education of some men.

In requiring women to care for the ill, other prescriptive books extended the domestic obligation of women through an ideal of female charity. Fray Martín de Córdoba, in his book *Jardín de nobles donzellas*, praises women

[30] Ibid., p. 207–19. See also Alison Klairmont Lingo, "Empirics and Charlatans in Early Modern France: The Genesis of the Classification of the 'Other' in Medical Practice," *Journal of Social History* 19, no. 4 (1986): 587–88.

[31] Sorapan, *Medicina*, p. 288.

[32] See María Helena Sánchez Ortega, "La mujer en el antiguo régimen: Tipos históricos y arquetipos literarios," in Durán, *Nuevas perspectivas*, 1: 114–16.

[33] Juan Luis Vives, *Libro llamado instrucción de la mujer cristiana* (1524), trans. Juan Justiniano (Madrid: Signo, 1936), p. 108, esp.

who are "obsequious, by which I mean that they are of gracious and consoling service. Thus says Solomon in the Proverbs," he continues: "that where there is no woman, the ill groan."[34] Woman demonstrates this virtue in three ways: "first, through devotion to God, then through compassion for her neighbor, and third, through love for her home." The woman's world, then, was not limited to the hearth; it extended to the church, to the hospital, to the houses of the poor, and to the streets where the poor fell ill.

Fray Martín de Córdoba praises Santa Monica, the mother of Saint Augustine, who "consoled the poor who were sick and dressed and cleaned the dead and protected orphans as her own sons; and when she saw paupers covered with sores, she washed and cleaned their sores, not showing any disgust whatsoever." Nevertheless, the good friar recognizes that caretaking tasks are not appropriate for everyone. He advises that "wellborn women" do not have the obligation "to provide care with their own hands; but they give alms that provide such necessities and induce other women to offer care when such need is apparent and even to make their almsgivers look for such poor people so that they can be cared for in the name and voice of the lady."

At the beginning of the sixteenth century, Catalina de Ribera transformed a house she owned in Seville into a hospital for poor women.[35] Although she was a "wellborn lady" and the mother of the duke of Medina Sidonia, she herself attended the ill. In fact, a historian of the city says that Catalina de Ribera inspired Queen Isabel to care for the sick personally in her hospital when she visited Seville.[36]

Generally, however, the "wellborn ladies" did not dedicate themselves personally to the care of the ill, and the work of healing and caring remained the task of other women. Thus, it was necessary to employ women from the lower classes in the hospitals and prisons of the city. We know of these women through reports in the municipal archive of Seville and through the *Historia de Sevilla* published by Alonso Morgado in 1587. Describing the hospitals of the city in his time, Morgado says that the Insigne Hospital de San Hermenegildo employed three women to wash and cook, assisted by six girls who each received nine thousand maravedís to help

---

[34] Fray Martín de Córdoba, *Jardín*, p. 203. The following quotations are on p. 205.

[35] Juan Ignacio Carmona García, *El sistema de hospitalidad pública en la Sevilla del Antiguo Régimen* (Seville: Diputación Provincial de Sevilla, 1979), pp. 54–59; José de Sigüenza, *Historia de la órden de San Jerónimo* (1464) (Madrid: Bailly, Bailliére é Hijos, 1907), p. 307; Alonso Morgado, *Historia de Sevilla* (Seville: Andrea Pescioni y Juan de León, 1587), p. 364; José Gestoso y Pérez, *Sevilla monumental y artística* . . . (Seville: La Andalucía Moderna, 1889–1892), 3: 107–10.

[36] Ortiz de Zuñiga, *Anales*, 3: 178–79.

preserve her virtue and also twenty thousand maravedís as a dowry.[37] Morgado does not describe their work as healing, but as the tasks that a woman does in the house. Again, the subtext reveals more of the work of women than the text, because it tells us that women's work of caring for the ill is easily subsumed in ordinary female work.

More clearly recognized as healers are the women who requested salaries from the city government. These are beatas, or women who dedicated their lives to God, making a vow of chastity, but not of poverty nor of obedience to any religious order.[38] María de la Cruz, for example, who describes herself as a "barefoot beata," requests alms from the city because she served in the hospital during the plague of 1599–1600 and was very poor with a daughter who was also impoverished.[39] Beatas who were employed by the city to work in the prison had the title of nurse and cared for the poor prisoners in body and soul.[40] Giving them food and medicines, they also exhorted them to live the life of a good Christian.

In this work, beatas served as the "other women" so essential to healing work, and they served for little or no money, sometimes paid merely with food or shelter, following the tradition of saints such as Santa Monica. The Sevillian painter Bartolomé Murillo represents this female ideal in the portrait *Saint Elizabeth of Hungary Healing the Sick*, which he painted for the Hospital de la Santa Caridad in the seventeenth century. In reality, the tradition of the holy healer grew in importance from the sixteenth to the seventeenth century, not so much because the city became more pious, but as a consequence of the urgent need for healers and, at the same time, through the growing number of women who needed a livelihood and asked salaries of the city.[41]

Holy healers appeared in great numbers in the chronicles and memorials of this period. In their catalogs of "illustrious sons of Seville," Arana de Varflora and Matute y Gaviria mention many nuns who were distinguished in the seventeenth century for healing the sick.[42] Sor Catalina de Nuestra Señora, for example, was noted for being especially tender with ill people, and sor Beatriz de Jesús took to her own cell sick women "so that she could

[37] Morgado, *Historia*, pp. 362–64.

[38] Mary Elizabeth Perry, "Beatas and the Inquisition in Early Modern Seville," in *Inquisition and Society in Early Modern Europe*, ed. Stephen Haliczer (London: Croom Helm, 1986), pp. 147–68. Also see chapter 5, below.

[39] AMS, Sección 3, Siglo XVI, Escribanías de Cabildo, Tomo 7, Número 17.

[40] AMS, Sección 4, Siglo XVII, Escribanías de Cabildo, Tomo 10, Número 26; Carlos Caro Petit, "La Cárcel Real de Sevilla," *Archivo Hispalense*, ser. 2, 12 (1945): 45; AMS, Archivo General, Sección 2, Archivo de Contaduría, Carpeta 13, Número 148, y Carpeta 16, Números 142 y 206.

[41] Perry, "Beatas," p. 153.

[42] Fermin Arana de Varflora, *Hijos de Sevilla ilustres en santidad, letras, armas, artes, o dignidad* (Seville: Vázquez é Hidalgo, 1791), esp. pt. I, pp. 76 and 64; pt. IV, pp. 99 and 19.

serve them with greater care." It was said that some nuns healed through miracles, like sor Tomasa de Santo Domingo, who "with making the sign of the Cross on the throat, and praying an Ave Maria completely healed" a kitchen assistant. Another holy healer, sor María de Salazar, was said to heal miraculously after her death, when a "a cloth that had absorbed the sweat" from her body was applied to a poor crippled woman, who "was instantly cured."

The papers of the Conde de Aguila in the municipal archive of Seville include descriptions of the beata madre María de Jesús, who founded the Beaterio del Pozo Santo and the Hospital del Santo Cristo de los Dolores, which cared for crippled women.[43] With the assistance of madre Beatriz de la Concepción, this beata cared in person for the sick. After her death, many "important ladies" continued her example of personally caring for and healing sick women in the hospital.

While appreciation grew for holy healers in Seville, another type of healer declined in favor. This was the wise woman or empiric who followed a long tradition of healing. Learning to heal by experience and from the advice of older wise women, these healers were noted especially for their knowledge of the healing properties of herbs. They used a medical tradition much older than that taught by doctors with a university degree. In rural districts and in neighborhoods where people lacked the money to pay a university-educated doctor, wise women played important social roles.[44]

Juan II had founded a tribunal for medical practice in 1477, and the Catholic Kings had established a *protomédico* to examine and license empirics in addition to doctors, surgeons, and pharmacists. It was another century, however, before the regulations of the protomédico were enforced. In 1593 a pragmatic of Philip II ordered salaries for more protomédicos, examiners, and inspectors. It also prohibited women from dispensing medicines.[45] Some thirty years later, the *asistente* in Seville decreed an examination for all people who dealt with medicine, including midwives.[46]

Midwifery, like many occupations of women, had a reputation both exalted and evil. In his *Libro del arte de las comadres o madrinas*, the first obstetrical text written in Castilian, Damian Carbon outlined the professional preparation and the moral qualifications that the midwife ought to have.[47]

---

[43] AMS, Sección Especial, Papeles del Señor Conde de Aguila, Libros en folio, Tomo 32, Números 1–3.

[44] Luis S. Granjel, *La medicina española del siglo XVII* (Salamanca: Ediciones Universidad de Salamanca, 1978), p. 62.

[45] AMS, Sección 3, Siglo XVI, Escribanías de Cabildo, Tomo 11, Número 78.

[46] Guichot y Parody, *Historia*, 2: 213.

[47] Damian Carbon, *Libro del arte de las comadres o madrinas y del regimiento de las preñadas y paridas y de los niños* (Majorca?: n.p., 1541). See also Granjel, *Renacentista*, p. 136, and María del Carmen Simón Palmer, "La higiene y la medicina de la mujer española a través de los libros (s. XVI a XIX)," in *La mujer en la historia de España (siglos XVI–XX)*, ed. María Angeles

Not only must this woman be an expert in her art; she should also be ingenious, moderate, well-behaved, good-humored, honorable, chaste, God-fearing, devoted to the Virgin Mary, and, finally, she should have a good complexion. However, Carbon, like so many men, acknowledged a mysterious and potentially threatening female world in his prescriptions for midwives. The midwife, after all, presided over the rites of birth, which must have seemed very magical in this period when most people had little scientific knowledge of human reproduction. She seemed to know the secrets of women's bodies and how to ensure life or death at the time of birth. Carbon asserts that the "most essential" quality of the ideal midwife is that she should be secretive because she sees so many things that she should not tell others "for shame and the damage that would result."[48] He advises that "for honesty," birth should be left "in the power of women."[49] Only when it was necessary to extract the fetus in pieces was a man called, preferably a surgeon and not a physician.

Many officials in the sixteenth and seventeenth centuries wanted a stricter rule for midwives, perhaps because birth usually remained in the hands of women. In 1538 and also in 1558, it was requested in the *cortes* that midwives be examined by "the justice or government of the . . . cities or villages where they would practice their offices, taking with them for the said examination two doctors of science and experience, who finding them competent will license them to perform the said offices, and that without it they cannot perform them, [without incurring] penalties, nor can the justices consent to it."[50]

Licensing was necessary not simply because midwives could be ignorant, but also because it was believed that they used sorcery and promoted immorality. Francisco Santos, for example, complained that midwives sheltered in their houses many women, not because they were poor, but because "past pleasures" had made them leave their own homes.[51] In his *Coplas de las comadres*, Rodrigo de Reinoso denounced the sorcery practices associated with midwives. Carbon warned his readers to beware of midwives who are old and mutter incantations.[52] Some associated midwives with the immorality and sorcery of *La Celestina*. It was believed that women in the actual world, just as in that of literature, learned from these

---

Durán, *Actas de las Segundas Jornadas de Investigación Interdisciplinaria* (Madrid: Universidad Autónoma, 1984), pp. 82–83.

[48] Carbon, *Libro*, p. iv.

[49] Ibid. Also see Juan Luis Morales, *El niño en la cultura española* (Madrid: Talleres Penitenciarios de Alcalá de Henares, 1960), p. 117, esp.

[50] In Granjel, *Renacentista*, p. 136.

[51] Francisco Santos, *Día y noche de Madrid*, discussed in Granjel, *Siglo XVII*, p. 64.

[52] Carbon, *Libro*, p. xxxviii.

midwives a medicine of contraception and abortion.[53] The sin of the midwives, then, was not their ignorance in matters of giving birth, but their knowledge, which seemed so close to magic and could facilitate illicit sex.

Morisca midwives were especially subject to suspicion. Christians believed that moriscos had a dissolute sexual tradition and also that moriscas contaminated infants at birth. In Granada, a regulation of 1565 ordered that "New Christian women in a parish or place where there was an Old Christian midwife not give birth with a New Christian nor of their generation."[54] During the persecution of moriscos, the reputation of Islamic medicine declined and came to be considered the practice of quacks. Moriscas such as María de Luna, imprisoned by the Inquisition in Cuenca, knew a great deal about medicine and taught it to their sons and neighbors who acted as doctors in the villages where there were no licenses.[55] Inquisitors in Seville asked Ynés Yzquierda, the wife of a morisco, about a book that she said a Moor had given her "for remedy of her illnesses . . . and with [which she] would heal and take away all illnesses."[56] When she had cured two women "very sick to the death," Ynés Yzquierda had asked for sheets, shirts, head-coverings, and warm water, but according to her these were to prepare the bodies for death. She had not even attempted to cure them, she said, much less to use sorcery or instructions from the book.

Moriscas practiced a medicine that appeared very similar to magic, curing through water baths and burning an article of clothing of the sick person. They also used fumigations that were closely connected with a demoniacal concept of illness. Moriscas believed not only that the fumigations created a suffocating atmosphere for demons, but also that the vapors of vegetable remedies could cure illnesses.[57] They projected curative power into an object such as an amulet or into certain secretions such as the healer's saliva.

The Inquisition took a great interest in these medical practices because it saw them as proof of heresy and sorcery. Wanting to preserve an orthodox Scholastic Christianity, inquisitors attacked devil beliefs in morisco culture and also the medical practices of moriscas.[58] Thus, inquisitors converted Islamic medicine into a persecuted tradition, investigating offensive

---

[53] Granjel, *Renacentista*, p. 140. For an example, see Francisco Delicado, *La Lozana andaluza* (1528) (Madrid: Editorial Castalia, 1969).

[54] In Luis García Ballester, *Los moriscos y la medicina: Un capítulo de la medicina y la ciencia marginadas en la España del siglo XVI* (Barcelona: Editorial Labor, 1984), p. 116.

[55] See the case of Roman Ramírez before the Inquisition in Cuenca, discussed in García Ballester, *Moriscos*, p. 82.

[56] AHN, Inquisición, Legajo 2075, Número 15.

[57] García Ballester, *Moriscos*, pp. 121–22. For a doctor who also believed in fumigations, although not for their power against demons, see Juan Alonso y de los Ruizes de Fontecha, *Diez previlegios de preñadas* (Valladolid: n.p., 1606), pp. 228ʳ–229.

[58] García Ballester, *Moriscos*, p. 143.

practices not only among moriscos, but also among Old Christians. They found them especially among women of the villages and rural areas around Seville.

Bárbara María del Espíritu Santo, for example, was a professed nun in the convent of the Nombre de Jesús in Jérez de la Frontera. Accused in 1624 of having made herself "spiritual mistress" of spiritual sons and daughters and clerics "who kissed her hand that she gave to them with much vainglory," she was also accused of following the heretical sect of the *alumbrados*.[59] Witnesses testified that she "gave them to understand that she had the gift of healing" and "cured some people, placing her hands on their pains and speaking some words between her teeth." Other women who had cured the ill did not concern inquisitors, but Bárbara María had presumed to be a "spiritual mistress," inverting the acceptable sexual order. Evidently, it was permissible for a woman to heal the sick, but not that she be seen with magical power.

Women who carried out healing work had to take care not to disturb the religious monopoly of clerics. Many wise women healed with a combination of prayers, invocations, and herbs. Male doctors used very similar practices, and many still believed in a medicine of miracles. In his *Fábrica universal*, the doctor Salvador Ardevines, for example, wrote of "illnesses and plagues, not having natural causes, neither can demons make them by their own virtue, but as instruments of God, or through divine will and permission." Thus, he concluded, "the prudent and good doctors will first attend to God, and will confess and supplicate that God withdraw his wrath and punishment."[60]

In the sixteenth and seventeenth centuries, physicians as well as healers believed in *aojamiento*, or illness caused by cursing. Pero Mexía warned of "persons, men and women, who have poison in their eyes, and who with looking at something intensely, visible rays intervening, inflict and make notable damage that is called aojar, especially in children."[61] Martín de Castañega explained the aojamiento as the expulsion of impurities from the body through the eyes and noted especially the woman who, "being with her [menstrual] flow," looks at a new clean mirror and "fills it with specks and rays that leave from her eyes."[62]

Given the beliefs of both groups, the practices of midwives do not appear any more superstitious than those of learned men such as Gregorio López, who recommended that mothers in labor place parsley in the mouth or on the thigh when the infant is crosswise in the womb and can-

---

[59] AHN, Inquisición, Legajo 2075, Número 31.
[60] Granjel has cited this book, published in 1621, in *Siglo XVII*, p. 116.
[61] Cited in Granjel, *Renacentista*, pp. 142–43.
[62] Quoted in Granjel, *Renacentista*, p. 143.

not enter the birth canal.[63] In his book that was reprinted many times in the seventeenth century, this doctor also prescribed sage and egg for the woman who could not conceive, but he warned that the recipe was dangerous for women of "warm temperaments." Women's medicine, just like that of learned men, included beliefs that we would consider superstitious, but in Seville officials punished only women for blasphemous or superstitious healing. While men, in published books, declared their medical practices official, the healing work of women was considered a potential danger that required special control. In the second half of the sixteenth century, this control grew with an intensified effort to enclose nuns, beatas, prostitutes, and married women.[64]

The Inquisition provided a very convenient forum for discrediting many female healers. Their practices of combining prayers with remedies caught the suspicions of inquisitors. Many men and women denounced them to the Holy Office, resentful of their demands for payment, or fearful of their powers. Diabolical beliefs that penetrated an official mentality as well as a popular tradition affected the work of women in particular because it was believed that women were most vulnerable to seduction by the devil.[65]

An Inquisition case of 1648 against four women accused of sorcery illustrates official male anxieties and also a female world of tradition and experience.[66] Three years earlier, the four women, who all came from the village of Ayamonte, outside Seville, were taken into custody by inquisitors. Six witnesses declared that one of them, the ninety-seven-year-old Ana Linda, "was a sorceress and that she taught other people certain prayers that they had to say after the stars faded so they could marry the persons they loved. . . . And that she also said certain prayers so that lost things would appear and sick people be healed and that when it did not work, she invoked demons, the moon, and the stars and the sea with which she stirred up the republic and scandalized the place." Ana Linda confessed that she had not invoked demons, but the Holy Trinity, and also that she healed the "mal de Rosa," that is, pellagra. She said other prayers for "males de ojo" and for sores, invoking the Holy Trinity and the Mother of God, and "she always said each one for the effect of healing the ill."

[63] López, *Tesoro*, p. 100. For the following quotation, see pp. 35–36. See also his book cited in Granjel, *Siglo XVII*, p. 113.

[64] Mary Elizabeth Perry, "Deviant Insiders: Legalized Prostitutes and a Consciousness of Women in Early Modern Seville," *Comparative Studies in Society and History* 27, no. 1 (1985): 138–58. See also chapter 7, below.

[65] Lingo, "Empirics," p. 594, discusses this mentality in France in the same period. Note that the Inquisition punished males for superstitious practices in other parts of Spain, but I have found no cases of male healers penanced by the tribunal in Seville.

[66] AHN, Inquisición, Legajo 2075, Número 38. Also see Sánchez Ortega, "La mujer en el antiguo régimen," pp. 111–12, for a discussion of women accused of witchcraft and sorcery before the Inquisition.

Whether holy healer or diabolical sorceress, Ana Linda represents a mixture of healing, sorcery, love magic, and the belief in supernatural powers, a combination that was common in this period. Perhaps she and others like her represented a female network whose power appeared to be growing; what is certain is that they represented a form of popular culture that witnesses considered diabolical and which inquisitors treated as superstition, blasphemy, or sorcery. Although they declared that they cured "el mal de madre" and "males del ojo," these women nevertheless confessed that they used remedies such as the hair of their husbands. It is not surprising, then, that they were sentenced to be penanced for sorcery in a public auto de fe and that they were exiled from Ayamonte, Seville, and Madrid.[67] Popular beliefs of this period indicate that ordinary people tried to enhance or control the sexuality of others through rather ordinary means. According to one proverb, for example, carrots that benefited the kidneys, stomach, and appetite were also credited with reminding the consumer of "madonna Venus."[68]

Women who combined healing with magic were condemned not only by male officials, but also by the people from rural areas who testified against them and by learned women, such as Luisa de Padilla, condesa de Aranda. Recognized by Manuel Serrano y Sanz as a most notable writer of the seventeenth century, the countess considered cures, magic, and witchcraft in her *Elogios de la verdad e invectiva contra la mentira*.[69] She warned in particular against sorcerers and magicians whom she described as "soldiers of the demon, and no less enemies of human nature than of the Truth." Crediting the Inquisition with protecting Spain, she said that in other parts of the world curses and spells kill almost as many people as illnesses do. Inquisitors had uncovered six thousand witches in Vizcaya and Guipúzcoa, she noted, and one woman in a small village who confessed that she had killed eight hundred people through evil magic. Moreover, the Inquisition of Zaragoza had punished a man who by himself had bewitched two hundred women in one mountain village and five hundred in another. Evil magic was to blame, according to Padilla, for "separating married couples, causing hatred among many, causing pregnant women to have miscarriages, and drying up the milk of nursing mothers." Yet inquisitors defused the power of those accused of witchcraft, defining their transgressions as blasphemy or ignorant heresy.[70]

---

[67] AHN, Inquisición, Legajo 2075, esp. Números 34 and 38.

[68] Sorapan, *Medicina*, p. 287.

[69] In Manuel Serrano y Sanz, *Apuntes para una biblioteca de escritoras españolas desde el año 1401 al 1833*, vols. 268, 269, 270, 271 of *Biblioteca de Autores Españoles* (Madrid: Atlas, 1975), 270: 107–13. Quotations are found on pp. 109 and 110.

[70] Gustav Henningsen, *The Witches' Advocate: Basque Witchcraft and the Spanish Inquisition*

As professions developed in the late sixteenth and seventeenth centuries, women's work became less the accomplishment of their own hands and more the subject of male regulation. This is clearly evident in the practice of medicine, which changed from a female world to a sphere dominated by men. If the work of healing continued as a domestic task of women in the home, the hospital, and the prison, it received positive recognition only when it was carried out with submission and obedience by women who were not paid.[71] From Inquisition prosecution of some female healers, women learned to doubt their healing tradition. They came to depend on male doctors, taking a subservient place in the developing modern patriarchy.[72] Praised as the care-giving sex, woman was confirmed as the emotional sex, clearly distinct from the sex gifted with reason.[73] Securely alienated from sites of public power, the healing work of women was seen as a labor different from that of the male doctor. Their value unrecognized and often unremunerated, women healers were carefully protected from arrogant pretensions. Thus, they formed part of a social structure in which a hierarchical order was established. Topped by male doctors and learned men, it relegated the women below, according to perceptions of their power, into the categories of sorcerer or saint.

(Reno: University of Nevada Press, 1980); and María Palacios Alcalde, "Hechicería e Inquisición en Andalucía," *Codice* 2 (1987): 43–65.

[71] See, for example, the midwife doña Ana, who founded a hospital in 1698, in AMS, Sección Especial, Papeles del Señor Conde de Aguila, Libros en folio, Tomo 32, Número 1. It should be noted that Michel Foucault's thesis of "the great confinement" can be applied to the work of women, who appeared to become more suspect and dangerous.

[72] Sánchez Ortega, "Antiguo régimen," p. 110; idem, "La mujer, el amor y la religión en el antiguo régimen," in Durán, *La mujer en la historia de España*, pp. 35–58.

[73] See this theme in Susan Griffin, *Pornography and Silence* (New York: Harper and Row, 1981); Carolyn Merchant, *The Death of Nature: Women, Ecology and the Scientific Revolution* (San Francisco: Harper and Row, 1980); and also in Ortner, "Is Female to Male as Nature Is to Culture?"

Chapter 2

VIRGINS, MARTYRS, AND THE NECESSARY EVIL

THE PRACTICAL ROLES of women in early modern Seville required them to participate actively in both public and private events of the city, but their symbolic roles became more restrictive especially after the mid-sixteenth century and served to diminish the significance of this participation. The most powerful symbols and legends that prescribed gender ideals for women came from religion: Mary, the Virgin Mother, and Justa and Rufina, the sister martyrs (see fig. 4). Praised in ballads and extolled in legend, Justa and Rufina became "the most principal patronesses" of Seville and the inspiration for countless churches, confraternities, convents, hospitals, chapels, and altars throughout the Iberian Peninsula.[1] Mary, the Virgin Mother, developed into a crucial link between God the Father and his mortal children. In Seville she was especially revered as Our Lady of Antiquity, a statue believed to have resided here from the Gothic period. Although the Virgin and the sister martyrs prescribed gender ideals that were considered universal and timeless, these symbols actually underwent significant historical change.[2]

In the third century, when Seville was known as Hispalis in the Roman province of Betis, Justa and Rufina had lived in Triana, a section of the city across the Guadalquivir River.[3] Archaeological remains corroborate their historical existence, which otherwise can be glimpsed only in legends and ballads. Such information must be used carefully as historical evidence, for it reveals more about perceptions of the sister martyrs than about their actual existence. Moreover, these perceptions change as needs develop for particular legends, especially stories of women that exalt their strength, constancy, purity, or obedience.

According to the legend common in the sixteenth century, Justa and Rufina were born to devoutly Christian parents who taught them to care for the ill and afflicted. The sisters, who supported themselves by selling earthenware in the public market, gave to the poor any profits that they did not need. One day when they had taken their earthenware to the mar-

---

[1] Arana de Varflora, *Hijos*, pt. 3, pp. 67–69.

[2] For the significance of gender symbols, see Scott, "Gender," pp. 1067–69. Morgado, *Historia*, describes Our Lady of Antiquity on pp. 350–51.

[3] Antonio Blanco Freijeiro, *La ciudad antigua de la prehistoria a los visigodos*, vol. 1 of *Historia de Sevilla* (Seville: Universidad de Sevilla, 1979), p. 105. See also Juan de Mata Carriazo, *Protohistoria de Sevilla en el vértice de Tartesos* (Seville: Guadalquivir Ediciones, 1980).

FIGURE 4. *Saint Justa and Saint Rufina with Giralda*, by Bartolomé Murillo (Museo de Bellas Artes, Seville).

ket, a procession of "infidels" came by, carrying a statue of Salambona, as the Syrians called Venus.[4] The infidels demanded that the sisters pay homage to the idol, giving them either alms or a lamp to light before it, but Justa and Rufina refused. They replied that they worshiped the one God who was maker of all and source of all goodness. Moreover, they added, the idol lacked life, virtue, and power, and they abhorred it with all their heart. Angrily, the infidels turned on the sisters and broke their earthenware vessels. Justa and Rufina quickly retaliated, seizing the statue and hurling it to the ground, where it broke into many small pieces.

The outraged infidels dragged the sisters before Diogenian, the Roman ruler of the province. Accusing Justa and Rufina of blaspheming their goddess and smashing their statue, they demanded that the sisters provide formal satisfaction. Diogenian tried to persuade the sisters to acknowledge and pay compensation for their wrongdoing, but Justa and Rufina refused and mocked the infidels. In addition, they proudly confessed their Christian faith and said that they were not afraid to die for it.

Infuriated, the Roman official determined to break their pride. He ordered several forms of torture. Even pulling off their fingernails and toenails and suspending them from poles, however, could not shake their declarations of faith. He ordered them chained in an underground prison without food or water, but Jesus appeared to them and gave them water from a well that legend says remains at this site, beneath the Church of the Most Holy Trinity. Diogenian next ordered them taken by foot and without shoes to the Sierra Morena. The sisters survived ice and snow and rocks, and they persisted in their asseverations of Christian faith. Imprisoned again, they received visits and consolation from Jesus and the angels. However, Justa died in prison on July 17, the date that would later become the feast day of the holy sisters. Her death, signaled by an earthquake, left Rufina alone to maintain her faith bravely, even when she was turned over to a lion in the city amphitheater. The lion was so impressed with her courage and piety that he bowed to her and would not touch her. Here, according to legend, the heathen finally beat her to death and burned her body.

The ashes and bones of Justa and Rufina became highly venerated relics in Seville. Although the body of Justa had been thrown down a well, the bishop of Seville later had it recovered and buried with Rufina's ashes in a cemetery that came to be called the Prado de Justa y Rufina. The devout

---

[4] Note that legends of Justa and Rufina vary in details. See AMS, Sección Especial, Papeles del Señor Conde de Aguila, Libros en folio, Tomo 60, Números 1 and 5; Luis de Peraza, *Vida de Santa Justa y Santa Rufina, vírgenes y mártires de Sevilla*, BC 83–7–6; Walter M. Gallichan, *The Story of Seville* (London: J. M. Dent, 1903), pp. 196–98; Blanco Freijeiro, *Ciudad*, pp. 167–69; and Arana de Varflora, *Hijos*, pt. 3, pp. 64–69.

placed wooden crosses here where "great celestial marvels" had been seen.[5] Earth from the Prado was said to have shed blood when held in the hands of the pope. San Isidoro revealed before he died in the seventh century that God did not want the relics of these saintly virgins to leave the city; rather, they were to remain in Seville to defend and guard it.

Stories and relics of the sister martyrs inspired Christian warriors who attempted to regain the city after it had fallen under Muslim rule. During the thirteenth century, legends of Justa and Rufina transformed the campaign under Ferdinand III from a secular power struggle into a holy crusade against the infidel. Feliciana Enríquez de Guzmán, who wrote poetry in Seville, described the glorious achievement of Ferdinand III in not only "liberating" the city from Muslim rule, but in seeking the "holy bodies" of Justa and Rufina.[6]

After Ferdinand III delivered Seville from its Muslim rulers in the thirteenth century, he dedicated a magnificent church and monastery on the site of the prison of Justa and Rufina. A rock in the crypt of this church is said to be the place where the sisters were scourged. The city's senate also erected a hermitage in their honor just outside the Córdoba gate, and a new church was built and named for them. An ancient brotherhood dedicated to venerating Justa and Rufina carried images of them in Corpus Christi processions. Christians all over Spain celebrated their feast day on July 17, but especially in Seville where the sisters were remembered with sermons and "great solemnity."[7] According to Alonso Morgado, who wrote a history of Seville in the late sixteenth century, Justa and Rufina provided infinite mercies because "our Lord works in this city through their intercession and patronage. Through which all its citizens confess they are very obliged to these glorious sisters."[8] He added that Spain's monarchs had also received special favors from God, who, through the intercession of Justa and Rufina, gave them victories against their enemies.

Clearly identified with both the Christian faith and the city of Seville, Justa and Rufina became significant symbols of local pride and religious strength. Their sacrifice served to explain the higher purpose of religious fidelity for early Christians who had to live with persecution. Both men and women could emulate the brave piety of the martyred sisters, but women, in particular, would find in Justa and Rufina examples of female

[5] Morgado, *Historia*, pp. 33–34.

[6] Feliciana Enríquez de Guzmán, "Censura de las antiguas comedias españolas," in *Biblioteca de Autores Españoles* (Madrid: M. Rivadeneyra, 1855), 42: 545.

[7] Arana de Varflora, *Hijos*, pt. 3, p. 67. Celebrations of Justa and Rufina gradually disappeared in other cities after the end of the sixteenth century, but in Seville the archbishop was still offering indulgences for those who kept this feast day in 1656. See AMS, Sección Especial, Papeles del Señor Conde de Aguila, Libros en folio, Tomo 60, Números 1 and 15.

[8] Morgado, *Historia*, p. 29.

heroines who transformed passive obedience into an acceptable defiance of established authorities. As one contemporary scholar has noted, the "moral toughness" of virgin martyrs resembled very clearly the strength and tenacity expected of male warriors.[9] It was in death, however, that the virgin martyrs had their greatest effect; and they changed the world not through their own actions, but through the men they inspired to act and the women who saw in their example that dying was the one form of heroism in which women did not have to challenge the gender order.[10] Moreover, women could learn from stories of Justa and Rufina to discount their bodies and their physical suffering.

The legends of Justa and Rufina show how women could best express passion and yearning. Women of wealth and status could dedicate their lives to God, using holy martyrdom as a strategy to become heroic "respectably" without challenging a gender order that valued female passivity, obedience, piety, and chastity.[11] Poorer women could look to the martyred sisters to infuse meaning into their own endurance of pain, sorrow, and suffering. In either case, Justa and Rufina provided a model for what one literary scholar has described as "a feminine mode of negative self-assertion," one of the few forms of self-assertion considered appropriate for women.[12]

Mary, the mother of Jesus, provided another model for women in Counter-Reformation Spain. Not even negatively self-assertive, Mary in the sixteenth and seventeenth centuries had become a passive, asexual figure of compassion, far different from earlier versions of this symbol. Some scholars believe that veneration of Mary developed out of earlier mother-goddess worship.[13] The Christian religion had to displace already existing gods and goddesses, a process that was facilitated when earlier deities could be transmuted into Christian forms. During the first few centuries of Christian development, martyrs provided these replacements. It is no accident that the legend of Justa and Rufina includes pagans worshiping Venus, whose image the sainted sisters broke. Later, as the Christian religion won official recognition, ascetics more often than martyrs replaced former

[9] Simon Shepherd, *Amazons and Warrior Women: Varieties of Feminism in Seventeenth-Century Drama* (Brighton: Harvester, 1981), p. 2.

[10] Shepherd, *Amazons*, p. 201; and Mary Ellen Lamb, "The Countess of Pembroke and the Art of Dying," in *Women in the Middle Ages and the Renaissance: Literary and Historical Perspectives*, ed. Mary Beth Rose (Syracuse: Syracuse University Press, 1986), p. 209.

[11] See Lamb, "Countess," pp. 207–26, for a unique example of a learned woman whose translations of literary works about dying became her own strategy for dealing with the heroic.

[12] Mary Beth Rose, "Gender, Genre, and History: Seventeenth-Century English Women and the Art of Autobiography," in *Women in the Middle Ages and the Renaissance*, p. 267.

[13] See, for example, Geoffrey Ashe, *The Virgin* (London: Routledge and Kegan Paul, 1976), pp. 7–32.

deities. For a religion based upon a male God and his Son, Mary provided the single most powerful female symbol that could supersede pagan goddesses. By the fifth century, she had been elevated to "Mother of God," and she was often portrayed seated in heaven, crowned by her Son at whose side she sat.[14]

Mariolatry appeared even stronger in the thirteenth century. The Queen of Heaven had become Our Lady, recipient of millions of prayers from the devout who believed that she alone could represent them before God. As intercessor, Mary did not simply sit on a heavenly throne; she intervened directly in the lives of mortal men and women. Moreover, she bore the fame of centuries of miracle making as the much loved Our Lady of Antiquity, the statue believed to have been in Seville since the time of the Goths and remaining here even during the period of Muslim rule.[15]

This active and heroic Mary appears very clearly in one of the most significant documents of the thirteenth century. Alfonso X, who ruled Castile in the later thirteenth century, wrote his *Cantigas de Santa María* to celebrate the miraculous adventures of the Virgin Mother. In this beautifully illuminated manuscript, which one modern scholar has called a "literary-musical monument," Alfonso sang praises not to a remote and passive saint, but to a thoughtful, clever, and innovative Virgin who directly intervened in earthly affairs to rescue an assortment of human beings.[16] The fourth cantiga, for example, described Mary's action to save a young boy who had been cast into an oven by his Jewish father for saying that he had taken the Christian communion. She saved a man condemned to hang, in another cantiga, supporting his feet as he hung by the neck until he could escape by climbing down the tree that had been his gallows. A nun who ran away from her convent repented and returned, to find that the Holy Virgin had quietly replaced her so that no one would miss her during her absence. And a foolish abbess who became pregnant prayed to Mary, who took the child from her as she slept and left a miraculous mark on her body to confound her accusers.

Seville had its own very active image of Mary. In the early fifteenth century, a noble lady and nobleman exchanged pledges of betrothal before the image of Our Lady of Merced. He, indulging his "carnal appetite," as the chronicle reports, refused to marry her, denying that he had ever promised marriage. When she told her story to a judge, he realized that the only witness to their betrothal was the image of Our Lady of Merced. Taking

[14] Manuel Trens, *María: Iconografía de la virgen en el arte español* (Madrid: Editorial Plus Ultra, 1946), pp. 397–413, discusses this Romanesque image of Mary enthroned.

[15] Morgado, *Historia*, pp. 350–51.

[16] *El 'códice rico' de las Cantigas de Alfonso X el Sabio* (Madrid: Edilan, 1979), p. 9. This is a very fine facsimile of the original manuscript and includes an introduction, comments, and glosses on the cantigas.

in tow the lady, the man, and, "at such a strange novelty, an innumerable crowd," the judge went to the convent that housed the image. There the lady addressed the image with sobs and entreaties. The head of the image then lowered, as though nodding in agreement with the woman. "Full of reverent fear," the nobleman confessed the truth, begged the pardon of Our Lady of Merced, and promptly carried out his promise of marriage, exchanging matrimonial vows before the image.[17]

In the fifteenth century enthusiasm grew for the belief that Mary had been born without stain of original sin. Franciscans promoted this belief, while Dominicans opposed it with the argument of Thomas Aquinas that the universality of redemption meant that Mary, too, had to be redeemed from sin.[18] While the controversy triggered theological debates throughout the sixteenth century and into the seventeenth, it also embroiled ordinary people who seized the symbol of Immaculate Mary as a cause to defend, even to the death. Boys stoned a Trinitarian in 1613, mistaking him for a Dominican, in the wake of a sermon against belief in the Immaculate Conception. In 1615 members of the Cofradía de Nuestro Padre Jesús Nazareno, Santa Cruz en Jerusalén, y María Santísima de la Concepción vowed to defend belief in the Immaculate Conception, "even to giving the life for it," with a fervor reminiscent of chivalric vows to protect the honor of a lady.[19]

The Holy Virgin of the sixteenth and seventeenth centuries appeared more often as an obedient girl or passively sorrowing mother than as the actively ingenious Mary of the *Cantigas*. Portrayed as the Immaculate Conception, Mary stood with the folded hands of a pure, obedient young girl, untouched not only by mortal sin, but by mortal activity, as well.[20] Figure 5 presents one of the many paintings in which Bartolomé Murillo depicted Mary as the pure Immaculate Conception.

The sorrow of Mary, which received increasing emphasis in the art and literature of this period, added a special poignancy to the purity and obedience of this female figure. Following her marriage as a modest maiden, Mary became the sorrowing mother, the mater dolorosa portrayed by many artists in the seventeenth century, such as the sculptor Pedro Roldán, whose *Sorrowful Image of the Most Holy Virgin* shows her with hands crossed, head raised and eyes fixed on heaven, with seven knives in her

[17] AMS, Efemérides, cuadro 2.

[18] Nancy Mayberry, "The Controversy over the Immaculate Conception in Fifteenth-Century Art, Literature and Society" (unpublished manuscript, 1989).

[19] José Bermejo y Carballo, *Glorias religiosas de Sevilla o noticia histórico-descriptiva de todas las cofradías de penitencia, sangre y luz fundadas en esta ciudad* (Seville: Salvador, 1882), pp. 59 and 202–3.

[20] Francisco Pacheco, *Arte de la pintura* (Sevilla: Simon Faxardo, 1649), pp. 482–484, discusses the manner in which painters should portray Mary as the Immaculate Conception.

FIGURE 5. *The Immaculate Conception of Escorial*, by Bartolomé Murillo (Museo del Prado, Madrid).

breast to represent "the affliction, the anguish, the pain most sharp."[21] Murillo's painting of the sorrowing mother appears in figure 6. Pain became purity in this image: the symbols of virgin and martyr merged in Mary, sanctifying the martyrdom idealized for women.

In this period long before development of mass media, religious symbols functioned as a common language recognized by most people as representing widely held beliefs and attitudes. Moreover, they acted to shape reality, setting expectations and interpreting reality in terms of these expectations.[22] During the sixteenth century, the Holy Virgin appeared in many books as a model for women. Writers such as Juan Luis Vives urged women to emulate the chastity, industry, silence, compassion, and obedience of Mary.[23] No mortal woman could truly attain such perfection as Mary, however, particularly in light of the belief that she herself was conceived without stain of original sin. Mary thus came to symbolize difference from mortal women, an Other to be venerated but also to remind women of their imperfection.

Earlier representations of Mary had shown her pregnant or nursing her Child, but in the sixteenth and seventeenth centuries she more often appeared as innocent maiden or sorrowing mother. Only a few, such as sculptor Luisa Roldán, portrayed her as an earthly mother with child.[24] Francisco Pacheco, who wrote a treatise on the careful illustration of theology in the seventeenth century, advised artists to depict her as the Immaculate Conception "not only . . . without the Child in her arms, but even without having given birth."[25] Suspended between heaven and earth, her feet on the moon, Immaculate Mary presented the antithesis of earthy, carnal Eve. As an idealization of female purity, Mary denied the sexuality of woman and promoted the belief that it was dangerous and sinful.

Ritual provided a way to celebrate Mary's difference and also to pro-

---

[21] Bermejo y Carballo, *Glorias*, p. 225.

[22] Carmelo Lisón Tolosana, *Invitación a la antropología cultural de España* (Madrid: Editorial Adara, 1977), p. 156, describes an "anthropology of perception" which studies the ways that beliefs culturally define reality.

[23] There are many examples, including Juan Luis Vives, *A Very Frvtfvl and pleasant boke called the Instruction of a christen woman, made fyrst in latyne, by the right famous clerk mayster, Lewes Vives, and tourned out of latyne into Englishe by Richard Hyrde* (London: Thomas Berthe, 1547), p. 15. I wish to acknowledge the kind permission of the Huntington Library to read this and many other volumes in the collection of Renaissance literature.

[24] María Victoria García Olloqui, *La Roldana: Escultora de Cámara* (Seville: Diputación Provincial de Sevilla, 1977), pp. 59–63, lists several works of this daughter of sculptor Pedro de Roldán that depict the Virgin with Child, feeding her child and giving birth.

[25] Pacheco, *Arte*, p. 482. Valentina Fernández Vargas and María Victoria López-Cordón Cortezo, "Mujer y régimen jurídico en el antiguo régimen: Una realidad disociada," in *Ordenamiento jurídico y realidad social de las mujeres*, ed. María Carmen García-Nieto París, Actas de las Cuartas Jornadas de Investigación Interdisciplinaria. (Madrid: Universidad Autónoma, 1986), p. 17.

FIGURE 6. *Virgin of Sorrows* (detail), by Bartolomé Murillo (Museo del Prado, Madrid).

claim human bonds with her. Anthropologist Carmelo Lisón Tolosana describes a mediating function of rituals, especially those of separation and integration.[26] Coming together to say the Rosary, to kiss the hands of images of Mary, or to present the stately sixteenth-century dance of the "Seises" before the high altar of the cathedral on the Feast of the Immaculate Conception, people of Seville overcame their differences and celebrated the special status of Mary even as they renewed their love and respect for her.

Confraternities, which especially proliferated after the mid-sixteenth century, venerated particular images that they carried in processions for feast days and Holy Week. Each of the confraternities established in Seville in this period had an image of Mary, but each had its own identity even though almost all of them represented Mary as the sorrowing mother. The seemingly endless variations of Mary functioned to allow each parish or confraternity to maintain its own separate identity while participating in a larger veneration of this figure.[27]

Anthropologist William Christian, who studied historical records of religious practices in Spain, has suggested that Mary and Jesus became symbols of cultural unity to replace the great diversity of local saints and extend Christianity into rural areas during the Reconquest.[28] Noting that patterns of venerating saints and icons changed along with a centralizing church and a developing state, Christian has emphasized the political function of religious symbols. Particularly appropriate for people dependent on agricultural success, the symbol of Mother and Child represented fertility and nurturing, or maternal protection.

By the late sixteenth century, when Seville had to import food to feed its people, the image of Mary less frequently appeared as a fertility symbol. The greater emphasis on her as an innocent maiden or protective mother seems to reflect a need for social control, a concern for order that rested squarely on gender prescriptions. A city undergoing great growth and change looked to its men to be loyal and its women to be obedient and sympathetic. The image of Mary as Our Lady of the Kings led processions when Seville suffered a drought in 1605, floods and dearth in 1626, and an epidemic in 1649. When rebellions broke out in nearby Portugal in 1640, Philip IV designated Seville's Our Lady of Antiquity as protector for his troops.[29]

[26] Lisón Tolosana, *Invitación*, p. 98.

[27] William A. Christian, Jr., *Local Religion in Sixteenth-Century Spain* (Princeton: Princeton University Press, 1981), p. 150.

[28] William A. Christian, Jr., "De los Santos a María: Panorama de las devociones a santuarios españoles desde el principio de la Edad Media hasta nuestros días," in *Temas de antropología española*, ed. Carmelo Lisón Tolosana (Madrid: Akal, 1976), pp. 60–66.

[29] Ortiz de Zuñiga, *Anales*, 4: 215, 316, 369–70, and 413–15.

Religious beliefs invigorated the impact of virgins and martyrs as gender symbols, for the people of Seville did not restrict religion to learned theological discussions, nor did they keep it within the walls of a parish church, carefully restricted to Sundays and feast days. In Seville, a city as noted for its piety as for its crime, religion functioned publicly and daily as a symbolic framework within which men and women could explain their lives and judge their neighbors. Religion provided not only a common symbolic language for these people; it also reassured them that a social order built upon the rock of true religion would withstand the storms and strains of social change. During Seville's rapid demographic and commercial changes of the sixteenth and seventeenth centuries, religion took on special significance for sanctifying gender definitions and preserving a social order in which gender expectations bridged the gaps between classes and differences between generations. Regardless of age or socioeconomic status, to be female in this city meant conformity to social expectations as a "good woman" or nonconformity as a "wicked woman."

Virgins and martyrs provided a standard of female perfection by which women were judged. Obviously, few mortal women could attain such perfection; and in this sense all women were deviants. Some were more deviant than others, however. Prostitutes, in particular, were not seen as simply falling short of female perfection; they represented a betrayal of the good that woman could be and the ultimate in female depravity. They broke not only the taboo against sexually active unmarried women, but also a taboo against women who made money from their sexuality. Unregulated, they appropriated the public space of the streets, an act of tremendous potential for subverting the social order.[30] Legalized prostitution defused the danger of women who claimed public space and broke taboos, and it thus permitted the toleration of regulated prostitution as a necessary evil. Contrasting these women with the purity of the Holy Virgin, legalized prostitution safely contained them in brothels and symbolically transformed their commerce into a version of the female self-sacrifice so exalted in the martyr-saints.

Over many centuries the prostitute had developed as a gender symbol along with virgins and martyrs. Concubines and "dishonest women" threatened the salvation of men such as Saint Jerome, whose temptations appear in female form in the painting by Juan de Valdés Leal in figure 7. These women also endangered social order to such a degree that they had been the subject of an entire section in city ordinances from the fourteenth century.[31] Prohibiting them from dressing as "honest women," the ordi-

---

[30] Angelina Puig and Nuria Tuset, "La prostitución en Mallorca (s. XVI): El estado un alcahuete?" in García-Nieto París, *Ordenamiento jurídico*, p. 74.

[31] AMS, *Ordenanzas*, fols. 63ʳ–64.

FIGURE 7. *The Temptation of Saint Jerome*, by Juan de Valdés Leal (Museo de Bellas Artes, Seville).

nances decreed that women "who do not want to be good and chaste, and want to sell their bodies" should be placed in the public brothel where they could be carefully regulated. Here women could be watched more closely than in the "monasteries of evil women, who use their bodies for evil in the sin of lust, and who have a director, in the manner of an abbess" and "carry out their lusts and evils, more covertly than in the public brothels."[32]

Religion and prostitution shared more connections in Counter-Reformation Spain than the use of the words *abbess* and *monasteries*. Close beside the prostitute, in fact, stood the Holy Virgin and female martyrs, an unlikely group that seems to contradict the moral condemnation of prostitution and official efforts to separate the sacred from the profane. Despite the common assumption that religion opposes sexual commerce, it actually provides an ideological basis for prostitution through symbols that sanctify perceptions of gender and sexuality. In Counter-Reformation Seville, the juxtaposition of prostitute with Holy Virgin and sister martyrs reflects a relationship far more complex than the simple polarities of Madonna and whore.

Images of the sorrowing mother and self-sacrificing virgins could be used in self-validation by women who became prostitutes to feed their children and serve the needs of men. Toleration of prostitution developed in order to preserve a gender order of arranged marriages, with males marrying later than females, and a sexual norm that placed great value on female chastity. This form of prostitution assumed that society requires females to be available to serve males, with prostitutes as a special class of women to provide sexual services for young unmarried men, sailors, and merchants.

A sexual double standard supported the city's legalized prostitution. People who believed that immoderate sexual activity could harm the body advised men to temper their sexual appetites through remedies such as the seed, leaves, or blossom of the hemp tree; they expressed no concern for the abuse that frequent sexual activity could work on the body of the prostitute.[33] Others, such as the sixteenth-century clergyman Francisco Farfan, spoke of the benefits of coitus in curing a variety of disorders, including headaches, fevers, myopia, and madness. Authorities like Farfan thus seemed to assume female cooperation as the means to provide these benefits for men. A sensuality that was believed to have developed during several centuries of Muslim rule combined with an austere Augustinian view that prostitution was a necessary evil. Farfan paraphrased Augustine's

[32] Ibid. Also see the royal letter to Seville in 1500, quoted in Guichot y Parody, *Historia*, 1: 375. Jacques Rossiaud, "Prostitution, jeunesse et société dans les villes du sud-est au xvᵉ siècle," *Annales, E.S.C.* 31, no. 2 (1976), p. 290, found that people in southeastern France also referred to brothel keepers as "abbesses."

[33] Sorapan, *Medicina*, pp. 416–27; cf. Sabuco, "Coloquio," p. 341.

statement: "The brothel in the city, then, is like the stable, or latrine for the house. Because just as the city keeps itself clean by providing a separate place where filth and dung are gathered, etc., so neither less nor more, assuming the dissolution of the flesh, acts the brothel: where the filth and ugliness of the flesh are gathered like the garbage and dung of the city."[34] Regarded as vessels to collect the filth of the flesh, prostitutes were seen as a necessary evil to prevent the worse sins of homosexuality, incest, rape, and seductions of honorable women.

Accepted because they played what was considered an essential social role, prostitutes nevertheless had to be kept within boundaries. City ordinances from 1500 provided for brothels where prostitutes could be regulated, but they also warned of "false monasteries" that purported to enclose women in orderly piety while actually selling their sexual services.[35] In order to prevent procuring on the streets, regulations required any woman who practiced prostitution to work within a brothel, and they attempted to prohibit free-lance prostitution, forbidding women to drink in taverns, where they might also solicit customers.[36] Brothels, as Farfan argued, provided appropriate "secret places" out of *vergüenza*, or shame, just as the husband clears the room of anyone else before he touches his wife.[37]

The brothel system developed in the city as an income-producing monopoly granted to certain individuals, almost always male and usually called "padres."[38] In most other European cities, prostitution remained a female-directed occupation; but by the sixteenth century the city of Seville appointed men only as brothel administrators. Owning the privilege of renting little cubicles in the town brothel to women who sold sexual services, these men looked upon prostitution as an enterprise, and they attempted to make even more money through renting out bedding and clothes, charging the women for cleaning and laundry services, and selling

---

[34] Francisco Farfan, *Tres libros contra el peccado de la simple fornicación: donde se averigua, que la torpeza entre solteros es peccado mortal, según ley divina, natural, y humana; y se responde a los engaños de los que dizen que no es peccado* (Salamanca: Heredetos de Matthias Gast, 1585), pp. 860, 730.

[35] These ordinances are reprinted in Guichot y Parody, *Historia*, 1: 375–77.

[36] AMS, *Ordenanzas*, "De las mugeres barrangas y desonestas," fols. 63r–64. See also Angel Galán Sánchez and María Teresa López Beltrán, "El 'status' teórico de las prostitutas del reino de Granada en la primera mitad del siglo XVI (las ordenanzas de 1538)," in Segura Graiño, *Las mujeres*, pp. 161–69. Cf. these examples from Spain with the system of prostitution discussed by Rossiaud, "Prostitution," pp. 290–91, esp.

[37] Farfan, *Tres libros*, p. 698.

[38] Legalized prostitution appears to have been widely accepted in many towns and cities of late medieval Spain. See, e.g., Angel Caffarena, *Apuntes para la historia de las mancebías de Málaga* (Málaga: Juan Such, 1968); Manuel Carboneres, *Picaronas y alcahuetes, o la mancebía de Valencia* (Valencia: El Mercantil, 1876); Enrique Rodríguez Solís, *Historia de la prostitución en España y América* (Madrid: Biblioteca Nueva, 1921).

them food and drink at high prices. No one outside the brothel was permitted to provide these services for prostitutes.

The exclusive monopoly granted to brothel padres received the protection of laws that prohibited pimps from taking money from women. The cortes that met in Ocaña in 1469, for example, complained that prostitutes, "through giving money to their ruffians or to other persons, become impoverished and owe some debts to the said padre or madre."[39] The solution, according to this assembly, was to require the prostitute to pay fees to the brothel padre before she paid anyone else. Regulations directed at pimps regarded them as illicit interlopers attempting to violate the commercial territory of brothel administrators. This form of early monopoly capitalism could preserve itself only at the price of constant vigilance against encroachments by male pimps and female procurers or free-lance prostitutes.

Traditionally, ordinances required prostitutes to distinguish themselves from nonprostitute women through their dress. Beginning in the fourteenth century prostitutes in Seville were to wear yellow head-coverings, and sumptuary laws prohibited concubines, that is, mistresses or "kept women," from wearing the long trains, furs, and other ornaments of honorable women. Increasingly city ordinances combined concubines in a single category with prostitutes, to be distinguished in dress from the city's respectable women.[40] This classification of women into good and evil defined them on the basis of their sexual availability to men, dividing women so that they felt more anxiety about losing their virtue than impetus to question gender inequity. And it warned women that expressing their sexuality outside the monopoly of ownership by father or husband would cause them to lose not only their virginity, but their classification as good women. For their fathers or husbands, it could mean the loss of male honor.[41]

Ordinances, of course, do not simply describe what happened in the past but express beliefs about what ought or ought not to happen. Ideally, according to these regulations, appearance should easily distinguish evil women from those with virtue. However, laws requiring prostitutes to wear a yellow headdress did not clearly distinguish them from respectable women because, according to a royal ordinance, "many women who are good, married, honorable, and honest" were wearing the yellow head-cov-

[39] Quoted in Galán Sánchez and López Beltrán, "Status," p. 167.

[40] Reprinted in Guichot y Parody, *Historia*, 1: 375–76.

[41] Joseph Pérez, "La femme et l'amour dans l'Espagne du xvie siècle," in *Amours légitimes, amours illégitimes en Espagne (XVIe–XVIIe siècles)*, ed. Augustin Redondo (Paris: Publications de la Sorbonne, 1985), pp. 20–21; and Julian Pitt-Rivers, *The People of the Sierra* (Chicago: University of Chicago Press, 1971), pp. 112–21.

erings prescribed for prostitutes.[42] A nineteenth-century historian suggested that respectable matrons wore the distinctive head-covering out of sympathy with stigmatized prostitutes, hoping to mitigate the harshness of restrictions on them.[43] Another possible explanation is that yellow head-coverings did not really become symbols of prostitution because prostitutes did not comply with the rule. It is also possible that nonprostitute women wanted to appear daring, or that they wanted to rebel against dress restrictions. Realizing their inability to define themselves if they simply conformed to official definitions of good women, they may have seized the power to define themselves through appearance. Officials did not try to explain this blurring of categories for women, but simply decreed in the late fifteenth century that prostitutes must henceforth distinguish themselves by adding a tinsel ornament to their head-coverings.[44] Both ecclesiastical and lay officials continued to tolerate prostitutes if they differentiated themselves from nonprostitute women and thus confirmed the dichotomization of women into good and evil.

Increasingly, women and men of the sixteenth century perceived poverty as a social problem, and they drew a distinction between immoral women who were willfully promiscuous and those who lost their virtue as a consequence of poverty. The Cofradía de los Niños Perdidos took on the task of sheltering poor and abandoned girls in Seville who "go wandering about and in danger of losing themselves," a euphemistic phrase for losing their virginity and virtue.[45] Members of this brotherhood venerated in their chapel a painting of the Holy Virgin holding out her mantle to shelter orphan girls.

Identifying poverty as a cause of prostitution, confraternities established charitable dowries in this period for young women who otherwise would not be able to marry or enter a convent. Churchmen founded houses to receive women who wanted to convert from prostitution, although their strict discipline appeared more punitive than supportive in this critical phase between ostracism and social reintegration, when errant women might try to resume respectability through roles different from that of the penitent whore.[46] Noting that harsh punishment deterred women from

[42] Reprinted in Guichot y Parody, *Historia*, 1: 375–77.

[43] José Velázquez y Sánchez, *Anales epidémicos: Reseña histórica de las enfermedades contagiosas en Sevilla desde la reconquista cristiana hasta de presente* (Seville: José María Geofin, 1866), p. 54.

[44] Guichot y Parody, *Historia*, 1: 376.

[45] AMS, Sección 4, Siglo XVII, Escribanías de Cabildo, Tomo 24, Número 1; see also Bermejo y Carballo, *Glorias*, p. 136.

[46] Turner has provided a broader social application of Arnold van Gennep's theory that initiands undergo a phase of liminality in rites of passage, and he and other anthropologists have emphasized liminality as a period offering the opportunity to create other relations and categories that can result in reintegration; see his *The Ritual Process: Structure and Anti-Struc-*

leaving prostitution, Augustinians and Jesuits established more kindly havens, such as the Convent of the Sweet Name of Jesus, which was established in the mid-sixteenth century for former prostitutes.[47]

Two saints, Mary Magdalen and Mary of Egypt, demonstrated that promiscuous women could be saved from their sin and become shining examples of God's mercy. Sexuality played a more direct role in their legends than in those of Justa and Rufina and the Holy Virgin. Mary of Egypt was believed to have been a Christian woman who sold herself to sailors in order to pay her way to the Holy Land, where she wanted to worship the True Cross. There she was turned away from the shrines as a sinner, but God recognized her holiness and directed her to a desert where he sustained her for many years. Jesus also recognized the holiness of Mary Magdalen, who was reputed to have been a prostitute before she met him and converted from her sinful life. He chose her to be the first to know of his Resurrection on Easter, but Church stories often omitted this demonstration of her importance to Jesus and, instead, emphasized her depravity before she met him and her subsequent penitence as depicted in figure 8.

People of Seville knew about these prostitute-saints through stories and pictures. Bones from each of them were among the relics held by the cathedral and carried in special gold and silver vessels during Corpus Christi processions.[48] Mary Magdalen became especially significant in efforts to convert prostitutes. On her feast day, preachers went to the brothel to preach, or they marched prostitutes to churches where they urged them to convert in rituals of sermons and prayer. Fray Luis de Rebolledo, noted for giving "the most ornate and best sermons of the city," preached so fervently on one such feast day that twenty-seven prostitutes who heard him decided to leave that life.[49]

Those who wanted to convert women from lives of prostitution provided dowries for them and tried to place them in convents or locate their parents or husbands. Historical records do not tell how difficult it was for former prostitutes to find husbands, nor do they describe problems these women had in returning to their families. Charitable dowries undoubtedly made the task of finding a husband easier, but it is likely that these women

---

ture (Ithaca: Cornell University Press, 1969). For more on charity in Seville, see Mary Elizabeth Perry, *Crime and Society in Early Modern Seville* (Hanover and London: University Press of New England, 1980), pp. 163–234. Pedro de León discussed the punitive nature of the Magdalen houses in Seville in his *Compendio de algunas experiencias en los ministerios de que vsa la Compª de IESVS con q practicamente se muestra con algunos acaecimientos y documentos el buen acierto en ellos* (Granada: n.p., 1619), pt. 1, chap. 5.

[47] See the report of the abbess and nuns of this house in AMS, Sección 3, Siglo XVI, Escribanías de Cabildo, Tomo 14, Número 7; and Morgado, *Historia*, pp. 465–66.

[48] Ortiz de Zuñiga, *Anales*, 3: 231.

[49] Francisco Pacheco, *Libro de descripción de verdaderos retratos, de ilustres y memorables varones* (Seville: Ayuntamiento, 1599), n.p.

FIGURE 8. *Penitent Magdalen*, by Bartolomé Murillo (Museen der Stadt, Cologne).

married less for affection or any personal feeling than to fulfill the expected gender role or simply to survive. Sympathetic treatment seemed more successful than punishment in convincing prostitutes to assume the kneeling, penitent position of Mary Magdalen, a position that acknowledged female sin and thereby justified male dominance and female submission.

Religious symbols played a major role in promoting female purity, but occasionally they fell into profanity through popular use. A letter to Philip II from Seville in 1590 complained about the royal order to reduce the number of hospitals in the city, pointing out that the hospital named for the sister-martyrs Justa and Rufina had been rented out as a tavern "where much dishonesty has occurred."[50] City residents might imagine the relics of the sisters shaking in horror, and yet the ideal of sacrificing the self and denying the body lived on in the sexual commerce of those who met in the shelter named for them.

[50] BC, 84-7-19, "Memorias eclesiásticas . . . ," "Carta al Rey Ntro Sr en su Real Consejo," dated 1590, fol. 52.

Chapter 3

PERFECT WIVES AND PROFANE LOVERS

MARRIAGE provided one of the few avenues to respectability for the women of Seville. Sixteenth-century clerics and moralists refined definitions of marriage so that it could promote social stability as a more effective institution of domestic enclosure. Secular and ecclesiastical officials in Seville worked together to promote their idealized notion of marriage through charitable dowries, catechizing the faithful, and prosecuting bigamists. They drew upon a growing body of literature that emphasized the sanctity of marriage for both social health and individual salvation.

Prescriptive literature of this period evoked the long tradition in Castile that presented marriage as the best antidote for illicit love. *Las Siete Partidas*, the code of law compiled under Alfonso X in the thirteenth century, defines marriage as a state necessary "to avoid quarrels, homicides, insolence, violence, and many other wrongful acts that would take place on account of women if marriage did not exist."[1] In this view, marriage could safely contain sexual expression, which otherwise would erupt in violent, antisocial behavior. Wedlock provided "a remedy," as a sixteenth-century cleric wrote, "for the flames of the flesh."[2] When a man married, he gained the sexual services of a wife, the possibility of producing heirs, and a respectable position of social stability. For women, marriage brought the honorable status of wife and mother. It also provided discipline and supervision as well as some economic support, neutralizing, it was believed, the conditions that caused "good women" to "lose themselves" in prostitution or promiscuity.

Juan Luis Vives, an early sixteenth-century Christian humanist who proposed both a system of caring for the poor and a program for educating women, recognized the close relationship among poverty, lack of supervision for females, and their loss of virtue. While acknowledging that some females had aptitude for learning, his plan for educating women aimed primarily to raise them to be chaste and industrious wives who would abhor idleness, dancing, books of gallantry, appearing and speaking in public, and adorning themselves with cosmetics. Even queens and princesses, he advised, should know how to spin and make things with their hands for

---

[1] *Las Siete Partidas*, ed. Samuel Parsons Scott (Chicago, New York, and Washington: Commerce Clearing House, 1931), p. 886.

[2] Farfan, *Tres libros*, p. 191.

the house because "the principal care of women" ought to be "the conservation of estate and honesty."[3]

As an antidote to immorality, marriage was carefully distinguished from love, especially carnal desire. Vives advised young women not to fall in love. Women are particularly susceptible to falling in love and letting it take over their lives, he wrote, and it becomes the same as casting oneself into a dungeon. The wisest course is to leave marriage arrangements to parents, for they who marry for love "shall lead their life in sorrow."

Nevertheless, Vives did not advocate that young women should be entirely without feelings of love. They should love God and Christ "as a spouse," the Virgin Mary and her mother, their earthly parents, and "holy mother Church." They should also love the saints and their own souls and virtue. Growing from "chaste and pure desires of honest and virtuous things," this love will not lead them into filthiness and sin, but into obedience "with all humility and meekness." Murillo's *Marriage of the Virgin* depicts this idealized love in figure 9.

In contrast with earthy and carnal desire, Vives called for a "heavenly love" between men and women, but this distinction sometimes blurred in the literature of the period.[4] Poets of Golden Age Spain described the sweet agonies of love between women and men, and religious writers, such as Teresa de Jesús and Juan de la Cruz, described their mystical experiences in terms so sensual that it was difficult to distinguish between physical and spiritual love. María de la Antigua, a lesser-known poet who lived in the province of Seville between 1566 and 1617, drew upon bodily images to move the reader to love Christ. In the poem "Canción," she vivified his bloody Passion with phrases that described the crucified body, his head punctured by thorns, his hair "stained and bathed" in blood, his "ravaged hands" and "lividly purple" lips, his wounded side "bubbling crimson."[5] The poetic presentation of Christ as a physical body to know through sight, touch, and sound implies that the body provides a significant vehicle for knowing spiritual truths.

A tradition of courtly love, which continued from centuries past, also blurred the distinction between physical and spiritual love. The service that a medieval knight pledged to his lady could be sexual love, and songs of the troubadours celebrated sensual feelings as well as passion for the beautiful and the true.[6] Under the influence of Christianity, courtly love became

---

[3] Vives, *Libro llamado instrucción*, p. 22. Quotations that follow are on pp. 94–95 and 83.

[4] Vives, *Libro llamado instrucción*, p. 83.

[5] The poem is reprinted in *La primeras poetisas en lengua castellana*, ed. Clara Janes (Madrid: Editorial Ayuso, 1986), pp. 69–71; see also p. 203 for a brief biographical sketch.

[6] Joan Kelly-Gadol, "Did Women Have a Renaissance?" in *Becoming Visible: Women in European History*, ed. Renate Bridenthal and Claudia Koonz (Boston: Houghton-Mifflin, 1977), pp. 141–45.

FIGURE 9. *The Marriage of the Virgin*, by Bartolomé Murillo (Reproduced by Permission of the Trustees, The Wallace Collection, London).

less sexual and developed into a respectfully distant reverence for Our Lady. Despite Church opposition to knightly tales, which clerics blamed for infecting young women with erotic desires, books such as *Amadís de Gaula* and *Florisande* continued to be printed and read in the sixteenth century. In Seville alone, seven separate editions of the first four books of *Amadís* were published between 1520 and 1547.[7] These books described erotic love as well as adventure, and they also presented an inversion of the gender order, with women frequently dominating men who asked only to serve them.[8]

Publishers in Seville in the first half of the sixteenth century issued thirteen editions of Fernando de Rojas's *Tragicomedia de Calisto y Melibea*, commonly known as *La Celestina*.[9] Condemned by Vives and other clerics for describing carnal love and the powers of love magic, *La Celestina* also warned of the dangers of erotic love enflamed with a passion unchecked by notions of duty and virtue. In the story, Celestina, an older woman who introduces the lovers, is eager to profit from their passion. Melibea and Calisto fall so desperately in love that it blinds them to reason. Melibea rebels against the marriage her parents have arranged for her and says that she cannot live without Calisto. Her sense of dependence develops out of the strong emotion that has overtaken her, rather than from an acceptance of woman's lesser position in God's "natural order"; and her rebellion tells more about the dangers of disobedience than about her strength of character. Rojas presents love not as the recognition of virtue, but as a warning of weakness all too easily exploited by a bawdy old woman who uses potions and superstitions to arrange trysts for her own enrichment.

Themes in *La Celestina* echo in many historical documents of the city. A Jesuit who worked with Seville's street children at the end of the sixteenth century condemned evil women who introduced young girls to prostitution.[10] The director of an orphanage for girls wrote of the need to protect them from older women who could transform their innocent virtue into commercial sex.[11] Inquisitors prosecuted some women who sold potions and spells and taught rituals and incantations believed to work love magic. Rojas's *La Celestina* undoubtedly reflected actual concerns in the social world of early modern Spain, but it also influenced the expression of these concerns by providing a character who symbolized the evil older woman profiting from erotic passions as the third party or go-between.

---

[7] Aurora Domínguez Guzmán, *El libro sevillano durante la primera mitad del siglo XVI* (Seville: Diputación Provincial de Sevilla, 1975).

[8] Mariló Vigil, *La vida de las mujeres en los siglos XVI y XVII* (Madrid: Siglo XXI, 1986), pp. 64–65.

[9] Domínguez Guzmán, *Libro sevillano*, p. 250.

[10] Pedro de León, *Compendio*, pt. 2, chap. 25, fols. 191–92.

[11] AMS, Sección 4, Siglo XVII, Escribanías de Cabildo, Tomo 22, Número 12.

Few women learned about erotic love from books such as *La Celestina*. Daughters of poor parents might never learn to read, and the middle- and upper-class women who learned to read from private tutors and nuns would have limited access to reading material other than books of devotion. The theater offered more opportunities for young women to learn about relations between the sexes, particularly in Seville, where outdoor theaters flourished in courtyards and plazas that filled periodically with eager spectators.[12] Love between a man and woman figured prominently in the dramatic plots of this period, and marriage usually provided the happy solution at the conclusion. Ana Caro Mallén de Soto, one of the most famous of Seville's seventeenth-century dramatists, described in *El Conde de Partinuplés* the unstable situation that results when the young empress Rosaura refuses to decide among her many suitors.[13] Happily for both playgoers and her kingdom, however, she chooses the count of Partinuplés and successfully uses various enchantments to make him fall in love with her. By the play's end, the count has declared that he is Rosaura's slave, and she has happily pledged that she is his.

The drama of this period did not present love and marriage as a simple partnership, however, and many dramatists contrasted "profane" with "honest" love. Feliciana Enríquez de Guzmán, who wrote *Tragicomedia: Los jardines y campos sabeos* in Seville in the early seventeenth century, presented the hero Clarisel as the victim of "perverted" and fickle Belidiana in part 1, so blinded by her beauty that he feels himself "in shackles and in chains."[14] In part 2, however, he has recovered from Belidiana and is now stronger than ever, buoyed by his love for Maya, who is "wise and beautiful" and returns his love with constancy and loyalty. Her beauty, rather than dazzling and entrapping Clarisel, is compared with that of the graces and the muses. Belidiana, on the other hand, is advised to

> leave the hunt, for the woman
> is better off in the house.

The "honest" love of Clarisel and Maya appropriately leads to marriage, while the profane love he felt for Belidiana is recognized as a warning that

---

[12] Celestino López Martínez, *Teatros y comediantes sevillanos del siglo XVI* (Seville: Diputación Provincial de Sevilla, 1940), pp. 24–25 and 60, esp.

[13] Ana Caro Mallén de Soto, *El Conde de Partinuplés* (1653), in *Biblioteca de Autores Españoles* (Madrid: M. Rivadeneyra, 1859), 49: 125–38.

[14] Feliciana Enríquez de Guzmán, *Tragicomedia: Los jardines y campos sabeos* (Lisboa: Gerardo de la Vinlea, 1624), pt. 1, act 1, sc. 2; quotations that follow are from pt. 2, act 1, sc. 6. It should be pointed out that Enríquez dedicated her play to her sister who was a nun, and she undoubtedly wrote it not so much to be performed as to be read, in response to dramatists who she believed were forsaking literary quality for popular appeal.

women must be enclosed, sent home from the hunt, so that they cannot imprison men in their own passions.

Writers of this period referred to overwhelming passions, such as Clarisel's love for Belidiana, as lust. Profane love imprisoned men in the chains and shackles of mortal sin, as one cleric wrote; and it also caused them to neglect their estates, to lose their reason and control over body movements.[15] It could lead to early death and certain damnation, and, in depleting the fluid proceeding from the cerebrum that causes hair to grow on the head, it could even result in baldness. Oliva Sabuco de Nantes Barrera, a remarkable woman who wrote a medical treatise on human nature in the late sixteenth century, also warned that lust could harm or kill the body.[16] She believed that lust caused the brain to release a fluid which went to the stomach, making it cold and weak, and disrupting the body's natural harmony.

Profane love also included the passions that a man could so arouse in a woman that she would "lose herself" and her virtue. Ecclesiastical authorities saw this as a problem of sin and salvation, while secular authorities viewed it as the cause of social problems such as abandoned women and illegitimate children. Illegitimacy reached its peak in the parish of San Martín at the end of the sixteenth century when one-quarter of all births reported in parish records were to unmarried women. By 1650, this fraction had declined to one-tenth, a rate that has also been found in parishes of Madrid in this period.[17] Extramarital sex for women threatened orderly inheritance, but even more serious in this period of the Counter-Reformation, it undermined limpieza de sangre, or the preservation of bloodlines free of contamination from non-Christian individuals.

Bastardy did not seem to concern aristocratic men, who could legally decide whether to make their illegitimate children heirs; but an illegitimate child for a woman of the middle or lower classes meant moral condemna-

---

[15] Francisco Farfan, *Regimiento de castos: Y remedio de torpes. Donde se ponen XXVIII remedios contra el peccado de la torpeza: Y por otras tantas vías se exhorta el christiano al amor de la castidad* (Salamanca: Cornelio Bonardo, 1590), pp. 212^r–224^r, 259–71, and 316^r–403^r. See also Michel Foucault, *The Use of Pleasure*, vol. 2 of *The History of Sexuality*, trans. Robert Hurley (New York: Pantheon, 1985), p. 16, esp.; and Michel Foucault, "The Battle for Chastity," in *Western Sexuality: Practice and Precept in Past and Present Times*, ed. Philippe Ariés and André Béjin, trans. Anthony Forster (Oxford and New York: Basil Blackwell, 1985), pp. 14–25.

[16] Sabuco, "Coloquio," p. 341.

[17] Gregorio García-Baquero López, *Estudio demográfico de la parroquia de San Martín de Sevilla (1551–1749)* (Seville: Diputación Provincial de Sevilla, 1982), p. 117. Note that this is one of several demographic parish studies which have been undertaken by a team of scholars working under Professor L. C. Alvarez Santaló, and it is the first to be published. Workers and transients especially lived in the parish of San Martín, so the illegitimacy rate for this parish should not be assumed accurate for parishes where the population had more wealth. Also, see Claude Larquié, "Amours légitimes et amours illégitimes à Madrid au xviie siècle," in Redondo, *Amours légitimes*, pp. 69–91.

tion.[18] Aware that unmarried mothers and illegitimate children could place an even greater strain on a system of charity already overtaxed, officials attempted to discourage extramarital sex by enforcing laws against common-law wives and concubines. They imposed fines to punish erring men, but they reduced the women involved to the status of prostitutes. In penalizing women more than men for illicit sex, these officials reinforced a double standard and the gender ideology that saw female sexuality as more dangerous and more in need of control.[19]

Class undoubtedly affected the complications of seduction and abandonment, and it also modified attitudes about them. Rarely do historical records describe cases of men seducing women from a higher social class. This may demonstrate the efficacy of upper-class protection for their daughters and the pattern of males considering as fair game females of a class inferior to their own; it also suggests that a patriarchal system usually views seduction and abandonment as a matter of economics rather than sexual exploitation. In Seville, officials regarded seduction and abandonment as one of the major causes for the problem of wandering women, particularly when the male seducer came from a higher class than the woman. According to the counsel of Martín de Azpilcueta Navarro, a priest who published a confessional manual in 1554, the man who seduced a woman with "false persuasions," even though he did not promise to marry her, was obliged to marry her "or satisfy her or pay damages." However, if he was of a higher class than she, "then one can presume that she pretended to be deceived," and the man should compensate her father, but he owed her nothing more than to give her some assistance in making a good marriage appropriate to her class.[20]

This moral prescription contrasts with actual cases of seduction. A man who seduced a young servant in the house of his father at the end of the sixteenth century, for example, put her to work as a prostitute instead of helping her make a good marriage.[21] He was sentenced to penal duty in the galleys when authorities learned that he was acting as her pimp. From prison he wrote her a note, reminding her that she was his "thing," as bound to him as he was to her. He drew a picture of a heart pierced with

[18] Domínguez Ortiz, "La mujer en el tránsito," p. 177.

[19] Keith Thomas, "The Double Standard," *Journal of the History of Ideas* 20 (1959): 195–216. Also see Martín de Azpilcueta Navarro, *Manual de confesores, y penitentes, que clara y brevemente contiene la universal, y particular decisio de quasi todas las dudas, que en las confesiones suelen ocurrir de los pecados absoluciones, restituciones, censuras, irregularidades* (Toledo: Juan Ferrer, 1554), p. 118, for the statement that a couple living together outside of marriage should not be absolved of sin as long as they continue doing so. The greater importance of chastity for women than for men is noted by Joseph Pérez, "La femme," pp. 21–25.

[20] Azpilcueta Navarro, *Manual*, p. 117.

[21] AMS, Papeles del Señor Conde de Aguila, Sección Especial, Cristóbal Chaves, "Relación de las cosas de la cárcel de Sevilla y su trato," Tomo B-C, pt. 2.

an arrow and placed between the figures of a man and a woman attached by chains. This message would not have surprised clerics and moralists of the period who warned of the dangers of sexual feelings, and it clearly reflected the folk wisdom of love magic and proverbs that cautioned men about deceptive women who could imprison them in blinding emotions.

As an antidote to dangerous sexuality, marriage also included a spiritual significance that grew during the sixteenth and seventeenth centuries. Chastity, of course, still represented the most perfect human state, but Erasmus and his followers believed that marriage could preserve chastity and provide the situation in which individuals realized their highest spiritual potential.[22] Erasmian thinking, however, fell out of favor with the Inquisition, and the idealization of marriage as a path to salvation gave way to a more pragmatic view: so many people lived in the married state that it had to be the subject of Church teachings even though it was a less perfect state than virginity or celibacy.[23] Artists of the later sixteenth and seventeenth centuries helped to idealize the sanctity of marriage in paintings such as *The Holy Family of the Little Bird* by Bartolomé Murillo (fig. 10).

Later sixteenth-century writings on marriage emphasized its function to reflect God's order on earth, with the husband's authority as the rightful ruler of the family softened by his obligation to love and care for his wife and children. In contrast with traditional misogynistic views of women as chattel, fray Vicente Mexía devoted the first treatise of his book on marriage to an argument that the order of nature required husbands to regard their wives as companions rather than slaves.[24] When God created Eve from Adam's body, Mexía wrote, he showed that the husband must love his wife very much "because she is so similar to him: she is almost another him." She was not created to be her husband's slave because she was not made from his feet, nor to be his servant because she did not come from his hands. However, she was also not intended to be his equal because she was not created from his shoulders or his head; instead, she was made from his rib, showing that she should be under his protection and shelter. He should love her and teach her and show her how to avoid error, advise her and correct her, defend her from all evil and danger.

Mexía referred to the wisdom of Church fathers as he described the appropriate power relationships within marriage. Neither slave nor servant, the wife was to become the mistress of her husband's house and estate, but

---

[22] See the discussion of Erasmus and marriage in Marcel Bataillon, *Erasmo y España: Estudios sobre la historia espiritual del siglo XVI* (Mexico and Buenos Aires: Fondo de Cultura Economica, 1950), 1: 335–36; and in Alban Forcione, *Cervantes and the Humanist Vision: A Study of Four Exemplary Novels* (Princeton: Princeton University Press, 1982), p. 95.

[23] Fray Vicente Mexía, *Saludable instrucción del estado de matrimonio* (Córdoba: Juan Baptista Escudero, 1566), dedication, p. 30; also see fray Luis de León, *La perfecta casada*, p. 211.

[24] Fray Vicente Mexía, *Saludable instrucción*, pp. 16, 44.

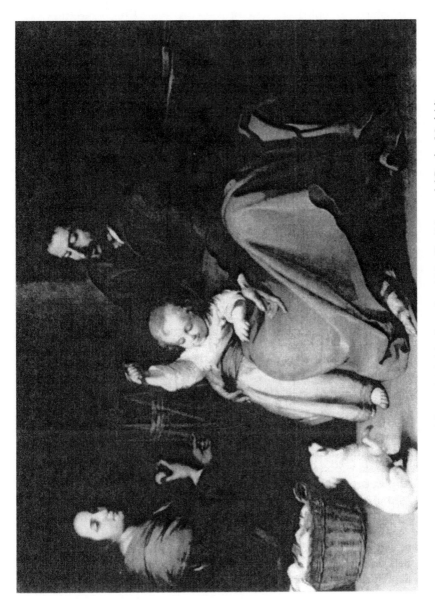

FIGURE 10. *The Holy Family of the Little Bird*, by Bartolomé Murillo (Museo del Prado, Madrid).

always subject to him. Her "state of perpetual subjection," according to Mexía, was justified by the fact that God created Adam before Eve. Moreover, natural law provides that "naturally the man is of greater ability and strength to be able to rule and support the wife." To allow the wife to rule the husband is a "disorder both great and ugly." A good wife will preserve the peace and harmony of the home, never presuming to contradict her husband, to disobey him or annoy him, always remembering that "to be a woman is [to be] less than her husband." On his part, the good husband will use moderation as a wise ruler, and he will follow four principles: he will treat his wife as a reputable person created by God, rather than as a slave or servant; he will not flee from her as something foreign, because she is flesh of his flesh; he will love her very much; and, finally, he will honor her as much as possible, but not to the extent of perverting the natural order.[25]

Mexía goes on to describe more intimate relations in marriage, or the "matrimonial act," explaining that he does so in order to instruct women, who are more "timorous" and more "inclined to have shame" and thus cannot easily ask questions about these things "without embarrassment." Sexual relations between husband and wife must be governed by reason rather than sensuality, he writes, and those who engage in sex for any purpose other than procreation, such as "appetite and vain happiness," are guilty of a "very grave sin." If a man wants relations with his wife only for sensuality and not for procreation, she has the right to refuse to obey him. Moreover, if he threatens her and tries to force her, she has the obligation to resist him, even to death. This is not a tragedy, however, the cleric advises, "because the crown of martyrdom in heaven will not be denied her, who . . . to avoid an offense to God is willing to die in this world."[26]

God has ordained sexual relations between a man and his wife, but only within a specific order for purposes of procreation. Couples sin very gravely, Mexía wrote, when they use different sexual positions to increase sensual pleasure or to avoid conception. The couple wanting to change "the natural order that God instituted for marriage" is guilty of "wanting to pervert the natural order." While admitting that there are some legitimate reasons for using positions other than the only one ordained by God, such as very pregnant women or debilitated men, Mexía warns that those who deliberately pervert this order will be punished because sinful sex results in offspring with "horrible defects, or monstrous things, or very grave illness."[27]

---

[25] Ibid., pp. 34ʳ–35ʳ, 43ʳ, 42ʳ.

[26] Ibid., pp. 122, 112, 122ʳ.

[27] Ibid., p. 116ʳ. However, note that Thomas Sánchez wrote that pleasure from marital sex was not sinful unless copulation was separated from its procreative function and engaged in for pleasure only. See Jean-Louis Flandrin, "Sex in Married Life in the Early Middle Ages:

To counter erroneous beliefs about the "marriage debt," Mexía points out that the Church permits either spouse to delay sexual relations for two months following their marriage while one or both decide whether to join the religious life instead. In addition, he outlines situations in which either may refuse to engage in sex, such as feast days or days of penitence or when the wife is very pregnant or is menstruating. Concerning menstruation, Mexía wrote that "it should not create a serious problem for husbands to let their wives rest for those few days that they are with that natural occupation and not to touch them: they know that through God's express command in his laws, there is no less than the punishment of death for those [men] who come to them when they are so disposed." God also commanded death for the woman who allowed a man to have sexual relations with her during her menstrual period. Acknowledging that some discount these commandments as merely ceremonial provisions of the "old law," Mexía argues that they are also sanctioned by natural law as "natural" and "virtuous." He closes this section of his book with the reminder that when a woman marries, she "makes herself subject to her husband . . . and is no longer owner of her own body."[28]

For women, the separation of self from the body could result not only from clerical prescriptions for marriage, but also from medical descriptions of pregnancy. Both learned and popular beliefs of this period emphasized the horrible and monstrous during pregnancy, perhaps an extension of fray Vicente's warning about the punishment for unnatural sex. Although Dr. Juan Alonso y de los Ruizes de Fontecha entitled his early seventeenth-century book *Diez previlegios de preñadas* (Ten privileges of pregnant women), he begins with a discussion of monsters rather than privileges.[29] Referring to an imperfect fetus as a "mole," Dr. Alonso assures the reader that a woman by herself can engender a mole, but she requires a man's participation to produce a perfect fetus. The doctor does not add a description of how a woman alone could engender a mole but simply says that this illustrates the imperfect nature of woman.

Dr. Alonso explains that his purposes in discussing the privileges of pregnant women are "the defense of good women, to teach them how to pass less badly their distressing pregnancies, and to facilitate their dangerous births." The privileges that he discusses refer less to a privileged status of pregnant women than to the authority of the doctor to excuse these women from religious fasting days or to allow them to be bled or purged. The fifth privilege, which he misleadingly entitles "How the pregnant woman can wear what she wants," actually refers to allowing her to wear

---

The Church's Teaching and Behavioural Reality," in Ariés and Béjin, *Western Sexuality*, p. 115.

[28] Fray Vicente Mexía, *Saludable instrucción*, pp. 135ʳ, 213.

[29] Alonso y de los Ruizes de Fontecha, *Diez previlegios*, p. 22, esp.

amulets or precious stones as protection against abortion or miscarriage. Class determines the finer points of this privilege, however, for poor women will be unable to wear diamonds or other precious stones for protection; they must not despair, for they can wear amulets of such materials as powdered roasted frogs or vegetable grubs, which, he says, are known to be effective.[30]

Dr. Alonso grants pregnant women the privilege to choose a midwife, but he cannot resist telling them what kind of a person they should choose. She should have "natural gifts and graces acquired through reasoning, work, and experience." She must also be "placid and tender, compassionate, cautious, modest, diligent, a peaceful worker, prudent, and not avaricious." Compassion is especially important in the person chosen, he adds, so that she will not "tear to pieces the tender and unfortunate infant between her fingernails." Declaring that the midwife must know how to assist the woman in labor, Dr. Alonso describes in gruesome detail several cases of neglect, such as that of the midwife who failed to remove from the womb a child who had died during labor. Years later when the mother died, doctors found within her the child, perfectly formed, but as hard and dry as wood, a "petrified fetus," as he calls it.[31]

Despite his own horror stories of birthing disasters, Dr. Alonso declares that the midwife must be able to sustain the woman in labor with broth and wine and cheerful stories of successful births. The midwife's optimism must convince the laboring woman that she can continue with her pains, persuading her to disbelieve, the good doctor adds, the proverbial wisdom that a long labor brings a daughter. Implying that a female child would not be considered worth the effort, Dr. Alonso urges the midwife to tell the woman in labor examples of women who, after long labor, had very lively and strong sons.[32]

In even greater detail, the doctor describes complicated births in which the midwife will have to assist the child and put her hands within the mother. He describes instruments that may be helpful and directs the readers to drawings in a book by Ambroise Paré. He instructs the midwife in how to deliver the child in pieces after it has died within the mother, but he adds that she may look for a surgeon to carry out this difficult task. "When a surgeon is not available to do this work: the poor pregnant woman is placed in the hands of some sheep butchers, well-experienced in slaughtering ewes, gathering the dead lambs and the live ones." These butchers then prepare to tie down "the sad and afflicted woman, as though she had done bad things and they wanted to torture her, making her suffer

[30] Ibid., pp. 6, 68ʳ.
[31] Ibid., pp. 108, 121ʳ.
[32] Ibid., 127ʳ–128.

what the martyrs suffered, although for another purpose, different enough."[33]

As if all this were not enough to discourage any woman from wanting to become pregnant and give birth, Dr. Alonso finishes his book with a long chapter on the terrible things that can happen to the child once it is born. He warns these new mothers in particular against "old women with their fragrances, prayers, and psalms" who say they can cure a child sickened by a spell. Not doubting for a moment the reality of aojar, as this kind of illness was called, Dr. Alonso warns against calling on the help of these old women, who he says appear to be "more lost than devout." Citing many authorities from antiquity as well as his own time, the doctor describes women who do not themselves appear ill but are able to sicken others with their "vapors." He argues that they can even kill "the tender infant," not through a pact with the devil, and "not only by the vapors that leave through the eyes, but much more [those] that leave through the mouth and [those that] are exuded throughout the body."[34]

Prudent mothers will protect their babies against these vapors with fumigations, especially those produced by a piece of iron boiling in vinegar. They will also prevent strange old women from looking at their babies, for one never knows when a child may sicken from their vapors. Dr. Alonso offers many recipes for potions and unguents, and he also advises the mother to fasten at her baby's neck precious stones or less costly items such as rock salt carved into a cross or a heart, or even a shell from the sea. Attempting to show that these beliefs are based on both piety and reason rather than pagan superstitions, the writer ends his book with the hope that if he has written anything offensive to the Church, it will be corrected.[35]

A similar mixture of piety and pragmatism appears in a treatise by fray Luis de León entitled La perfecta casada, in which he argues that marriage is a biological and social necessity.[36] His pragmatic view of marriage presents it as providing a means to preserve the human race, propagate new servants for God, honor the land, and bring glory to Heaven. He also shows that marriage could bridle the independence of women and harness their energies for an economy of domestic production. For this cleric, the most significant "marriage debt" is not the sexual relationship described by Mexía, but the preservation and increase of material wealth.

---

[33] Ibid., p. 155ʳ.

[34] Ibid., pp. 178, 185, 189ʳ. Sabuco, "Coloquio," p. 347, also described the sickening and deaths of young children and animals through a venom that was passed by adults full of bad humors that they expelled through the eyes, mouths, or noses.

[35] Fray Vicente Mexía, Saludable instrucción, pp. 223ʳ–225, 230.

[36] Fray Luis de León, La perfecta casada, p. 211. See also María Angeles Durán, "Lectura económica de fray Luis de León," in Durán, Nuevas perspectivas, 2: 257–73.

Fray Luis prescribed a work ethic for wives that coincided with actual conditions in all but the most wealthy families. Urging wives to be the first to rise in the household, to supervise servants as captains oversee an infantry, and to work with their own hands throughout the day, shunning any idleness or self-indulgence, the friar's exhortation prescribed behavior that necessity pressed on many women. It also condemned wealthier wives who wanted to begin the day more leisurely, spending time and money on adorning themselves with cosmetics, dress, and jewels. He accused these women of simply wanting to imitate the self-indulgence of noble women, implying that the latter performed no domestic labor at all, and ignoring the possibility that middle-class husbands would want their wives to cultivate appearance and leisure which could demonstrate their rising fortunes.

Unpaid domestic work provided the backbone of the family economy in most homes of sixteenth- and seventeenth-century Seville. Many women had already learned this work as girls when they were apprenticed out as servants from ages as young as seven years. Those for whom they worked made contracts with their parents, agreeing to teach them not only domestic skills, but also "good manners and customs."[37] For their work, which could be contracted out for up to twelve years, the girls received board, room, clothing, and, at the end of their contract, a payment that was meant to provide part of a marriage dowry. This sum was not always clearly stated; instead the provision appeared in the contract as a phrase such as "what appears in God and in your conscience, in money as in goods."[38] These contractual agreements provided very cheap domestic help, and they also relieved families from the expenses of keeping their own daughters or providing their dowries.

During this period, the dowry played a very significant role in marriage arrangements for all except the most destitute women. Notarized letters, which specified the dowry promised as well as that received, indicate that even the daughters of unskilled workers and small artisans brought money, goods, or property to their marriages. In poorer families, daughters sometimes depended for a dowry entirely on the money or goods that they received at the end of their domestic service contracts. Some parents included as part of the daughter's dowry a building in which they continued to reside for the rest of their lives, along with the newly married couple.[39]

Charitable practices underscore the essential nature of the dowry, with private individuals as well as confraternities providing money so that young women from poor families could marry. A cathedral confraternity of some six hundred men and their wives, for example, awarded dowries

---

[37] Morell Peguero, *Mercaderes*, pp. 63–73.

[38] Letter of service notarized for Juan Moreno, trabajador, in APS, Oficio 20, Legajo 2 of 1540, quoted in Morell Peguero, *Mercaderes*, p. 73.

[39] Morell Peguero, *Mercaderes*, p. 47. Husbands could also use similar letters of agreement to pay *arras*, the small and traditional gift that the bridegroom paid to the bride.

to some thirty or forty young women each year who were poor, but legitimately born, and at least sixteen years old. On the birthday of the Holy Virgin, confraternity members accompanied the recipients in a procession to the cathedral where each young woman received a silken purse containing fifteen thousand maravedís.[40] Pedro de León, the Jesuit who worked with prostitutes at the end of the sixteenth century, convinced one wealthy woman to provide dowries for those prostitutes who wanted to change their lives.[41] Two wealthy sisters of the city, Ana and Juana Nuñez Pérez, established a fund that, following their deaths, was to provide dowries for "virtuous maidens" to marry or enter a convent.[42] Administered through the Hospital de las Cinco Llagas, which had previously been established for the care of poor women, these charitable dowries were intended for young women who worked in the hospital, for those who lived in the sisters' parish of the Magdalen, and for legitimate descendants of their own family, as well as those of specific persons who had served the sisters during their lifetimes.

The dowry system encouraged parents and other family members to regard marriage as an economic arrangement in which they should participate directly. Families of wealth could exert considerable pressure on a young woman to marry a particular propertied suitor or, if the family lacked enough wealth to provide the dowry for a suitable match, to forgo marriage in favor of the convent, which usually required a lesser dowry. Parents played a critical role in making these arrangments. They had to consider the marriage of their sons and daughters as a strategy for safeguarding or enriching the family estate.[43] At the same time, they were advised to consider the wishes of their sons and daughters, who did not always agree to the parents' arrangements. Some young women who insisted that they wanted to become nuns rather than wives cut their hair and told their parents that they had already taken a vow of chastity.[44]

A case from Inquisition records of 1620 illustrates the complexity of marriage arrangements. Catalina de Mesa, the only child of a lay official of the Inquisition, realized as her father lay mortally ill that his will committed her to a marriage she did not want.[45] Lacking a son to inherit his Inquisitional office, her father had won agreement from the Holy Office that his son-in-law would inherit the post, and his will named Diego de Villanueva

---

[40] Morgado, *Historia*, pp. 320–21.

[41] Pedro de León, *Compendio*, pt. 1, chap. 4, fols. 10–14; chap. 5, fols. 14–15.

[42] ADPS, Hospital de las Cinco Llagas, Libro 11, contains the will of Juana Nuñez Pérez, dated December 15, 1617, and two codicils dated May 8, 1620, and November 2, 1622.

[43] Morell Peguero, *Mercaderes*, pp. 166–68.

[44] For example, see the women listed in alphabetical order by Justino Matute y Gaviria, *Hijos de Sevilla* (Seville: El Orden, 1886–1889).

[45] AHN, Inquisición, Legajo 2056, Número 2 contains the criminal process of Diego de Villanueva against Catalina de Mesa in 1620.

as the prospective son-in-law. Catalina enlisted the help of her sympathetic mother, and the two of them reported after the death of her father that they had found a letter from him which named Bernardo de Azme rather than Diego de Villanueva as his rightful son-in-law. Although this man was at that time in the Canary Islands, Catalina and her mother arranged a marriage by proxy. Outraged at being nudged out of a lucrative and respectable position, Diego de Villanueva filed a complaint that protested the marriage and accused Catalina and her mother of forging the letter they said they had found.

As inquisitors investigated the case, it became clear that the real issue was not who should inherit the office, but whether Catalina and her mother had demonstrated female obedience or female treachery. They decided it was the latter, but they did not declare Catalina's marriage void, nor did they attempt to grant her father's position to Diego de Villanueva. Instead, they focused their wrath on her mother, whom they blamed for lying and forgery. While Bernardo took up the position he had supposedly inherited as husband of Catalina, inquisitors sentenced her mother to perpetual prison. The resolution of the dispute succeeded in restoring order, with the widow imprisoned for the rest of her life and her daughter safely enclosed in marriage.

The case of Catalina de Mesa demonstrates the growing alarm about women outside the enclosures of marriage or convent who were able to escape male authority. As an unmarried woman who had not entered a convent and now lacked a father, Catalina had an anomalous position of potential danger. Not only could she slip through the webs of discipline and enclosure; she could also escape male control unless she married or took religious vows. As a widow, her mother represented an even greater social danger. She evidently inherited enough property that she would not have to remarry or accept the direction of any male. Inquisitors were able to correct this situation by subjecting her to enclosure in perpetual prison.

Prescriptive literature extolled enclosure as the natural state for women and warned against talkative and footloose females. Just as nature made women to be enclosed, according to fray Luis de León, "so it obliges them to close the mouth." The loquacious and wandering woman, he wrote, "perverts her very nature." A prudent husband should enclose his wife and prohibit her from receiving visits from other women, because allowing women to talk together "always leads to a thousand evils." Evoking nature, he cited the often-used simile, pointing out that the fish which swims in peace and security in water cannot live outside it; in like fashion, the good woman lives in peace and security within her house, but outside she becomes obscene and whorish.[46]

---

[46] Fray Luis de León, *La perfecta casada*, pp. 239, 241, 228, 241. Other examples of prescriptive literature addressing this point include Juan de la Cerda, *Vida política*, and Diego

Wandering women free from enclosure in marriage or convent worried many who saw them as the most potent symbol of disorder. One response, fired by impatience with women who did not conform to prescriptions for enclosure, called for establishing a workhouse to confine the many "lost" and vagabond women who wandered about Seville.[47] Another response appeared in the proliferating books that prescribed enclosure and shame in socializing young girls, calling upon parents to guard "as dragons" the purity of their daughters.[48] Discussions at the Council of Trent of the sacrament of marriage and the cloistering of nuns underscored their gravity and developed an earlier trend toward enclosure that took on greater momentum under the impact of urban growth and social dislocation in the sixteenth and seventeenth centuries.[49]

The decision at Trent to require strict enforcement of marriage as a sacrament followed discussions that condemned "clandestine marriages" for allowing men to pretend to marry gullible women and later to abandon them.[50] The explanation that these women did not realize they were being duped presents a patronizing attitude about women, ignoring the possibility that some women may have willingly agreed to such "marriages" as a protest against the business negotiations that accompanied the sacrament of marriage. However, the distinction between a promise to marry, "words of the future" (which could be a simple pledge without any witnesses), and "words of the present" (the declaration of marriage before witnesses) should be noted. Many believed that without the safeguards of public banns, witnesses, and a priestly blessing, marriage became a mockery, and, as a result, "honest maidens," in the words of a sixteenth-century cleric, lost their honor.[51]

After the middle of the sixteenth century, the Inquisition in Castile increasingly considered cases of bigamy, justifying their jurisdiction with the argument that remarriage while a previous spouse still lived challenged the sanctity of the sacrament of marriage. The Church had already affirmed at the end of the fifteenth century that marriage is perpetual and indissoluable and cannot be ended by simple abandonment.[52] Now since the Tridentine

---

Pérez de Valdivia, *Aviso de gente recogida* (1585) (Madrid: Universidad Pontífica de Salamanca y Fundación Universitaria Española, 1977).

[47] AMS, Papeles Importantes, Siglo XVI, Tomo 9, Número 1.

[48] Juan de la Cerda, *Vida política*, p. 242ʳ.

[49] Domínguez Ortiz, "La mujer en el tránsito," p. 172.

[50] Farfan, *Tres libros*, pp. 954–55. See also James Casey, "Household Disputes and the Law in Early Modern Andalusia," in *Disputes and Settlements: Law and Human Relations in the West*, ed. John Bossy (Cambridge and New York: Cambridge University Press, 1983), pp. 189–217; and Ricardo García Cárcel, "El fracaso matrimonial en la Cataluña del Antiguo Régimen," in Redondo, *Amours légitimes*, pp. 121–32.

[51] Farfan, *Tres libros*, pp. 957–59.

[52] In 1480 Alfonso Carrillo, archbishop of Toledo, had convened a synod which decided that marriage is perpetual and indissoluble. See Jean-Pierre Dedieu, "Le modèle sexuel: La

discussions, ecclesiastical authorities called for more vigorous prosecution of bigamy cases, using theological arguments to make a vigorous defense of Christian marriage.[53] Secular officials supported this defense, although they saw bigamy less as a theological issue than as a challenge to social order that compounded the very severe social problem of what to do with abandoned wives and children.

According to Inquisition records, bigamy consisted of making a false statement when contracting another marriage. The tribunal in Seville prosecuted 164 people for bigamy between 1559 and 1648. Bigamists were accused of swearing falsely either that they had never been married before or that they had proof of the death of the previous spouse. In some cases, their friends swore with them and were subsequently prosecuted for giving false testimony. All of the cases appear to have been abandonment, perhaps by mutual agreement, although men were accused of abandoning wives in three-quarters of the bigamy cases considered by the tribunal in Seville. Geographically more mobile than women and less restricted by the care of children, men could simply disappear. Some assumed new names and preserved their new lives for many years.

Accused bigamists appeared to be "small fish," rather than the wealthy merchants and conversos sometimes assumed to be the primary target of the Inquisition.[54] With only three exceptions, accused bigamists who listed their occupations were laborers or artisans. Of the exceptions, two were scribes, and one had a position as a squire in a wealthy house and also worked in the mint.[55] The accused probably did not have enough wealth to maintain one marriage, let alone two or more. Juan de Herrera, however, had married three times and explained to the inquisitors that he had not done so out of disrespect for marriage, but because he was "a poor man."[56] His testimony does not say whether his wives helped to support him, or if he used the term "poor" to refer to his vulnerability as a man afflicted by a fatal fascination with the opposite sex. Ages for those accused of bigamy ranged from twenty-one to eighty years.

Inquisition reports follow a consistent formula. After stating the name, origin, residence, age, and occupation or social status of the accused, the report gives the number of witnesses who testified against this person, usually with their sex and whether they were adults or minors. A clear majority of witnesses were adult males, perhaps because inquisitors considered these

---

défense du mariage chrétien," in *L'Inquisition espagnole XVᵉ–XIXᵉ siècle*, by Bartolomé Bennassar et al. (Paris: Hachette, 1979), pp. 314–15. See also Philippe Ariés, "The Indissoluble Marriage," in Ariés and Béjin, *Western Sexuality*, pp. 140–57.

[53] Dedieu, "Le modèle sexuel," p. 317.

[54] An example is Kamen, *Inquisition and Society*.

[55] AHN, Inquisición, Legajo 2075, Números 11, 12, and 20.

[56] Ibid., Número 14.

witnesses more credible than women and minors. Some witnesses were spouses of the accused or the mothers of women whom the accused had married. Their motivation to denounce a person to the Inquisition is easier to understand than that of other witnesses. A possible explanation, similar to that used by Alan Macfarlane in his study of witchcraft in England, is that these ordinary people used the Inquisition, an extraordinary and official institution, to settle old scores and neighborhood grievances.[57]

When inquisitors received testimony accusing a person of bigamy, they allowed a short period in which the accused could come forward and voluntarily confess to them. In most cases, however, inquisitors ordered the accused bigamists imprisoned and then called each into a first hearing without divulging the charges or denunciations. The many accused who confessed to bigamy in this hearing demonstrate very clearly the power of the Inquisition to elicit information even without the use of torture, which is recorded in only one bigamy case.

The explanations that the accused offered for their offense reveal more about what they believed inquisitors wanted to hear than what actually had happened. They usually declared that "some man" or "some people" had told them of the death of the first spouse. Juana Bautista, alias de Torres, who said that she had only married a second husband after hearing the testimony of a witness who swore that her first husband was dead, had even paid the witness six ducats.[58] Francisco Muñoz, alis Ruiz, tried to blame a notary for writing down erroneous information about his marriage.[59] Two other men explained that they had married their first wives in order to help these women leave the brothel in Madrid and their lives of sin; the women disappeared, then, and both men had subsequently remarried.[60] Antonio Robalo confessed that he had married his first wife out of fear of her friend, a law officer, then had fled, changed his name, and married another woman.[61] Miguel de Robledo, alias Sánchez, testified that his first wife had left him. He looked for her for two months, moved to another town, returned twice in the next five years to continue the search, and finally married another woman. After eight years of marriage to his second wife, he received a letter from his first wife reminding him that she was his wife. He replied that she was not his wife, but his "amiga"; she denounced him to the Inquisition and had him imprisoned.[62] María González confessed that she had fled from her first husband because he was a

[57] Alan Macfarlane develops this theme in his *Witchcraft in Tudor and Stuart England* (New York: Harper and Row, 1970).

[58] AHN, Inquisición, Legajo 2075, Número 16.

[59] Ibid., Número 8.

[60] Ibid., Número 10 for Alonso Hernández, and Número 12 for Joan Martín.

[61] Ibid., Número 12.

[62] Ibid., Número 14.

thief. In another city she had lived as a concubine with a Negro, who married her after nine years. Her past caught up with her, however, when seven witnesses swore that she had another husband who was still alive in another town.[63]

Testimony of the accused suggests that marriage did not automatically mean an orderly life. It is true that some marriages lasted for a long period of time before a spouse disappeared. María Rodríguez, for example, said that her husband had left after thirteen years of marriage, but inquisitors did not ask her about the quality of her marriage before his departure.[64] María Escudera testified that her parents had married her to Juan López when she was only ten years old. Because she was so young, she said, she did not live with him as a wife. They went to Carmona to escape an epidemic, and there Juan López disappeared. For five years she had not heard anything from him. She married Bernardo Alonso after a woman told her that Juan López had died. When they found Juan López alive, Bernardo Alonso disappeared, and María Escudera finally entered into a conjugal relationship with Juan López.[65]

Once the accused had confessed to bigamy, inquisitors directed them to appear in a ceremony of penitence, the auto de fe. Usually held in a church, the auto began with a procession of penitents through the streets and plazas of the city. Accused bigamists customarily wore the *corona*, a tall peaked cap, and the *sanbenito*, or penitential sacklike garment, marked with insignias of multiple marriage. During the ceremony, penitents heard their charges and sentences read aloud in a ritual that publicly and solemnly labeled them as bigamists. They then had to respond by renouncing their offenses in an *abjuration de levi*. Male bigamists invariably received one hundred lashes and a sentence of not more than six years in the galleys. Female bigamists might also receive a whipping, but in place of galley service they were generally exiled from Seville or their place of residence. One woman was excused from a whipping because she was nursing a child.[66] Several bigamists received one hundred lashes in the streets of Seville and were then taken to the place of their first marriage, where they received another one hundred lashes.

Marriage in these cases clearly did not provide an orderly resolution for the problems of relations between the sexes. Authorities who tried to make marriage into an institution of stability assumed that relationships between women and men could be orderly if they were sacralized, but not even the

---

[63] Ibid., Número 16.

[64] Ibid., Número 14.

[65] Ibid., Número 20. The parallels between this case and that of Martin Guerre should be noted; see Natalie Zemon Davis, *The Return of Martin Guerre* (Cambridge, Mass. and London: Harvard University Press, 1983).

[66] AHN, Inquisición, Legajo 2075, Número 14.

powerful Church or Inquisition could eliminate abandonment or adultery. In the seventeenth century Francisco Martínez de Mata decried the economic problems that prevented men from marrying and encouraged foreign men to marry women of Spain for the profits they could reap before simply leaving their wives and returning to their homelands.[67] On two occasions, in 1565 and in 1624, wronged husbands called on the ancient secular law that permitted them to publicly execute adulterous wives and their lovers, but these two single cases cannot provide a basis for estimating the numbers of unfaithful wives nor the numbers of men who simply abandoned their wives because they had taken lovers.[68] Although the law and custom were more tolerant of adultery by married men, it is impossible to know how many men took lovers and how many wives responded by leaving them. Obviously, women with several children who depended on husbands for survival would have much less freedom to choose to leave.

María de Zayas y Sotomayor, who published two books about the relationships between women and men in the seventeenth century, recognized that the double standard for sexual behavior depended on more than the economic vulnerability of women and children.[69] Designated by their titles as "love stories," her books actually describe the violence and grief resulting from love, with women invariably suffering the most. In "La fuerza del amor," for example, Zayas tells of the jealousy that strikes the newly married Laura after her husband begins to have an affair with another woman.[70] They quarrel violently, and she considers suicide, crying out, "Woe to the woman who believes in [men], for in the end she will find the cost of her love, as I find it. Who is the foolish one who wants to marry, seeing such things and such pitiful examples?" She blames herself for lacking courage to end her life, but then she lashes out at those who have made the laws and customs so oppressive to women: "Why, vain legislators of the world, do you tie our hands for vengeance, deeming strength impossible to us in your false opinions, for you deny us letters and weapons? Aren't our souls the same as those of men? Well, if it is this that gives

---

[67] *Memoriales de Martínez de Mata*, p. 159.

[68] AMS, Sección Especial, Papeles del Señor Conde de Aguila, Tomo 64, Libros en folio, Número 3.

[69] *Novelas amorosas y exemplares* (Zaragoza: Hospital Real de Nuestra Señora de Gracia, 1637); and *Parte segunda del Sarao y entretenimiento honesto* (Zaragoza: Hospital Real y General de Nuestra Señora de Gracia, 1647). The second book is often referred to as *Desengaños amorosos*. For more on Zayas, see Elizabeth J. Ordoñez, "Woman and Her Text in the Works of María de Zayas and Ana Caro," *Revista de Estudios Históricos* 19, no. 1 (January 1985): 3–15; and Lena E. V. Sylvania, *Doña María de Zayas y Sotomayor: A Contribution to the Study of Her Works* (New York: Columbia University Press, 1922); and Alicia Yllera's critical edition of *Desengaños amorosos* (Madrid: Ediciones Cátedra, 1983).

[70] Reprinted in *Biblioteca de Autores Españoles*, vol. 33 (Madrid: M. Rivadeneyra, 1902). The quotations that follow are my translations from pp. 565–66.

courage to the body, who obligates us to such cowardice? I assure you, if you understood that there is also in us courage and strength, you would not make fun as you do; and so, by making us subjects from our birth, you weaken our strength with fears about honor, and our understanding with the caution of shame, giving us spindles for swords, and instead of books the sewing cushion."

Zayas recognized that her society had made women into a subject class, vulnerable not only in their economic dependence, but also in an emotional, an intellectual, and a social dependence that prevented them from being equals with men in love, marriage, or any other association. Unusual for her consciousness of gender oppression at this time, Zayas cannot really be considered a "feminist" in the modern sense, for she did not call for a change in the patriarchal system that she blamed for oppressing women. At the end of "La fuerza del amor," Laura does not demand an equal education nor a set of rules that would apply equally to her husband and herself. Instead, she declares that she will leave her husband and enter a convent, where she believes that God will be "a more agreeable lover" than her husband. Zayas's solution for Laura repudiates the traditional association of women with disorder, even as it reflects the Counter-Reformation emphasis on purity and enclosure. In her story, the convent offers an alternative to marriage, another form of enclosure for women—not, however, to prevent their sinfulness from spilling over onto others, but to provide women with a safe haven.

Chapter 4

WALLS WITHOUT WINDOWS

WOMEN OF SEVILLE could live within religious rather than domestic enclosure, making their homes within the convents that formed quiet islets in the teeming urban landscape. A few nuns lived in the *emparedamientos*, or walled-up houses, that since the thirteenth century had provided absolute seclusion. By the sixteenth century, however, most nuns who had lived in these shelters had either died or been absorbed into convents. Only three emparedamientos survived: one attached to the parish church of San Miguel, another to the church of San Ildefonso, and a third attached to the church of Santa Catalina.[1] Far more convents provided refuge for nuns in Counter-Reformation Seville. As table 4.1 indicates, twenty-eight convents had been founded in this city and still survived into the seventeenth century.

Not so large as some of the monasteries, convents followed the same pattern as so many other buildings in Seville in presenting to the streets a face without windows. Behind the walls women lived out their lives observing the rules of a religious order and the directions of male confessors. It would be easy to assume that nuns were the most oppressed of all women in this patriarchal society, but to view them as victims ignores the ways that many women in religious orders found increased opportunities for self-expression. Nuns empowered themselves through community, chastity, enclosure, and mystical experiences.[2] Accomplishing this within an authoritarian and hierarchical context that could be very hostile, these women clearly demonstrate not only female strategies for survival, nor merely female participation in patriarchy, but women's subversiveness in expressing and asserting themselves.

Living in a community could empower nuns, for each convent had a founding legend that enhanced the position and prestige of its members. Those in the Convent of San Clemente de Real, for example, knew that no lesser person than Ferdinand III, the "liberator" who was later canonized, had founded their convent on the very day that he delivered Seville from the Muslims in 1248.[3] Established on the site of a royal palace of the Mus-

---

[1] Morgado, *Historia*, p. 472.

[2] Elizabeth A. Petroff, *Medieval Women's Visionary Literature* (New York and Oxford: Oxford University Press, 1986), pp. 32–36, esp. See also Rudolph M. Bell, *Holy Anorexia* (Chicago and London: University of Chicago Press, 1985), pp. 54–55.

[3] AMS, Sección Especial, Papeles del Señor Conde de Aguila, Libros en folio, Tomo 15, Número 1.

TABLE 4.1
Convents in Seville, 1620

Convent	Order	Parish	Date of Founding
S. Clemente	Cistercian	S. Lorenzo	1248
Sta. María de las Dueñas	Cistercian	S. Juan de la Palma	1251
S. Leandro	Augustinian	S. Ildefonso	1295
Sta. Clara	St. Clare	S. Lorenzo	1298
Sta. Inés	St. Clare	S. Pedro	1376
Sta. María la Real	Augustinian	S. Vincente	1403
Concepción de S. Juan	Franciscan, tertiaries	S. Juan	1475
Sta. Paula	Jeronimite	S. Marcos	1475
Madre de Dios	Dominican	S. Nicolas	1476
Sta. Isabel	Comendadore de S. Juan	S. Marcos	1490
Nta. Sra. del Carmen[a]	Carmelite	S. Gil	1513
Sta. María de Jesús	Franciscan, barefoot	S. Esteban	1520
Nta. Sra. del Socorro	Franciscan	S. Marcos	1522
Regina Angelorum	Dominican	S. Pedro	1522
Sta. María de Gracia	Dominican	S. Miguel	1525
Nombre de Jesús	Augustinian	S. Vicente	1550
Espíritu Santo	Franciscan, Pauline	Triana	1563
Nta. Sra. de Consolación	Franciscan	Triana	1566
Asunción de Nta. Sra.	Mercenarian	S. Vicente	1567
Nta. Sra. de la Paz	Augustinian	Sta. Catalina	1571
S. José	Carmelite, barefoot	Sta. Iglesia	1574
Victorias	Franciscan	Triana	1585
La Pasión	Dominican	S. Nicolas	1587
Encarnación	Carmelite	S. Pedro	1591
Concepción de Nta. Sra.	Carmelite	Magdalena	1594
Nta. Sra. de los Reyes	Dominican, barefoot	Santiago Viejo	1611

Source: Alonso Morgado, *Historia de Sevilla*, passim; and Diego Ortiz de Zuñiga, *Anales eclesiásticos y seculares de la muy noble y muy leal ciudad de Sevilla*, passim.

[a] Name subsequently changed to Encarnación and Belén.

lims, the convent became a burial place for royal bodies. Wives, sisters, and daughters of monarchs entered this convent over the years, and many other "principal persons" endowed it with income-producing property. Nuns in San Clemente knew the self-confidence of belonging to a community of well-born women whose convent was reputed to be the city's richest and largest in the sixteenth century.[4]

Convents also gained prestige through association with a sacred image. The Convent of Santa María de las Dueñas was originally established in 1251 as a congregation of only two nuns that had been endowed to pray each Monday for the soul of their benefactor.[5] It quickly grew in size and fame, however, when it became the home of the image called Nuestra Señora de Bulto de Marmol. According to legend, this marble statue of Mary had been hidden when the Muslims took over most of the Iberian Peninsula. Then, several centuries later, after Christians defeated the Muslims in Seville, a shepherd found the image in the trunk of a tree and took it to the parish church of San Juan de la Palma. However, that night the image returned to its hiding place and spoke to the shepherd as he prayed to tell him that he must take it to the Convent of the Dueñas. There it attracted many gifts and endowments for the convent as stories spread of miraculous feats attributed to the image.

Augustinian nuns founded the Convent of San Leandro in 1295 at a site reputed to be the hermitage of the martyred sisters Justa and Rufina. Because it was outside the walls near the gate of Córdoba, opinion grew that it should be moved. A manuscript described the great aggravation and damage that this convent suffered and attributed these misfortunes to its vulnerability outside the protective walls of the city.[6] Later the convent moved into the city when it received from the king some houses that he had confiscated from a woman who had said "certain free words against his royal person."[7] Such evidence of royal favor ensured that daughters of noble families would choose to enter this convent and that it would continue to enjoy the protection and financial support of well-placed nobles.

Nuns of Santa Clara came from Guadalajara to establish a Franciscan convent in Seville in the thirteenth century. Founded some forty years earlier in Italy by a devoted disciple of Saint Francis, this order observed strict

---

[4] Morgado, *Historia*, pp. 436–38.

[5] Ibid., p. 449; AMS, Sección Especial, Papeles del Señor Conde de Aguila, Libros en folio, Tomo 15, Número 13.

[6] Quoted in Antonio Ballesteros, *Sevilla en el siglo XIII* (Madrid: Juan Pérez Torres, 1913), p. 141; see also Marcelle Bernstein, *Nuns* (London: Collins, 1976), p. 55, for an explanation of the need for convent walls; and Morgado, *Historia*, p. 452, for the ancient site. Note that Ortiz de Zuñiga, *Anales*, 5: 65, gives the founding date as 1310.

[7] AMS, Sección Especial, Papeles del Señor Conde de Aguila, Libros en folio, Tomo 15, Número 15.

enclosure and perpetual discipline. Emphasizing poverty, the Poor Clares in Italy sometimes had "extern sisters" who begged food from door to door so that their cloistered sisters could devote all their time to prayer.[8] In their community in the Plaza de San Francisco in Seville, these nuns worked and prayed and developed a reputation for the special holiness of poverty. Doña María Coronel, who disfigured her face with boiling oil to escape the unwanted passion of the king, founded and endowed the Convent of Santa Inés for nuns of the Order of Saint Clare in 1376 and died as its abbess. Followers of Saint Clare founded a third convent, that of Santa María de Jesús, in 1520.[9] All of these communities shared the unique status granted to those who sacrificed worldly wealth in order to devote their lives to God.

More than half the convents still existing in Seville by the middle of the seventeenth century had been founded in the sixteenth century. Counter-Reformation zeal for monastic life accounts for some of this activity, but it also resulted from population increase in the sixteenth century and from the continuing desirability of placing daughters in convents when marriage did not seem suitable. None of these convents provided for an active vocation outside the cloister, as the Ursulines and Daughters of Charity did in Italy and France. Obeying the Tridentine directive to enforce cloistering of all female religious, Spanish convents followed a broader prescriptive order that valued enclosure for women of the middle and upper classes more than their public service in nursing, education, and charity.

Many of the convents had been founded by noble women for women of their own class. In 1522, for example, doña Juana de Ayala from a noble house in Seville founded the Convent of Nuestra Señora del Socorro for twenty noble women, stipulating that preference be given to descendants of her and her sister, doña María de Ayala.[10] The five oldest convents of the city had been intended for the daughters of nobles, and more than one hundred noble women had lived in each of them at various times. Before cloistering became more strictly enforced in the mid-sixteenth century, these noble nuns often attended services in the cathedral and prayed at sepulchers. Most convents founded for noble women received enough wealth in dowries and bequests that their nuns could live in some comfort.

---

[8] Ballesteros, *Sevilla*, pp. 143–45.

[9] Gil González Dávila, *Teatro eclesiástico de las iglesias metropolitanas, y catedrales de los reynos de los dos Castillas* (Madrid: Pedro de Hornay Villanueva, 1647), 2: 38; Morgado, *Historia*, pp. 441–47, discusses the legendary doña María Coronel. Francisco M. Tubino, *Pedro de Castilla: La leyenda de doña María Coronel y la muerte de d. Fadrique* (Madrid: Principales Liberías, 1887), also discusses her role in founding the convent, but his interpretation of the legend exonerates Pedro.

[10] Ortiz de Zuñiga, *Anales*, 3: 329.

However, even these nuns were reported to go out sometimes to sell their threads and handwork at respectable places.[11]

Poverty, however perceived as holy, posed a very real problem of survival for less wealthy convents. Resentment increased against nuns dependent on charity in the later sixteenth century as new convents sprang up, population density increased, and townspeople felt beleaguered by hands held out for alms from every direction. Unable to depend upon alms from city residents, some nuns worked to earn money and provisions for their convents, particularly in silk weaving and embroidery. As noted earlier, stricter enforcement of sumptuary laws and the influx of French-made products into the market undercut the earnings of Spanish nuns.[12]

A natural disaster, such as a flood or epidemic, was especially catastrophic for convents that functioned close to a subsistence level. The Convent of Santa María la Real, for example, petitioned the king in 1597 for funds to help rebuild their church and dormitories damaged by flooding.[13] So poor that it could feed its people on only three days of the week, the convent noted that it was impossible to make the necessary repairs without some outside help. Fortunately, the king agreed, but he gave only three hundred of the nine to ten thousand ducats that the convent estimated it needed.

Convents seeking extra income took in secular boarders, usually girls, whose families paid for their board and education. The addition of these paying guests seemed to dilute the rules of the religious orders as it brought nuns into more contact with the external world. They received presents from their tenants and shared diversions with them, and some nuns even left the cloister for several days at a time and visited or carried out their work away from the convent. Ecclesiastical authorities who believed that any contact with the secular world weakened the discipline of religious orders argued at the Council of Trent that nuns should be strictly cloistered.[14] The Council approved this position and even agreed that bishops should call upon help from "the secular arm" when necessary to en-

[11] Ibid., 5: 65–66.

[12] See chap. 1, above. For the effects of sumptuary laws, see Domínguez Ortiz, *Orto y ocaso*, p. 80; the depression of silk weaving is noted in *Memoriales de Martínez de Mata*, pp. 194–95; and in Antonio Domínguez Ortiz, *El estamento eclesiástico*, vol. 2 of *La sociedad española en el siglo XVII* (Madrid: Consejo Superior de Investigaciones Científicas, 1970), p. 119. See idem, *Golden Age of Spain*, p. 186; and his *Orto y ocaso*, pp. 34–36 and 84.

[13] AHN, Consejos, Legajo 4415, Número 128.

[14] Domínguez Ortiz, *Estamento*, pp. 121–22; *Canons and Decrees of the Council of Trent*, trans. H. J. Schroeder, O.P. (St. Louis and London: Herder Books, 1941), pp. 220–21. Catholic reformers called for cloistering before the Council of Trent, and they also prescribed it for certain male orders. According to Domíngez Ortiz, however, cloistering was more strictly enforced following Trent, and it was more severely imposed on nuns.

force cloistering regulations. In a bull of 1566 Pope Pius V formally abolished any privileges or customs contrary to cloistering.

Contact between nuns and secular people continued to cause consternation. The presence of servants or slaves in convents belied the urgency for contributions to the nuns and, at the same time, incurred boarding expenses that consumed the convents' wealth. In 1591, for example, eight black women were purchased for the Convent of the Incarnation to replace eight servants who had died, but very shortly economic difficulties beset this convent. It became apparent that overspending had depleted the original endowment to such an extent that the convent could not support itself.[15] Some convents assigned their lowly chores to tertiaries or lay sisters, as well as secular women. Only the reformed Carmelite convents forbade the use of any servants whatsoever.[16] Occasionally servants embroiled convents in sordid crimes, such as the scandal that resulted in 1597 in the hanging of one maid and the whipping of two others.[17]

Even more damaging to nuns' reputations were the so-called *devotos*, or men who chose young and attractive nuns as objects of devotion. Either clerics or secular, these men made signals to them in church and sent messages and gifts to them when they could not see them. Luis Góngora and Francisco de Quevedo satirized the devotos' worship of nuns as a threadbare form of courtly love, a sacrifice of consummation for "sugar candy," to become "do-nothing lovers."[18] Ecclesiastical authorities saw no humor in the situation and tried to prevent the nuns from being seen by their devotos. In 1613 Rome received denunciations that nuns in the Convent of Santa Paula in Seville were being courted by a group of prebendaries.[19] When Jeronimite monks of the city intervened to punish the nuns and make them install a protective grille, the prebendaries made their own denunciations against the Jeronimites' relations with the nuns. The Spanish ambassador to the Vatican wrote of his distress that the scandal could divulge the weaknesses of certain nuns from noble families. He might have added that the problem of devotos could harm the reputation of all nuns, who were supposed to be chaste and spiritual, with their eyes on a heavenly spouse.

Female chastity was considered so important in this society that the vow

[15] Domínguez Ortiz, *Estamento*, p. 126; P. Andres Llorden, O.S.A., *Apuntes históricos de los conventos sevillanos de religiosas agustinas* (Escorial: Imprenta del Monasterio, 1944), pp. 41–42, esp.

[16] Antonio Gil Ambrona, "Entre la oración y el trabajo: Las ocupaciones de las otras esposas. Siglos XVI–XVII," in Matilla and Ortega, *El trabajo de las mujeres*, p. 61.

[17] Pedro de León, *Compendio*, appendix 1 to pt. 2, case 241.

[18] Quoted in José Deleito y Piñuela, *La vida religiosa española bajo el quarto Felipe: Santos y pecadores* (Madrid: Espasa-Calpe, 1952), pp. 116–21.

[19] Domínguez Ortiz, *Estamento*, pp. 124–25.

of chastity empowered all women who became nuns, regardless of their economic class. It provided practical advantages such as independence from the dangers and demands of childbearing, and a psychic freedom from the expectations of marriage. Because many in early modern Spain praised chastity as the highest state for a Christian, it also increased the status of these women as symbols of purity. One friar who wrote a book about women declared that chastity originated in heaven. He said that God granted the gift of prophecy to the sibyls, virtuous women in the ancient world, as a reward for their chastity. This virtue, in his words, was "the beauty that is most splendid in woman."[20] In addition, chastity was believed to strengthen women: "Zeal for holy chastity and virginity makes a weak young woman or woman of whatever sort stronger than many men, and than the whole world, and than all hell; and when men see such extreme energy and force, they are afraid and jump back dismayed."[21] Although some women entered religious orders as widows, most became nuns as virgins, and their virginity ensured them, in the words of another cleric of the early sixteenth century, lives as angels.[22]

Prescriptive literature for nuns, however, suggests that angelic lives did not come easily. The Franciscan Juan de la Cerda, for example, emphasized the importance of the mistress of novitiates and charged her to teach the novices absolute and immediate obedience. He also gave careful instructions for how the nun must behave in choir, in the refectory, and especially in her cell where she must be always busy "so that the devil does not find her unoccupied." Nuns should speak only to the abbess and mistress of novitiates, unless ordered to speak to others, and then they should say only a few words that must be "meek, low, and brief." It is true that men were also expected to keep silence in certain monasteries, but Cerda noted that silence for women became a "precious virtue" as he repeated the classic misogynistic warning against women who speak all the time and never keep a secret.[23]

In the convent, safely closed away from the temptations of the world, the nun could live the life of the angels, according to Cerda, yet she lives in a "mortal and dirty body." True chastity requires her to closely guard her heart and five bodily senses through which "the soul dies," and she

---

[20] Juan de la Cerda, *Vida política*, pp. 63ʳ–69ʳ. For the view of chastity as a defense against marriage, see the introduction to *Beyond Their Sex: Learned Women of the European Past*, ed. Patricia H. Labalme (New York and London: New York University Press, 1980), p. 4. See also in the same volume Margaret L. King, "Book-Lined Cells: Women and Humanism in the Early Italian Renaissance," p. 78.

[21] Pérez de Valdivia, *Aviso*, p. 666. Marina Warner, *Alone of All Her Sex: The Myth and the Cult of the Virgin Mary* (New York: Vintage, 1983), p. 72, discusses the long tradition of attributing strength to sexual purity.

[22] Fray Martín de Córdoba, *Jardín*, p. 271.

[23] Juan de la Cerda, *Vida política*, pp. 117ʳ, 115ʳ, 118ʳ, 119ʳ.

must never touch or look at her own body except when absolutely necessary. Discipline and mortification, the friar continues, curb the flesh and its appetites, but the "major sign of true mortification is obedience." "O, how securely lives she who lives beneath the yoke of obedience," Cerda exclaims. Nuns must obey priests, not merely when they are good and just, but even when they are evil, because Christ said that the priest rules in the place of God. "One does not have to look at the vices and faults that there are in the priest, but at the jurisdiction and authority that he has."[24]

Fragile and subject to temptations that disguised Satan as "an Angel of light," nuns had to protect themselves by working with all their strength "to uncover the heart and all the temptations and thoughts to the confessor."[25] This directive became the seed of very significant relationships as oral confession became more widely practiced after the mid-sixteenth century. The priest to whom the nun confessed held a position of considerable power over her, in translating to her the Church's teachings and God's judgments of her soul. The ritual of confession placed her on her knees and required her to examine herself for her transgressions. From a position of subjection, however, she could say things within this ritual that would otherwise be unspeakable, and she could also know that the confessional provided one place where her words would be taken seriously. Here she not only could break the rule of silence; she was expected, indeed obligated, to speak. Not a few nuns developed close relationships with their confessors, and some attained considerable influence over them.

Confession seemed to require nuns to describe individual mystical experiences that flourished in the sixteenth century and threatened the tranquillity of the convent from within. Not far from Seville, reports of ecstasies and visions among nuns of the Convent of Santa Isabel de los Angeles in Córdoba so troubled ecclesiastical authorities that they made a special investigation.[26] They focused in particular on sor Magdalena de la Cruz, who had been elected prioress in 1533, 1536, and 1539.[27] After she had been placed in the convent by her parents at the age of seven, this woman had developed a great reputation for holiness, disciplining herself with long and rigorous fasts and always wearing a hair shirt. She claimed to have powers to know the unknown, and she said that she could transport herself all over the world with the aid of a staff she had first seen, as she prayed, reaching from the ground to the heights. Many people believed she was a

[24] Ibid., pp. 145, 126ʳ–127, 226, 123ʳ, 235ʳ.

[25] Ibid., p. 122.

[26] Marcelino Menéndez y Pelayo, *Historia de los heterodoxos españoles* (Madrid: Biblioteca de Autores Cristianos, 1956), 2: 176–77.

[27] Letter of Luis de Zapata, reported in Jesús Imirizaldu, *Monjas y beatas embaucadoras* (Madrid: Editorial Nacional, 1977), pp. 33–34; see also Sánchez Ortega, "La mujer, el amor y la religión," pp. 52–53.

saint; when Prince Philip was born, her vestments were used to wrap him and thus defend him from the devil.[28]

Church officials became alarmed as other nuns in sor Magdalena's convent reported having visions. Her visionary experiences appeared to have become contagious, and in the ensuing epidemic some of the nuns began to believe that these visions came from the devil rather than God. They reported among other things that they saw many black goats at the head of sor Magdalena's bed. Once accusations of diabolical possession were made, the Inquisition entered the investigation and convinced sor Magdalena to confess that for forty years she had been a servant of the devil, who appeared to her as an elegant man. He had promised to give her more fame and celebrity than any other woman in Spain. Through the devil's help, she said, she had been able to see the battle of Pavia and to describe the imprisonment of the king of France. Sentenced to appear in a public auto de fe gagged and holding a candle, with a rope around her neck, and then to be banished from her convent to reclusion where she was forbidden to talk with anyone without permission, sor Magdalena could no longer cause trouble among her sister nuns. Yet the problem persisted: the Church might enforce a strict enclosure of nuns to protect them from harmful outside influences, but it was more difficult to regulate the inner lives of these cloistered nuns.

Mysticism, which blossomed in the sixteenth century, provided an avenue for vivid individual experiences that could not be easily controlled. Within the framework of daily mental prayer and meditation, convent life contained opportunities for mystical experiences that male confessors and strict prioresses could not always restrain. The nun who saw visions and heard God or Christ or the Virgin speak to her directly may have felt her unworthiness, but she also must have felt the great power of knowing that she could communicate with heaven directly, independent of priestly intercessors. Male clerics became devoted followers of "spiritual mothers," as they called these visionary women whose special gifts prompted an inversion of the customary gender positions.[29]

The religious habit provided some license for women to speak out if others believed that God was speaking through them. Breaking through the usual repression of women's public voices, female visionaries cried out in exaltation. Others listened with more attention if they spoke with emotion rather than reason, and from sensual experience rather than intellectual learning, for gender beliefs proscribed women's engaging in public

---

[28] Testimony of Francisco de Encinas, in Imirizaldu, *Monjas y beatas*, pp. 37–38.

[29] One of these cases of the spiritual mother and her clerical son is discussed in depth in Angela Selke, *El Santo Oficio de la Inquisición: Proceso de fr. Francisco Ortiz (1529–1532)* (Madrid: Ediciones Guadarrama, 1968); see also Sánchez Ortega, "La mujer, el amor y la religión," pp. 55–57.

debates. Increased attempts to enforce strict gender prescriptions undoubt-edly promoted irrational outbursts from visionary women, who had few other ways to express themselves publicly.

Inquisitors in Seville remained very skeptical of "spiritual mothers," de-crying especially their "arrogance" in assuming the right to teach and ex-plain points of dogma. Francisca de Chaves, a professed nun in the Con-vent of Santa Isabel, had been condemned as a heretic by the Inquisition in 1560 after thirteen witnesses accused her of "Lutheran teachings."[30] Given the opportunity to recant and "return to the body of the Holy Ro-man Church that like a pious mother always has its arms open to receive her," this nun declared that she could not do or say anything that was against her conscience. Inquisitors told her that what she thought was from her conscience was "of a false spirit," and that the experience she be-lieved confirmed her ideas was merely "illusion and not revelation." To this, Francisca responded "with great liberty" and declared that what she understood to be true "was written with the finger of God," and she knew this with more certainty "than all the learned men in the world." The In-quisition agreed to have learned people speak with her to persuade her of the error of her beliefs, but the nun remained adamant and died as a here-tic.

Teresa de Jesús, one of the most noteworthy of the spiritual mothers of Counter-Reformation Spain, came to Seville in 1575 with a little band of six nuns to found a reformed Carmelite convent.[31] Here, as in other towns and cities of the period, some residents opposed the founding of more convents within urban space that they perceived as already overcrowded.[32] Teresa listened to Archibishop Rojas's objections that another convent would overtax the city's financial support, but she was able to win his sup-port. She faced even stronger opposition from the unreformed Carmelite monks who resented her insistence on restoring the "primitive rule" of poverty, labor, and silence.[33] Accusing her of causing schism and destruc-tion, the unreformed monks made such a commotion on the very day that those agreeing to the reform were to declare their obedience that Teresa nearly despaired. God intervened, according to one of the reformed nuns,

---

[30] AHN, Inquisición, Legajo 2075, Número 3.

[31] See *The Complete Works of Saint Teresa of Jesus*, trans. E. A. Peers (London and New York: Sheed and Ward, 1957), vol. 3, *Foundations*, chaps. 24 and 25; and also Pedro M. Pinero Ramírez, *La Sevilla imposible de Santa Teresa* (Seville: Ayuntamiento de Sevilla, 1982).

[32] Domínguez Ortiz, *Estamento*, p. 77. For more on the urban response to Teresa's reforms, see Jodi Bilinkoff, *The Avila of Saint Teresa: Religious Reform in a Sixteenth-Century City* (Ith-aca: Cornell University Press, 1989).

[33] María Luisa Cano Navas, *El Convento de San José del Carmen de Sevilla. Las Teresas. Es-tudio histórico-artístico* (Seville: Universidad de Sevilla, 1984), pp. 20–21.

and scolded Teresa: "Oh, woman of little faith! calm yourself for it is going well."[34]

Even more disturbing than the expected opposition of unreformed monks, a woman of saintly reputation in Seville entered the convent that Teresa had founded and subsequently denounced the members to the Inquisition. The first prioress of the convent wrote that when the woman found she could not endure the rigors of life in the convent, this "poor little one" accused the nuns of immoral practices and beliefs of the alumbrado heresy.[35] Inquisitors began to come and go at the tiny convent, questioning the nuns and writing reports of their suspicions to superiors.

Isabel de San Jerónimo, one of the nuns who came with Teresa to found her convent in Seville, caused many anxious moments during the inquisitors' investigation because Teresa realized that the mystical enthusiasms of this nun could be associated with the alumbrado heresy. Three years earlier, Teresa had written to another nun of her concern about the "illness" of Isabel de San Jerónimo and her hope that Juan de la Cruz could cure her, using his gifts to cast out devils from afflicted people.[36] Despite her constant effort to monitor this nun whose behavior could look so suspect to inquisitors, Teresa had not been able to prevent them from suspecting that Isabel's statements implicated Teresa herself in "novel, superstitious doctrine, of tricks and similarity with the alumbrados of Extremadura."[37] Teresa stated, in fact, that she feared that her visions were the devil's work or the product of her own "womanish imaginations."[38] Finally satisfying the inquisitors that Isabel represented neither the nuns of the convent nor her own beliefs, Teresa left her new convent in hopes that it would be able to survive the "injustices that are protected" in Seville and "the little truth, the duplicities," of the people she had met there.[39]

María de San José, the first prioress of the convent, found herself embroiled in another problem after Teresa's departure in 1576. The cleric

[34] BN, MS 2176, María de San José, *Ramilleta de Mirra*, pp. 102ʳ–103; see also excerpts from her *Libro de recreaciones*, in Serrano y Sanz, *Apuntes*, 270: 344–50.

[35] *Ramilleta*, pp. 103ʳ–104.

[36] Quoted in Pinero Ramírez, *Sevilla imposible*, p. 76. For more on the alumbrado heresy, see Antonio Márquez, *Los Alumbrados, orígines y filosofía, 1525–1559* (Madrid: Taurus, 1972), and also chap. 5, below.

[37] Quoted in Pinero Ramírez, *Sevilla imposible*, p. 74.

[38] This is in her Relación 7, p. 394 in *The Life of St. Teresa of Avila, Including the Relations of Her Spiritual State*, trans. David Lewis (Westminster, Md.: Newman Press, 1962); see also AHN, Inquisición, Legajo 2072, Número 43, for denunciations of Teresa before the Inquisition, including accusations of the alumbrado heresy.

[39] Her letter to her niece, María Bautista, quoted in Pinero Ramírez, *Sevilla imposible*, p. 78. For more on Teresa's uneasy relationship with the Inquisition, see Enrique Llamas Martínez, *Santa Teresa de Jesús y la Inquisición española* (Madrid: Consejo Superior de Investigaciones Científicas, 1972).

assigned as confessor to the nuns of the convent began to have long conversations with Isabel de San Jerónimo and Beatriz de la Madre de Dios, sometimes together and at other times apart. According to the prioress, their confessions might go on for three or four months.[40] She saw the cleric as "ignorant, confused, neither educated nor experienced," a man whose counsel to the two nuns increased their beliefs that anything which entered their imaginations was a direct communication from God. María de San José tried to limit the time he spent with Isabel and Beatriz, but she sensed that she would be the loser in the ensuing power struggle with the confessor. When she appealed to Teresa for help, her mentor advised her to endure the aggravation and conceal it, knowing that the Lord in this way allowed demons to afflict them for their greater perfection.

Finally in the summer of 1578, María de San José dismissed the cleric as confessor, but the Carmelite provincial who came to visit the convent then ordered him reinstated. Now both Beatriz de la Madre de Dios and a novice joined the cleric in writing testimony against the prioress, which they gave to the visiting provincial. Whether in irony or in humility, María de San José wrote that their "ignorance" helped her to purge herself of her sins; it also prompted the Carmelite provincial to remove the prioress from her position. In order to completely humiliate this audacious woman, he replaced her with Beatriz de la Madre de Dios.

María de San José was ordered imprisoned in her convent, with strict orders that no one was to speak to her, neither anyone from outside nor anyone from within the convent. The provincial and others made such lying accusations that her sisters feared for her safety. When men came to take her before the provincial, the deposed abbess wrote, her sisters began such a sobbing that one would have thought she was being called before a hanging judge. The harsh words spoken against her grieved her, she recalled, naming her a Judas among the apostles and a wolf in sheep's clothing, a troublemaker "and other worse things with such cries that made one tremble." They threatened her with excommunication and her convent with destruction, and they returned her to her cell "deprived of voice and place." When she fell ill during her imprisonment, the doctor ordered her to eat meat. She could not, however, saying that "we were not used to such gifts."[41] Enraged, the provincial ordered her to eat, calling her a hypocrite and a fake who preached penitence and ate only vegetables.

"The black vicaress," as Teresa described Beatriz, held the office of prioress throughout the winter of 1578 and the early months of 1579.[42] When a new provincial for the reformed Carmelites ruled that María de

---

[40] María de San José, *Ramilleta*, p. 106r.

[41] Ibid., pp. 114, 114r, 115r.

[42] See chap. 26 of her *Foundations* and also p. 127 of Pinero Ramírez, *Sevilla imposible*.

San José should be reinvested with her office as prioress in June of that year, this woman who knew so well the tribulations of the position tried to refuse. "This is not simply the business of your reverence," Teresa reprimanded her, "but of the entire Order."[43] Teresa also asked her to be kind to the nun whose denunciations had deposed her, suggesting that "the devil must be at the back of this," and that "she is not so much to blame as we thought she was, just as no blame attaches to a madman who really gets it into his head that he is God the Father so that nothing will drive the idea out again."[44]

Despite her ordeal in the new convent in Seville, María de San José maintained her innocence and preserved a remarkable sense of freedom. She gathered strength, she wrote in her *Ramilleta*, from knowing her own "free and pure conscience," and she knew that in the midst of the tempest at Seville, Jesus would "extend his powerful hand and free us." Later when she was again accused of wrongdoing as abbess in Lisbon, she wrote that she saw her enemies as "priests discontented that we enjoy this holy freedom." The abbess cautioned her sisters, however, that the freedom she spoke of was not liberty to say or do as each wished. "To some of us no fear appears, and to others the much more vain pretensions make us fall from the heaven of truth to the abyss of lies, where we do not live free as we think, but as vile slaves of a thousand whims." Their enemies accused the Barefoot Carmelites of inventing lies through heretical liberty, she warned, but she also insisted that they had found true freedom in their poverty and faith.[45]

María de San José, like many other women who became nuns in this period, found not only personal freedom from the cares of the world, but freedom to think and to write and to redefine reality. This woman, whom Teresa called "my lettered one," wrote beautiful prose and poetry about the Carmelite reform and her own inner state, but she did not write about obedience or subjection to male clerics.[46] In contrast to Teresa who called upon nuns to submit themselves in obedience to the counsel of "learned men,"[47] María de San José wrote of clerics as "ignorant and blind men." She described their opposition to her as opportunity to strengthen herself through humility, but also through clarification of her own sense of purpose. Identifying her opponents as agents of the devil, she fortified her resolve to resist them, warning her sisters that "the ancient serpent has

---

[43] Quoted in Pinero Ramírez, *Sevilla imposible*, p. 128.

[44] *The Letters of Saint Teresa*, trans. and ed. E. Allison Peers (London: Burns, Oates and Washbourne, 1951), Letter 274, May 3, 1579, p. 648.

[45] María de San José, *Ramilleta*, pp. 122, 137ʳ, 144–144ʳ, 145ʳ.

[46] Cano Navas, *Convento*, p. 18.

[47] See, e.g., in *Complete Works*, Teresa's prologue to her *Foundations*, 3: 42; and *Conceptions*, 2: 362.

raised against us such a war."[48] And she felt her strength in a martial sense, writing that she was surrounded by "a squadron of virgins" who carry "valorous arms against the common enemy."[49] "Do not be weak," she urged her sister nuns, "lose the fear that has gripped you." She reminded them that they were "witnesses of our fervent hearts, and of some burning words with which you have uncovered the ardent desire to die for Christ your Spouse." Martyrdom for this woman required strength, not surrender, and a tenacious will to fight.

Again and again María de San José writes of freedom and liberty that come not from human will, but from God's mercy. Describing her many sins, she adds, "Glory be to my Lord, who freed me from them." She calls upon God to free her from the infamies and tribulations of the world, and she affirms her faith that God will free those who wait on him.[50] When she was again imprisoned in 1593 in the convent in Lisbon, she wrote to her sisters that they should not be concerned for her, even though "all doors are closed of human means for my liberty," because through prayer all of them could provide her with the greatest support in presenting her to God.

María de San José found personal freedom through the inspiration of Teresa de Jesús. In a poem entitled "Elegía," she elevated Teresa to divine status, describing her as "the sublime goddess of Carmel." She used the metaphor most often reserved for Christ in the same poem as she called Teresa "sweet shepherdess" whose sheep enjoyed "the freest leap in the meadow."[51] Throughout her writings, María de San José referred to Teresa as "our holy mother," a title not unlike "holy father" for the pope.

Through writing María de San José found an acceptable way to express her passion. "Call me to be Queen in an eternal Kingdom," she besought God, "with a spouse in whose hands are life and death, honor and dishonor." "Oh, King, and spouse of mine," she wrote with ardor, indicating how his love empowered her to lose timidity, "whom I now call with less shame and more spirit." "This sweetest spouse, this only desire of my soul," she continued in the sensual style so reminiscent of Teresa, "I have you as a bunch of myrrh between my breasts."[52]

Convent life provided the opportunity to meditate on feelings, as long as they had to do with God, and on ideas that could be used to explicate the Bible and other holy writings. Another nun, Constanza Ossorio, who had entered the Convent of the Dueñas in Seville in 1573 when she was eight years old, learned to emulate the piety of the Virgin, shown in figure

[48] María de San José, *Ramilleta*, p. 170.
[49] BN, MS 3537, "Carta que escribe una pobre, y presa descalça consolándose, y consolando a sus Hermanas, y hijas que por berla asi estaban afligidas, del año 1593."
[50] María de San José, *Ramilleta*, pp. 169, 166ʳ–167.
[51] Ibid., pp. 130ʳ, 133ʳ–135.
[52] Ibid., pp. 165ʳ, 166, 168.

11 as a child. In addition, she learned Latin without a teacher and became so proficient in music that after taking holy orders she served as director of the chapel for both choir and organ for forty years.[53] During her lifetime, she also published *Exposición de los Psalmos*, which contained a preparatory exercise to be used before the hourly observations, translations into prose and poetry of several psalms, discourses on chapters 19 and 53 of Isaiah, and explications of concepts such as the *Gloria Patri* and the *Invitatorio*. In her *Huerta del celestial esposo*, published after her death, Constanza Ossorio did not hesitate to write her own explanation for the Trinity.

Women who lived in convents had a unique opportunity to develop the autonomy that most married women lacked. In contrast with earthbound husbands, the heavenly spouse of nuns appeared to them in individual visions that validated their special status. Life in the convent provided nuns the opportunity to learn and to write down their experiences and knowledge with a self-confidence that must have been much more difficult for women living in the homes of their husbands. Becoming a nun, as a present-day scholar has pointed out, permitted a young woman to simultaneously rebel against her social condition in the secular world and recapture her individual reality and self-sufficiency.[54] Energy that married women had to expend on childbirth and childrearing could be devoted by nuns to reading, writing, and music. It is not surprising that some women vehemently insisted, over protests of family members who wanted them to marry, that they preferred to become nuns rather than wives.[55]

Yet not all nuns became accomplished scholars, nor did all married women fail to develop self-confidence. Ana de Jesús, who married a widower with six children when she was only sixteen or seventeen years old, later wrote that in a vision God had directed her to marry rather than become a nun.[56] She followed her husband to the war in Portugal and then to Seville, where they were extremely poor. When a person gave them a little bread, Ana took it into her hands and raised it up to consecrate it. Acting the role of a priest, she said to God, "Lord, receive this bread into your hands." Then she divided it and gave it to all those with her, and, in a miracle like that of the loaves and the fishes, she gathered up enough leftover bread to feed her children the next day. In everyday dialogues with

---

[53] Serrano y Sanz, *Apuntes*, 270: 90–93.

[54] Petroff, *Visionary Literature*, pp. 3–59. Also see the very fine article by Electa Arenal, "The Convent as Catalyst for Autonomy: Two Hispanic Nuns of the Seventeenth Century," in *Women in Hispanic Literature*, ed. Beth Miller (Berkeley and Los Angeles: University of California Press, 1983), pp. 147–83.

[55] Sánchez Ortega, "La mujer, el amor y la religión," p. 44; see also chap. 2, above.

[56] I want to thank Professor Darcy Donahue, who discussed this person with me and showed me her manuscript. This and all other information about Ana is from her *Vida de la Venerable Ana de Jesús escrita por ella misma*, BN, MS 13493. See also Serrano y Sanz, *Apuntes*, 269: 545–46.

FIGURE 11. *The Virgin as a Child in Ecstasy*, by Francisco Zurbarán (The Metropolitan Museum of Art, Fletcher Fund, 1927).

God and Jesus, this very poor married woman learned that she had the gifts of healing and of prophecy. Devastated though she was by the deaths of her children and her husband, Ana grew stronger in her faith and, despite her lack of a dowry, was allowed to profess as a nun just before she died in 1617. Her religious calling undoubtedly played a much greater role than the economic and psychological motivations that prompted many other widows to enter a convent.[57]

More often, a woman became a nun as an adolescent, bringing with her a dowry that provided an essential economic base for the survival of the convent.[58] Repeatedly, Teresa had written to her convent in Seville cautioning them not to take postulants without dowries. Earlier she had accepted some without dowries "provided they are spiritual persons, and then the Lord sends me others with dowries, which puts things right."[59] By the time she had founded the convent in Seville, she believed that five hundred ducats was enough as a dowry to get a young girl accepted into any convent, but by 1620 wills provided one thousand ducats as charitable dowries for young women who sought to become nuns.[60] Young postulants frequently took their vows after spending a childhood in the convent. Letters of payment from Seville show that parents paid dowries to convents for daughters as young as four years, although the acceptable age for becoming a postulant was sixteen.[61]

Valentina Pinelo, the daughter of wealthy Genoese parents in Seville and the niece of Cardinal Dominico Pinelo, entered the Augustinian Convent of San Leandro in Seville when she was only four years old.[62] Having received her education from the nuns, she later took vows. In the routine of the convent, Pinelo was able to pursue her love of Latin and biblical study. An "excellent poet," according to the late seventeenth-century historian Ortiz de Zuñiga, Pinelo wrote highly esteemed verse.[63] In 1601 she published in Seville a book of praise for Saint Anne entitled *Libro de alabanzas y excelencias de la Gloriosa Santa Anna*, which is one of the few writings by

---

[57] Sánchez Ortega, "La mujer, el amor y la religión," pp. 49–50.

[58] For official concerns that nuns who only took simple vows could withdraw their dowries from convents and that some convents were consuming their dowries too rapidly, see Ruth P. Liebowitz, "Virgins in the Service of Christ: The Dispute Over an Active Apostolate for Women During the Counter-Reformation," in *Women of Spirit: Female Leadership in the Jewish and Christian Traditions*, ed. Rosemary Ruether and Eleanor McLaughlin (New York: Simon and Schuster, 1979), pp. 141–42.

[59] Letter 19, January 17, 1570; also letter 114, September 26, 1576.

[60] See Teresa's letter 121, October 21, 1576; and the will of Juana Nuñez Pérez and the autos made for the foundation established by her and her sister, in ADPS, Hospital de las Cinco Llagas, Legajo 242, Libro 11.

[61] Morell Peguero, *Mercaderes*, p. 167.

[62] Serrano y Sanz, *Apuntes*, 2: 132.

[63] Ortiz de Zuñiga, *Anales*, 4: 186.

women in this period to present theological exegesis rather than mystical experience.[64] Citing classical texts as well as Holy Scripture and the writings of Church Fathers, Pinelo used her learning to rewrite the story of Anne, the mother of Mary. As artists of the late sixteenth and seventeenth centuries emphasized, Anne fulfilled a major role in the genealogy of Christ, especially in giving miraculous birth to a daughter born without original sin and then in teaching her to read (fig. 12). Pinelo, after apologizing that she had no learned degree in Sacred Scripture, proceeded in her book to ask why the genealogy of Christ in the Gospel of Matthew is traced through the male line when the Church taught that Joseph did not father Jesus. She then cited the law and custom of the Jews and concluded that the requirements of patriarchy had eclipsed the female line of Jesus. However, writing in the context of a society obsessed with inheritance, Pinelo also argued that Mary played the crucial role in the genealogy of Christ because she was the only heir of her parents.

Gregoria Francisca de Santa Teresa, who took vows in the later seventeenth century as a Barefoot Carmelite in the convent founded in Seville by Teresa, also published writings, but hers were poems based on mystical experiences.[65] According to Matute y Gaviria, who included her in the *Hijos de Sevilla*, her poetry won the applause of "intelligent men," but the ire of her superiors in the convent.[66] They opposed her writing to such an extent that they even burned some of her verses.

The surviving writings of this nun provide some striking insights into the consciousness of those who entered convents. Almost entirely focused on inner experience, Gregoria Francisca's poetry speaks freely of feelings. In "La ovejuela," she writes of her

> Sufferings, distress and afflictions,
> Travails, fears and mortal danger.

Her breast breathes out sighs as she longs to see the beautiful face of her "Sovereign Shepherd." Her soul "sad and tearful," she cries out, "Do not deny me your loving glance."

In "Fuego de amor," Gregoria Francisca describes her lovesick heart with images very similar to those that Teresa de Jesús used to explain her

---

[64] Lola Luna, "Sor Valentina Pinelo, intérprete de las sagradas escrituras," *Cuadernos Hispanoamericanos*, no. 464 (February 1989): 91–103. I am indebted to Dr. Luna for sharing her research and insights with me.

[65] Gregoria Francisca (de Santa Teresa) de la Parra Queinoge, *Poesías de la Venerable Madre Gregoria Francisca de Santa Teresa Carmelita Descalza en el convento de Sevilla* (Paris: Librería de Garnier Hermanos, 1865); see also *Vida exemplar, virtudes heróicas, y singulares recibos de la V. Madre Gregoria Francisca de Santa Theresa* (Salamanca: Antonio Villarroel y Torres, ca. 1738); and Serrano y Sanz, *Apuntes*, 290: 379–83.

[66] Matute y Gaviria, *Hijos*, 1: 359–60.

FIGURE 12. *Saint Anne Teaching the Virgin to Read*, by Bartolomé Murillo (Museo del Prado, Madrid).

mystical ecstasies. Burning with heat so intense that she feels her heart "penetrated" with "the fire of Love," she also feels it "suffocated" from "the inner conflagration." Her breast can scarcely contain her rapidly beating heart and keep it from flying to God. "This divine violence," she writes, "is of such exalted beauty" that she feels whatever relieves it is travail and whatever increases it is "a great favor."

The nun speaks again and again in her poetry of her love relationship with Christ, whom she describes as her spouse, her lover, her shepherd and master. She longs for this lover and laments his absence from her. She calls out for his arms, his face, his "tender embraces." Whether she had ever read fray Luis de León's description of the love relationship between the human and the divine, Gregoria Francisca refined with sweet anguish this recurring theme of Spanish mystical writers.[67]

This poet uses martial language to describe her inner state as one of conflict and struggle, rather than mere passive sensation. In "Mándale a una alma resista a Dios y se queja amorosamente," she writes of fighting against her feelings and emotion in a "new combat," of resisting the lover whose "invincible arm shakes the mountains." Then, in a sudden and striking change, she ends the poem with the question:

> Well, how could I,
> Poor, lowly little worm,
> Deny myself the strong love
> Of such a wise and robust power?

In "La tortolilla" Gregoria Francisca urges the soul grieving for her absent divine lover to "struggle manfully," and "gallantly," with a "shield of obedience." With such strong armor, she writes, the soul defeats the devil and will win a "major victory" against the strongest resistance. The victory will be celebrated with song and the victors crowned with laurel:

> And to the Great God of battles
> You repeat happy praises
> For having given you the strength
> To conquer such armies.

In four poems Gregoria Francisca invokes the image of a lost and foundering ship to describe her need for divine direction. She declares in "La tortolilla" that faith can be the north star,

> With which, humble and reverent,
> Your shipwrecked boat
> Takes permanent port.

---

[67] Alexander A. Parker, *The Philosophy of Love in Spanish Literature, 1480–1680*, ed. Terence O'Reilly (Edinburgh: Edinburgh University Press, 1985), pp. 87–90, esp.

She acknowledges her perplexity and doubts, however, and in "La ove-juela" describes herself as a boat lacking sail and oars that bobs up and down in the sea. "I want to drown in the gulf of love," she writes in "El mar de amor," imagining herself in a little boat that breaks loose from the bank and is swept onto the high sea.

> In complete tranquillity
> My poor boat navigates,
> With a blind obedience,
> Without fear of tempest.

After desciribing her little boat beset with storms in "La navecilla," she con-cludes with a joyous *estribillo* (refrain):

> Awaken, my Lover,
> Order the seas
> To quiet, and the wind
> Then to calm;
> Let your two stars
> Vanquish the darkness;
> And let heaven and earth
> Praise you in admiration.

Gregoria Francisca's poetry describes her faith and inner feelings through images from nature, none more moving than the little bird that soars into heaven. She describes herself in "Pajarillo" watching it with envy as it evades the wind and circles upward to the "region of fire." "My anxious love follows you," the poet tells the bird,

> With impatient feelings,
> That the sad prison of the body
> Is harsh imprisonment for the soul.

Using more images of flight and imprisonment, she sees herself as a little dove in a cage whose trills and songs become laments:

> Through love and through captivity,
> Twice imprisoned, I suffer:
> Oh, who could break
> The shackle from the chains!

Then, overcoming her envy of the small bird, she transforms her anxie-ties into feathers and her sighs into flights. She drowns in the "immensity" of the light from the sun; her understanding is absorbed in its "gulfs of clarity." "Climb higher, if you can," she tells the bird,

> And you will be my messenger,
> You will give a loving remembrance
> From my sad sufferings
> To the inaccessible light
> Of the Sun of Eternal Justice.

She asks the little bird to have pity on her anxieties and sufferings and to request from her "sweet loving master" her liberty. "Leave this harsh prison," she cries,

> This long captivity,
> Where I sadly weep, and grieve
> My prolonged exile.

Although Gregoria Francisca notes her unhappiness, her suffering, and her imprisonment in an earthly body, she nevertheless had found an escape through the effortless flight of the tiny bird. Watching it, she became lost in the vastness of God, blinded and pierced by his beautiful rays. In her vision she cries out at the glory of being overcome by the impossible for which she yearns. No earthly cares can distract her from what she has determined is the meaning of her life. Surely, in a sense, she too soared over the convent walls and felt the fire of the burning sun.

Chapter 5

CHASTITY AND DANGER

RELIGION empowered another group of women in Seville, but they seldom lived within convents until later in the seventeenth century when ecclesiastical officials tried to enclose all female religious in cloisters. Known as beatas, these women enjoyed a status similar to Beguines or members of Third Orders.[1] They had taken a vow of chastity and dedicated their lives to serving God. Frequently they wore religious habits, but they rarely followed the rule of any religious order. Tertiaries, their closest male counterparts, usually had a closer association with a monastery or religious order and took vows of obedience and poverty that beatas did not.

In Seville beatas had become an established tradition, living here "since time immemorial," according to one sixteenth-century historian.[2] They usually retreated into private houses, often next to parish churches so that they could see the altar directly through a grille and hear mass without leaving the house. The three emparedamientos attached to the parish churches of San Miguel, San Ildefonso, and Santa Catalina continued to shelter beatas as well as nuns in the sixteenth century. Records for Seville do not indicate the numbers of women living as beatas in the sixteenth and seventeenth centuries, but one historian has estimated that thousands lived in the provinces of Andalusia and Extremadura. This number probably increased as development of the New World depleted the male population

---

[1] For Beguines and Beghards, see Norman Cohn, *The Pursuit of the Millennium: Revolutionary Messianism in Medieval and Reformation Europe and Its Bearing on Modern Totalitarian Movements* (New York: Harper Torchbooks, 1961), pp. 66–67, esp.; Lina Eckenstein, *Women under Monasticism: Chapters on Saint-lore and Convent Life between A.D. 500 and A.D. 1500* (New York: Russell and Russell, 1963), p. 331; Ernest W. McDonnell, *The Beguines and Beghards in Medieval Culture* (New Brunswick, N.J.: Rutgers University Press, 1954); Dayton Phillips, *Beguines in Medieval Strasburg: A Study of the Social Aspect of Beguine Life* (Stanford: Stanford University Press, 1941); and R. W. Southern, *Western Society and the Church in the Middle Ages* (Harmondsworth, Middlesex: Penguin, 1970), pp. 318–25. For more on tertiaries, see Pedro de Salazar, *Crónica y historia de la fundación y progreso de la provincia de Castilla, de la Orden del diaventurado padre San Francisco* (Madrid: Imprenta Real, 1612), pp. 395–96; and Vida Dutton Scudder, *The Franciscan Adventure: A Study in the First Hundred Years of the Order of St. Francis of Assisi* (London, Toronto, and New York: J. M. Dent and Sons, 1931), pp. 12–35, esp.

[2] Morgado, *Historia*, p. 471; Ballesteros, *Sevilla*, p. 147; Domínguez Ortiz, *Estamento*, pp. 113–14. I am indebted to Professor Julian Bueno for sharing his knowledge of beatas in an earlier period, and to William A. Christian, Jr., for sharing his research on beatas.

of Seville and reduced the real value of property held by families needing to provide their daughters with marriage or convent dowries.[3]

Early records show that a variety of women became beatas. Some of these women had turned to religious life when they were widowed, while others became beatas as adolescents, lacking a dowry for convent or marriage. Some beatas lived in their family homes and supported family members, others stayed together in an enclosed house, and still others joined a Third Order associated with a Franciscan or Augustinian monastery. In a few cases, beatas were exposed as fraudulent visionaries or phony prophets, but usually the community showed them respect.

As mysticism grew into a major religious movement in the sixteenth century, the influence of these women appeared to increase. *Recogimiento*, or withdrawing from the world and looking into the self to seek God, had already flourished among the Franciscans in the late fifteenth century and persisted through the sixteenth and seventeenth centuries.[4] Emphasizing internal spiritual experience, it attracted thousands of people dissatisfied with automatic and formulaic religious observance. These people hoped to find a more meaningful religion through direct experience of God. For spiritual exercises that enabled the soul to attain union with God, they consulted the writings of clerics such as Francisco de Osuna, the Franciscan from whom Teresa de Jesús said she first learned the art of recogimiento.[5]

This inward turning supported a "feminization" of religion. Assuming that women as well as men could reach union with God, its focus on the interior self undercut male-dominated ecclesiastical hierarchies with a form of spiritual egalitarianism. Its concentration on experience displaced formal theological learning with individual feeling, so that women became renowned for their "familiar simplicity" in teaching the love of God.[6] The devout, according to a popular devotional manual, did not need to know words, "but only feelings and interior movements of the heart."[7] Mysticism

---

[3] Alvaro Huerga, *Predicadores, alumbrados e inquisición* (Madrid: Fundación Universitaria Española, 1973), p. 53.

[4] Melquiades Andrés Martín, *Los recogidos: Nueva visión de la mística española (1500–1700)* (Madrid: Fundación Universitaria Española, 1975), pp. 12–13. See also Selke, *Santo Oficio,* pp. 231–39; and Bataillon, *Erasmo,* 1: 195–97.

[5] Teresa described spiritual exercises especially in her *Way of Perfection;* she said that she had learned the art of recogimiento from the *Tercer abecedario espiritual* of Francisco de Osuna, first published in 1527 and printed in *Nueva Biblioteca de Autores Españoles,* 16: 319–587, *Escritores místicos españoles* (Madrid: Librería Editorial de Bailly, 1911).

[6] Bataillon, *Erasmo,* 1: 207. For further discussion of this tradition in Spanish religion, see William A. Christian, Jr., *Apparitions in Late Medieval and Renaissance Spain* (Princeton: Princeton University Press, 1981), pp. 4–5 and 208–12. Broader discussions of religious leaders appear in Jeffrey B. Russell, *Dissent and Reform in the Early Middle Ages* (Berkeley and Los Angeles: University of California Press, 1965), p. 8, esp.; and Max Weber, *Sociology of Religion,* trans. Ephraim Fischoff (Boston: Beacon, 1963), pp. 2 and 238, esp.

[7] Osuna, *Tercer abecedario,* p. 378.

may have attracted women in particular because they had less worldly power and intellectual learning to give up as they surrendered themselves to the love of God.[8]

Mysticism provided an escape from many restrictions on the thought and behavior of women. Developing a personal relationship with God, beatas could completely avoid the ecclesiastical hierarchy. In contemplation and mental prayer, they could explore an interior world rich in possibilities of meaning and satisfaction. They entered trances, saw visions, and received revelations. Some saw in purgatory people who had already died and wanted the living to pray for them. Others received revelations of divine justice awaiting the living, and they felt justified to warn these people of certain punishment awaiting them if they did not mend their ways.

Women provided spiritual inspiration for those who wanted to revitalize religion. In early sixteenth-century Spain political and religious leaders listened to the words of María de Santo Domingo, the "beata of Piedrahita," who had many visions and ecstasies.[9] Later the beata Juana de la Cruz became associated with the miracles at the shrine in Illescas and won renown for her prophetic powers.[10] Mary the mother of Jesus became much more clearly defined as a symbol of hope for personal communication with God, a trend that culminated in the early seventeenth century with the proclamation in Spain of the Immaculate Conception.[11]

Their vow of chastity freed beatas from childbirth and from the stigma

[8] Carol Christ, *Diving Deep and Surfacing: Women Writers on Spiritual Quest* (Boston: Beacon, 1980), pp. 17–18.

[9] Jodi Bilinkoff, "Charisma and Controversy: The Case of María de Santo Domingo" (Paper delivered to the Society for Spanish and Portuguese Historical Studies, Vanderbilt University, 1988); Geraldine McKendrick and Angus MacKay, "Visionaries and Affective Spirituality during the First Half of the Sixteenth Century," in *Cultural Encounters: The Impact of the Inquisition in Spain and the New World*, ed. Mary Elizabeth Perry and Anne J. Cruz (Berkeley and Los Angeles: University of California Press, 1991); Bataillon, *Erasmo*, 1: 81; Henry Charles Lea, *Chapters from the Religious History of Spain Connected with the Inquisition* (Philadelphia: Lea Brothers & Co., 1890), pp. 219–21; Menéndez y Pelayo, *Heterodoxos*, 2: 174. See Selke, *Santo Oficio*, for a discussion of another very influential beata.

[10] Richard Kagan, "Prophecy and the Inquisition in Late Sixteenth-Century Spain," in Perry and Cruz, *Cultural Encounters*.

[11] Popular enthusiasm for the Immaculate Conception is recorded in "Memorias eclesiástics y seculares de la muy noble y muy leal ciudad de Sevilla," BC 84-7-19, fols. 195–97. Antonio Domínguez Ortiz, "La Congregación de la Granada y la Inquisición de Sevilla (un episodio de la lucha contra los alumbrados)," in *La inquisición española: Nueva visión, nuevos horizontes*, ed. Joaquín Pérez Villanueva (Madrid: Siglo Veintiuno de España, 1980), pp. 638–43, esp., discusses the support of alumbrados for the doctrine of the Immaculate Conception. See Nancy Mayberry, "Dramatic Representations of the Immaculate Conception in Tirso's Time," *Estudios* 156–57 (1987): 79–86. For the significance of symbols of purity, see Mary Douglas, *Purity and Danger: An Analysis of Concepts of Pollution and Taboo* (New York and Washington: Frederick A. Praeger, 1966). A broader study of the veneration of Mary and the saints is in William A. Christian, Jr., "De los Santos."

of female sexuality. It gave them an exalted status because many believed that chastity was the preferred status for both men and women, and it was frequently praised as the most precious virtue in women.[12] Regarded by many as "brides of Christ," the term used for nuns, beatas received admiration as symbols of purity.[13]

Worldly matters did not have to concern beatas. Wearing a simple habit, these women did not have to spend time or money on costume and appearance. Diego Pérez de Valdivia, a priest who wrote a book for beatas, advised them to wear simple, practical shoes, "very honest, high and broad, not shiny, but all enclosed, so that in no way can part of the foot be seen."[14] He said that they should wear natural-colored woolen skirts "more of necessity than of indulgence." Of ruffs, gaiters, and hoopskirts, this priestly adviser exclaimed, "God protect me! Did Jesus Christ our Lord your Spouse or the blessed Virgin wear either the one or the other?" Emphasizing practicality, he told them to cut their hair every two months and cover it with a veil because long hair takes time to wash and comb.

Her independence from so many material restrictions strengthened the beata's status in a world that seemed increasingly conscious of wealth. It is true that simplicity could humble feminine pride in personal appearance, but it also freed beatas from being judged by the material standards that were becoming so important in this commercial center of early modern Spain. Their voluntary poverty gave them a special status; it permitted them to devote themselves to the prayer and good works expected of them, and it associated them with a traditional Christian asceticism that many believed necessary to know God.[15] Beatas represented a pure simplicity that appeared to be above worldly pride. People who wanted to preserve the tradition of holy poverty supported beatas with alms and gifts. Rich donors might even repudiate their wealth at death, requesting burial in the simple rough garments worn by monks and beatas.[16]

[12] Juan de la Cerda, *Vida política*, pp. 63^r–69^r.

[13] Pérez de Valdivia, *Aviso*, p. 221. Mystics often used this term for holy women, according to Lea, *Chapters*, p. 248. See also Selke, *Santo Oficio*, p. 55; and Warner, *Alone of all Her Sex*, p. 128.

[14] Pérez de Valdivia, *Aviso*, p. 754. His discussion of clothing and appearance for beatas is on pp. 753–57.

[15] Ibid., pp. 755–57. Cohn, *Pursuit of the Millennium*, p. 162, points out that the poor could gain respectability by assuming voluntary poverty in a religious group. For a Jesuit view of asceticism, see Camilo Mª Abad, S.I., "Gil González Dávila, S.I., Sus Pláticas sobre las reglas de la Compañía de Jesús," in *Corrientes espirituales de la España del siglo XVI*, ed. Juan Flors (Barcelona: Universidad Pontificia de Salamanca, 1963), p. 370. A sociological discussion of poverty and religion is in Weber, *Sociology of Religion*, pp. 213–17.

[16] Blanca Morell Peguero, *Contribución etnográfica del Archivo de Protocolos* (Seville: Universidad de Sevilla, 1981), pp. 150–51, discusses such burial requests. Julio Caro Baroja, *Las formas complejas de la vida religiosa: Religión, sociedad y carácter en la España de los siglos XVI y*

Independence from the dowries required for either marriage or convent strengthened the status of beatas. These women did not have to be concerned with the fact that economic dislocations had made it more difficult for many families to provide enough as dowries for their daughters to make suitable marriages.[17] Nor did they have to find the sums of money that convents required of their novitiates, nor worry that these sums had to be increased as money declined in value and as French competition undercut the silk weaving that supported some convents.[18] The greater visibility of beatas in Seville during the first two decades of the seventeenth century may simply reflect an increasing number of women who became beatas as marriage and the convent became less attainable for them.

Religious enthusiasm permitted beatas to break free from convention. It explained their daring to criticize religious observations, asserting, as did one beata, that saying the Rosary was nothing more than a ringing of cowbells.[19] Under the cover of religion, beatas could laugh and shriek and cry. They could read the gospel aloud in formal groups and audaciously present their own interpretations of it. They shared intimate experiences with males and other females, and they hugged and kissed them. One group of beatas danced so vigorously after mass that they lost their veils and fell into a heap with their legs uncovered. Filled with rapture, they sang to the Holy Sacrament, "Oh, my little fat and round-faced one!"[20] A priest and a beata who had neglected their liturgical duties excused themselves as "drunk with the love of God."[21] Their enthusiasm resembled that of Saint Francis and his followers who had come to be known as the "minstrels of the Good Lord" in an earlier time.[22]

Undisciplined by husband or convent director, beatas enjoyed more freedom of movement and expression than most women. The Council of Trent decreed in the later sixteenth century that nuns must live enclosed in convents.[23] Despite official efforts to subject beatas to enclosure or regu-

---

XVII (Madrid: Akal, 1978), discusses the conflicts of materialism and religion in this period, pp. 363–87, and the tradition of holy poverty, pp. 445–61.

[17] As an example, see *Memoriales de Martínez de Mata*, p. 129.

[18] Perry, *Crime and Society*, pp. 214–15. Economic problems of convents are described in Domínguez Ortiz, *Estamento*, pp. 114–23; and in Teresa of Jesus, *Letters*, Letters 19, 114, and 121.

[19] AHN, Inquisición, Legajo 2962, Tomo 2.

[20] Ibid., Tomo 9.

[21] AHN, Inquisición, Legajo 2075, Expediente 31. It should be noted that religious enthusiasm permitted unconventional behavior for men as well as women. See the case of Fernando Méndez, a cleric in Seville, who fell into trances and uttered "terrible roars" during mass, reported in Henry Charles Lea, *A History of the Inquisition of Spain*, 4 vols. (New York and London: Macmillan, 1922), 4: 29–30.

[22] Scudder, *Franciscan Adventure*, p. 50.

[23] *Canons and Decrees of the Council of Trent*, pp. 220–21.

lation, these women did not have to vow obedience to a rule or person. Pérez de Valdivia recognized this freedom in his book of advice, warning beatas against the dangers of wandering and talkative women. He urged them to entrust themselves to a "good master" and accept his advice for their own mortification and perfection.[24] However, he left to each woman the choice of this master, and he acknowledged the difficulty of finding a good one. Beatas who formed congregations sometimes agreed to subject themselves to a particular male cleric, but they could choose whether to make a vow of obedience.[25]

After the Church officially renewed the rule of enclosure for nuns in the later sixteenth century, beatas performed the supportive and charitable work no longer possible for nuns and of increased importance for Seville, where a population of marginalized people continued to grow. Beatas who resisted enclosure for a time worked actively in the city. They received young girls rescued from procuresses who tried to sell them on the streets. When priests converted so many prostitutes that Magdalen houses had no more space to receive them, they took them to beatas who counseled them, gave them spiritual guidance, and saw that they were safely returned to husbands or parents, or placed as servants in respectable homes.[26] Ironically, these women, whose vow of chastity closed to them the avenue of biological motherhood, assumed the role of universal mother in protecting and nurturing others. People gave the title "madre" to three of the beatas interrogated by the Inquisition in Seville between 1609 and 1623, but this title may have indicated respect more than recognition of maternal work.

In the women's prison of Seville beatas filled a salaried position. Violante de Jesús set a good example for the female prisoners, according to a Jesuit who worked in the Royal Prison of this city at the end of the sixteenth century.[27] In her little "sermons" to the prisoners, she told them of the lives of the saints. She tried to keep them away from the grille of the

---

[24] Pérez de Valdivia, *Aviso*, pp. 146, 225, and 347–52. The fact that Diego Pérez wrote this book for beatas and included many Latin passages suggests that he believed many beatas were literate. He also advised them to write out their confessions so that they would take up less time with the priest in the confessional, p. 398. Note, however, that he cautioned against too much reading and knowledge as "a snare of the devil," p. 425.

[25] AHN, Inquisición, Legajo 2962, Tomos 6–13 suggest that beatas were under the direction of male clerics, but Tomo 1 states that all members of the alumbrado sect in Seville swore obedience to Catalina de Jesús. Padre Méndez, a cleric who directed many beatas, is described in Menéndez y Pelayo, *Heterodoxos*, 2: 195–96. Morgado, *Historia*, pp. 471–72, wrote that beatas in the medieval period had vowed obedience to a monastery, and he declared that women in beaterios, or houses of beatas, had to obey an older beata, called madre beata.

[26] Pedro de León, *Compendio*, pt. 1, chap. 4, fols. 10–14; pt. 2, chap. 25, fols. 191ʳ–192. See also Claire Guilhem, "L'Inquisition et la dévaluation des discours féminins," in Bennassar et al., *L'Inquisition espagnole*, pp. 197–240; p. 215, esp.

[27] Pedro de León, *Compendio*, pt. 2, chap. 12, fols. 142–142ʳ.

door where male friends of "evil interest" called to them. Taking care to speak to each one of the prisoners, this beata urged the women to voluntarily turn themselves over to the two institutions for contrite women. The city government paid a salary to the beata who provided spiritual and physical healing in this office. According to city records, Augustina de la Cruz, a beata and healer in the prison, was to receive twelve thousand maravedís in salary in both 1636 and 1639.[28] Occasionally petitions for supplies and repairs for the women's prison came from the beata holding this post.[29]

Even the beatas who remained enclosed in their houses were able to carry on charitable work through hospitality. In the village of Cuellar, beatas administered an institution for poor women established in 1572.[30] Endowed by a will, this convent of Franciscan Tertiaries was to provide an annual income to support fifteen lay women under the direction of five beatas. One beata acted as madre, supervising all the women, while another beata, the *ministra*, directed the work and care of the lay women. The latter were to be selected from among those who had no other means of support. A similar system worked in the emparedamientos of Seville, where beatas provided hospitality and shelter for women involved in marriage disputes and for devout lay women who wanted to live completely enclosed.[31]

All charitable work of beatas remained carefully confined. No report describes beatas out on the streets rescuing orphans from their adult exploiters, nor do records tell of beatas entering brothels to preach to prostitutes. The Church protected the homiletic privilege, and priests carefully avoided the word *preach* when they described the work of the beatas as "teaching" or giving inspirational chats. One beata observed this restriction so well, according to a Jesuit, that she merely "indoctrinated" her converts and then called in Jesuits to give the actual homilies.[32] Beatas who observed the boundaries of their social work and the restrictions on their power won the praise of clergy.

However, beatas who became charismatic leaders broke through these limits and developed broader spheres of power. Believed to be able to enter states of holy ecstasy, they commanded the respect of people who accepted

---

[28] Caro Petit, "La Cárcel Real," p. 42; salaries for Augustina de la Cruz are in AMS, Archivo General, Sección 2, Archivo de Contaduría, Carpeta 13, Número 148, and Carpeta 16, Números 142 and 206.

[29] For a petition for repairs and supplies, see that of Francisca de Jesús, "beata de la cárcel Real," in 1616, AMS, Sección 4, Siglo XVII Escribanías de Cabildo, Tomo 10, Número 26.

[30] B. Velasco, "Fundación del convento de terciarias franciscanas de Santa Isabel en Cuellar," *Archivo Ibero-Americano*, ser. 2, 31 (1971): 477–81. This study is based on documents in AHN, Clero, Legajo 6246, del convento de Santa Ana.

[31] Morgado, *Historia*, p. 472. Note that they received women involved in marriage disputes whom justice officials wanted to keep in protective custody.

[32] Pedro de León, *Compendio*, pt. 1, chap. 4, fols. 11ʳ–12. Pérez de Valdivia, *Aviso*, p. 425, warned that women should avoid preaching, "which is a very great snare of the devil."

their claims that they were in direct communion with God. Many, in fact, looked to them as religious leaders. As these beatas became more visibly and publicly influential, ecclesiastical officials became very disturbed. Two inquisitors wrote in December 1575 of "the inconveniences that result from permitting some women to go about in the habit of beatas, living in houses by themselves, without keeping themselves cloistered, nor living in community," and concluded by asking if it would be "suitable" to prohibit their manner of living.[33] As the Holy Office in Seville began to investigate these women, it reported that "usually they go around as vagabonds through pueblos where they live with more freedom than other women of their quality."[34] Wearing a religious habit permitted them to come and go as they pleased, clerics reported, "and they leave the service of their fathers and care of their houses, and many of them dare to take communion each day, and sometimes not with suitable reverence, and as they do this with the title and in the name of holiness and religion, no one cares to stop them."[35]

Between 1609 and 1645, the tribunal of the Inquisition in Seville penanced twelve beatas. As table 5.1 indicates, these beatas were prosecuted for heresy and false religious experiences. However, Inquisition records suggest that a major concern was to curb popular religious figures who had developed so much power independent of lay or ecclesiastical discipline.[36]

These proceedings cannot be dismissed as merely the case of an official institution opposing "the people," however, for they include statements of hundreds of witnesses who gave testimony against beatas as well as in support of them. Motivated by fear or class antagonism, witnesses against beatas also expressed resentment at their assumption of powerful leadership roles that overturned traditional gender positions.[37] The tumult of the Counter-Reformation empowered beatas for a time, but it did not permanently transform gender roles.[38] In fact, Inquisition records indicate

[33] Huerga, *Predicadores*, p. 54.

[34] Ibid.

[35] Ibid. See AHN, Inquisición, Legajos 2962 and 3716.

[36] AHN, Inquisición, Legajo 2075, Números 19, 22, and 31; Legajo 2962; AMS, Sección Especial, Papeles del Señor Conde de Aguila, Tomos 4 and 20 en folio. Bossy, "The Counter-Reformation," p. 52, describes official attempts to impose a "parochial conformity " on religious observance. See also Bataillon, *Erasmo*, for a broader discussion of tensions in Spanish religion at this time. Jaime Contreras, *El Santo Oficio de la Inquisición de Galicia: poder, sociedad y cultura* (Madrid: Akal, 1982), discusses more fully the role of the Inquisition in imposing official control over traditional beliefs in rural areas.

[37] Kamen, *Inquisition and Society* p. 45. Ricardo García Cárcel, *Orígines de la inquisición española: El tribunal de Valencia, 1478–1500* (Barcelona: Ediciones Peninsulas, 1976), pp. 181–82, points out that this popular testimony could very well have been grounded on fear.

[38] Natalie Zemon Davis, "City Women and Religious Change," in her *Society and Culture in Early Modern France* (Stanford: Stanford University Press, 1977), pp. 65–95, esp. For a discussion of women and religious sects in seventeenth-century England, see Keith Thomas,

that proceedings against beatas served to reintegrate them into the traditional gender order.

The example of beatas demonstrates not only how religion could increase the influence and status of women, but also how it checked their power. According to anthropologist Clifford Geertz, religion serves not merely to preserve beliefs and conserve a social order; it also acts as a dynamic cultural system that both motivates and justifies change.[39] Beatas became sacred symbols to those who believed that they could directly contact the spiritual source of all meaning. To religious officials, however, beatas represented the danger of heresy, of power received through the body, and of power protected in inner spaces of the mind. During the early seventeenth century official intolerance of these women mounted, and it found popular support in testimony before the Inquisition.

The most celebrated beata prosecuted by the Holy Office in Seville was madre Catalina de Jesús, who wore a Carmelite habit but did not follow the rule of any religious order. She taught and wrote and preached and prophesied. Unfortunately, none of her writings can be found, and most evidence about her comes from Inquisition records and chronicles of the period.[40]

On the night of February 27, 1627, so many people crowded the streets that led from the Inquisition's prison that officials had "great difficulty" moving their fourteen penitents through the throngs to the Church of San Pablo, where the auto de fe, or ceremony of penitence, was to be held the next morning.[41] Some had already taken their places along the route of the procession by midnight on the night before, and hundreds remained in their places all day, hoping for one more glimpse of those penanced by the Inquisition. They waited, in particular, to see two penitents: madre Cata-

---

"Women and the Civil War Sects," *Past and Present* 13 (1958): 42–62; see also Eleanor McLaughlin, "Women, Power and the Pursuit of Holiness in Medieval Christianity," in Ruether and McLaughlin, *Women of Spirit*, pp. 99–130.

[39] Clifford Geertz, *The Interpretation of Cultures* (New York: Basic Books, 1973), pp. 90, 129, and 146, defines religion as a cultural system, "a cluster of sacred symbols," which can change even as civilization continues. His definition of a symbol as a "vehicle for conception" suggests that its primary function is to give meaning to social and psychological reality, both by adapting itself to reality and by shaping that reality, pp. 91–93. Gustav Henningsen, "El 'banco de datos' del Santo Oficio: Las relaciones de causas de la Inquisición española (1550–1700)," *Boletín de la Real Academia de la Historia* 174 (1977): 547–70, discusses other anthropological approaches in using Inquisition records.

[40] Contreras, *Santo Oficio*, pp. 20–21 and 575, discusses problems of using Inquisition records as evidence. Henningsen, *The Witches' Advocate*, pp. 20–22, emphasizes the problem of false confessions made to inquisitors.

[41] "Relación de un auto de fee que se celebró en el Oficio de la Inquisición de la Ciudad de Sevilla en el Conv^to de S^n Pablo . . . el último día del mes Febreo del año de 1627," BC, 74-7-118. See also AMS, Sección Especial, Papeles del Señor Conde de Aguila, Tomo 4 en folio, Número 47, for another account.

TABLE 5.1
Beatas Appearing before the Tribunal of the Holy Office, Seville, 1559–1645

	Beata	Source	Charge; Verdict
1559	María de Borborques	AHN, Inq. 2075, #4	Lutheran heresy; relaxed, burned
1609	Madre Bárbara Beata Resident of Seville	AHN, Inq. 2075, #19	Led ecstatic prayer meetings of women; case suspended
1609	María Beata Resident of Utrera	AHN, Inq. 2075, #19	Religious enthusiasm; case suspended
1609	María Ximenez Resident of Moron	AHN, Inq. 2075, #19	Implicated with Bárbara Beata; case suspended
1609	Ynes de Jesús Resident of Xerez	AHN, Inq. 2075, #19	Prophecies, revelations; case suspended
1612	Juana de la Cruz Resident of Seville 20 years old	AHN, Inq. 2075, #22	False ecstasies, alumbrado heresy; 4 years' reclusion
1612	Madre Catalina de Jesús Resident of Seville 47 years old	AHN, Inq. 2075, #22	False ecstasies, alumbrado heresy; case suspended
1622	Same as above	AHN, Inq. 2962, Letters	Imprisoned for alumbrado heresy; penanced 1627, 6 years reclusion
1623	Bárbara de Jesús Resident of Cadiz 30 years old	AHN, Inq. 2075, #31	False ecstasies, Free Spirit heresy; 2 years' reclusion
1623	Catalina de Jesús Native of Xerez 30 years old	AHN, Inq. 2075, #31	False visions, Free Spirit heresy; 2 years' reclusion
1623	Madre Mariana de Jesús Resident of Seville Native of Aguilar	AHN, Inq. 2075, #31	False visions; alumbrado heresy; 4 years' reclusion, exile
1624	Antonia de S. Francisco Resident of Xerez 30 years old	AHN, Inq. 2075, #31	False revelations, alumbrado heresy; public auto, warning
1624	María de Jesús Resident of Seville 36 years old	AMS, sec. Especial Tomo #20	False revelations and stigmata; public auto
1645	María de Concepción Resident of Mairena	AHN, Inq. 2061, #12	False prophecies, creating uproar; verdict unknown

lina de Jesús, the leader of a local sect, and her lieutenant, Juan de Villapando, a priest who had been her first disciple.[42]

Although most historians have dismissed Catalina de Jesús and other beatas as weak and hysterical women, archival evidence indicates that they exercised powerful functions as traditional symbols of holiness in the sixteenth and early seventeenth centuries.[43] According to Inquisition records, nearly seven hundred people in Seville and thirty nearby villages obeyed the directives of Catalina de Jesús.[44] Her followers believed that God spoke to her in visions and ecstasies. Venerating her life of holiness, they gave her the reverential title "madre." They knelt to kiss her hand when they met her in a church or on the street, and they told stories of miracles, such as the conversion of a young rake when he merely touched the hem of her garment. Many cherished bits of her clothing and hair as relics, and they prized her portraits that were inscribed "Santa Catalina."[45] Followers were said to venerate her words as "oracles from Heaven."[46] They believed that because she was always in God's presence she did not have to submit to

[42] "Memorial de la secta de los alumbrados de Sevilla y de sus doctrinas y delictos y de la complicidad que en ella se ha descubierto," AHN, Inquisición, Legajo 2962, Tomo 1. Note that archival sources refer to several women who were called Catalina de Jesús. To my knowledge, this particular woman is the only Catalina referred to as "madre." Villapando is sometimes spelled "Villalpando," as in Lea, *Chapters*, who describes Villalpando as the leader and Catalina de Jesús as the first disciple. However, his version may have been influenced by his own belief that "the impressionable female nervous system" suited women to be emotional religious intermediaries, but not leaders to whom people swore obedience. See especially pp. 233, 252, 260n, 300–308, 360. The memorial in AHN, Inquisición, Legajo 2962, states, "And in Seville and its surroundings the alumbrados have for their principal head and spiritual teacher madre Catalina de Jesús, and for their second Villalpando."

[43] Historians who have dismissed Catalina de Jesús and other beatas include Lea, *Chapters*, pp. 307–8; Menéndez y Pelayo, *Heterodoxos*, 2: 174 and 198–99; Deleito y Piñuela, *La vida religiosa*, p. 300; and Juan Antonio Llorente, *A Critical History of the Inquisition of Spain* (Williamstown, Mass.: John Lilburne Co., 1967), p. 504. A notable exception to these examples is Guilhem, "L'Inquisition et la dévaluation." More recently, Jodi Bilinkoff has discussed the significance of these holy women in "The Holy Woman and the Urban Community in Sixteenth-Century Avila," in *Women and the Structure of Society: Selected Research from the Fifth Berkshire Conference on the History of Women*, ed. Barbara J. Harris and JoAnn K. McNamara (Durham, N.C.: Duke University Press, 1984), pp. 74–80; and María Helena Sánchez Ortega has discussed them in "Flagelantes licenciosos y beatas consentidores," *Historia 16* 14 (1981): 37–54, and in "La beata de Villar del Aguila," *Historia 16* 74 (1986): 23–34.

[44] AHN, Inquisición, Legajo 2962, Tomos 1, 15, 17.

[45] Ibid. See also AMS, Sección Especial, Papeles del Señor Conde de Aguila, Tomo 4 en folio, Número 47. Although the latter report is not an official document of the Inquisition, it should not be seen as independent corroboration of the findings of the Holy Office, as the anonymous writer was undoubtedly getting much of his information from the Inquisition.

[46] AHN, Inquisición, Legajo 2962, Tomo 2; note that this and the following information report what people said about Catalina de Jesús under inquisitorial questioning and may better reflect the Inquisition's view of her. Weber, *Sociology of Religion*, pp. 2–3, 46, and 238, esp., discusses charisma.

human discipline. They accepted her claim that she had a special gift to save souls, believing that God revealed to her whom he would punish after death. They obeyed her when she said that a vision had told her to teach them how to pray, what to eat, how to dress.[47]

Followers of madre Catalina believed that she was the spiritual successor to Teresa de Jesús with a divine mission that placed her in authority over men as well as women. In this inversion of the usual gender positions, men listened to Catalina, obeyed her directives, and some even said they would sacrifice their lives for her. They believed that God had sent her to reform the Third Orders of both males and females, and they published her revelations, which they said were as holy as those of the recently canonized Teresa.[48]

Madre Catalina's claim that she had the gift of prophecy increased her influence and enabled her to grant power to others. From ecstatic visions, she said that she learned what was to happen in the future. She believed in predestination and asserted that she could look into the interior of people to see whether they would be blessed by God. One whom she identified as predestined to reach the summit of human perfection was Juan de Villapando, a cleric who became second in command of the illuminist sect that madre Catalina directed. Calling him her "spiritual son," madre Catalina granted him a position of authority.[49] Her position of leadership did not shock contemporaries who believed that God often worked through common, lowly people, even women. Teresa de Jesús expressed this belief when she referred to herself as "a dunghill" on which God had "made a garden of flowers so sweet."[50]

Most beatas did not develop the influence and independence of madre Catalina, however, held back by a combination of several factors. A search for security prevented many women from transforming potential power into actual power. Even though they could choose whether to submit to ecclesiastical direction, many subjected themselves to monks and priests

[47] AHN, Inquisición, Legajo 2962, Tomos 1, 13, and 15.

[48] Menéndez y Pelayo, *Heterodoxos*, 2: 198–99, 238–40; Bennassar, *L'Inquisition espagnole*, pp. 215–16; AHN, Inquisición, Legajo 2962, Tomo 15. Evidently Catalina wrote, as the Inquisition ordered the confiscation of all her writings, both published and in manuscript form; see AMS, Sección Especial, Papeles del Señor Conde de Aguila, Tomo 4 en folio, Número 47. To my knowledge, none of these writings has survived.

[49] AHN, Inquisición, Legajo 2962, Tomo 17. More information on alumbrados is in Andrés Martín, *Recogidos*; Márquez, *Alumbrados*; Flors, *Corrientes espirituales*; and Selke, *Santo Oficio*. Spiritual kinship is discussed in Julian Pitt-Rivers, *The Fate of Shechem, or the Politics of Sex: Essays in the Anthropology of the Mediterranean* (Cambridge: Cambridge University Press, 1977), chap. 3, although he is more concerned with roles of traditional godparents.

[50] Teresa of Jesus, *Life*, p. 66. Caro Baroja, *Formas complejas*, pp. 90–91, also discusses the tradition of lowly laypeople becoming miracle workers and objects of veneration. Bataillon, *Erasmo*, 1: 81–82 and 206–9, discusses women religious leaders.

whom they believed to be "good masters." Aware of their vulnerability outside an established hierarchy, they chose security over independence, tradition over self-assertion.[51]

Seville's economic decline in the seventeenth century affected the vulnerability of beatas. Those who lived on the income from property they owned felt their economic base crumble as prices rose, property rents fell, and money became devalued. Beatas without individual property depended on alms or what they could earn from the work of their hands. By the 1670s it was clear that working women could earn only one-fifth of the sum required for their daily food.[52] Since city law and Tridentine policy forbade beatas to beg in the streets, they had to beg privately or by petition. "I am poor and have an unmarried daughter who is also poor and needy," beata María de la Cruz told the city government.[53]

Officials regarded the poverty of these women as a metaphor for disorder rather than for holiness. If some saw their asceticism as a repudiation of the world of material wealth, others saw it as a criticism of it, particularly in the case of madre Catalina, who was said to have told one woman that she would go to hell because she wore silk and finery.[54] Poverty in this case signified a threat to the values of a mercantile culture, a disreputable condition closer to the devil than to God. Secular and ecclesiastical authorities who wanted to keep beatas respectably enclosed had to find ways to feed them, and their attempts to keep them in convents or charitable institutions led to many complaints about expense and discipline.[55]

Even more troubling, beatas could live independent of most formal regulation, engaging in personal forms of mysticism unrestrained by any discipline. Pérez de Valdivia warned of the dangers of this position in 1585 when he wrote his book of advice for them: "Through the liberty and occasions that they have, and through being fragile by nature, [beatas] need doctrine that teaches all modesty, and guards and keeps vigilance in their mode of life."[56] This priest discussed twenty "dangers" for beatas in the nearly seven hundred pages of part 4 of his book. He urged beatas in particular to avoid visions: "I exhort and admonish the brides of Jesus Christ, and all people devoted in the name of this same Lord, that they zealously call on him that he not give them visions, nor revelations, nor ecstasies, nor

---

[51] Teresa of Jesus, *Foundations*, pp. xxi and 42, discusses the blessings of obedience.

[52] "Consulta theológica, en que se pregunta si será justo y conveniente que se apliquen las obras pías de esta ciudad al remedio de la necesidad pública que al presente ay en esta ciudad de Sevilla," in *Papeles varios*, BC, 83-7-14, fol. 109.

[53] AMS, Sección 3, Siglo XVI, Escribanías de Cabildo, Tomo 7, Número 17.

[54] AMS, Sección Especial, Papeles del Señor Conde de Aguila, Tomo 4 en folio, Número 47; and AHN, Inquisición, Legajo 2962, Tomo 13.

[55] AMS, Sección 4, Siglo XVII, Escribanías de Cabildo, Tomo 24, Número 41; and Perry, *Crime and Society*, pp. 182–85.

[56] Pérez de Valdivia, *Aviso*, p. 344.

transportations, nor any such thing that singles out one from the others." Warning that "spiritual arrogance" could bring on false visions, he described in conventional language how it could transform the devil into an "angel of light."[57] Earlier Teresa de Jesús had expressed this same dismay about visions, praying that God would deliver her from ecstasies and visions that caused "much talk," from "womanish imaginations" that carried out "the devil's work."[58]

Submission to a confessor or spiritual director could not allay these concerns about beatas, for some clerics acted as "bad masters," whom Pérez de Valdivia described as "frogs, that give cries as they call, and when somebody comes, they jump into the water."[59] More serious than abandoning their obligations, bad masters could also act as tinder so that the ardor of beatas would leap into flame and become a fire out of control.[60] An Augustinian friar warned of the beatas' "strange liberty," which was a "knife that slits their throats."[61]

Mystical experiences enflamed many beatas so that they dared to teach and preach, activities that challenged the usual assumption of male dominance. Earlier the Inquisition had complained that "nowadays everyone presumes to be theologians, even the women."[62] Madre Bárbara, one of the beatas discussed in a 1609 report of the Inquisition in Seville, had been denounced for leading prayer meetings of women who entered trancelike states. Witnesses said that this beata not only led the women into undisciplined ecstasies; she also justified their unconventional behavior, explaining that the Holy Spirit had caused them to grimace and gesture with their arms and "all the body," and to fall upon the ground.[63]

Inquisition records, the only available descriptions of beatas' visions, present an official version of the symbolic language of mysticism in this period.[64] None of the visions reported was experienced collectively, yet

[57] Ibid., p. 334. Caro Baroja, *Formas complejas*, discusses contemporary cases such as those of more than 250 women who became "possessed" under the leadership of one dominant man in Aragon in this period, pp. 67–68, and that of padre Méndez in Seville who had women "swarming" around him like bees, p. 480.

[58] Teresa of Jesus, *Life*, p. 394.

[59] Pérez de Valdivia, *Aviso*, p. 344.

[60] Ibid., p. 334.

[61] Juan de Soto, *Obligaciones*, p. 67.

[62] AHN, Inquisición, Legajo 4520, Número 4.

[63] AHN, Inquisición, Legajo 2075, Número 19.

[64] Inquisition records report visions for five beatas examined in Seville between 1612 and 1627, but they report none for the three beatas examined and dismissed in 1609. The five and their records include Juana de la Cruz, AHN, Inquisición, Legajo 2075, Número 22; Bárbara de Jesús and Catalina de Jesús (not the madre), and María de Jesús, all reported in AHN, Inquisición, Legajo 2075, Número 31, and also in AMS, Sección Especial, Papeles del Señor Conde de Aguila, Tomo 20 en folio; and madre Catalina de Jesús, in AHN, Inquisición, Legajo 2962, Tomo 4, as well as AMS, Sección Especial, Papeles del Señor Conde de Aguila,

several shared striking similarities. God or Jesus Christ or the Virgin Mary spoke directly to the beata as an individual and showed her favor by granting her the special gift of prophecy or the ability to speak to the souls of people who had died. Similarity in messages received during the visions may be the result of inquisitors' asking an official set of questions that elicited the same information about them. It is also possible that the frequency with which people spoke of visions formalized them unconsciously so that certain images became part of a collective symbolic language.

Inquisitors found appearances by the devil or demons in the visions of all the beatas except madre Catalina de Jesús. Handsome young men in the visions were recognized to be the devil when they exposed their genitals. In Bárbara de Jesús' vision, the devil wore blue and gold and a hat with many feathers. María de Jesús had to beat off the devil in her vision, and he then leaped out as a cinder that burned a hole in her blue mantle. Animals spoke to the women: a lamb representing God addressed madre Catalina; while Bárbara de Jesús saw demons as insects, toads, lizards, and snakes.

The visions contained so many sensory details and recognizable religious symbols that they must have deeply impressed the beatas who reported them and the people who heard of them, regardless of whether they were genuine or pretended, as the Inquisition concluded. María de Jesús felt the ring of her Holy Spouse pressed upon her finger, and madre Catalina "burned" with the fire of God and "drowned" in his divinity. Madre Catalina was reported to have said that Jesus appeared to feed her the Host with his own hand, and God told her that the suffering she felt in her breast had made milk so that she could have a close communion with all the souls she met.

Spiritual favors granted during these visions emboldened beatas denounced to the Inquisition. Earlier Teresa de Jesús had used humility to defend her visions from critical clerics, not only accepting the notion that "women should be directed with much discretion," but also that "we women and those who are unlearned ought always to render [God] unceasing thanks—because there are persons who, by labors so great, have attained to the truth, of which we unlearned people are ignorant."[65] Her humility contrasts with the "spiritual arrogance" of beatas such as Bárbara de Jesús, María de Jesús, and madre Catalina. Each of these women had assumed a position of authority and treated clerics as her "spiritual sons."

Tomo 4 en folio, Número 47. Contreras, *Santo Oficio*, pp. 571–80, esp. discusses methodological problems with Inquisition sources. Caro Baroja, *Formas complejas*, pp. 61–67, presents several women's visions reported in this period.

[65] Teresa of Jesus, *Life*, pp. 90 and 174.

Insisting that others must listen to her, each of these beatas presumed to direct men and to release women from obedience to their husbands.[66]

In their criticisms of conventional religious practices, beatas appeared to present ideas dangerously close to those of the alumbrado heresy. Isabel de la Cruz, a beata in the early sixteenth century, acted as the "true mother and teacher [maestra] of all the alumbrados," working through small groups of people who sought direct religious experience.[67] These people believed that salvation came through grace alone, rather than good works or pious observations. They wanted all people to be able to read the Holy Scriptures, but they emphasized experience over learning. Focusing on internal spiritual truth, they steered perilously close to the centuries-old heresy of the Free Spirit, which taught that individuals could attain a state of perfection placing them above all human authority.[68]

The Inquisition continued to find evidence of the alumbrado heresy after defining its erroneous beliefs and sentencing Isabel de la Cruz to perpetual prison.[69] In Seville a memorial of 1625 to the Holy Office asserted that 695 people had been found guilty of the heresy in the city and nearby villages.[70] Many witnesses and the confessions of the accused themselves had implicated Juan de Villapando and Catalina de Jesús in the alumbrado heresy, inquisitors claimed; but madre Catalina argued that one inquisitor in particular had written her confession for her, moving her with "smooth reasons" and putting words into her mouth and those of other witnesses.[71] When the Inquisition called for denunciations of heretics, the Edict of Grace that it issued acted as a guide in eliciting evidence of the heresy that it sought.[72] The prohibition in October 1625 against cults for any person

---

[66] AHN, Inquisición, Legajo 2962, Tomo 17, Número 35. See the descriptions of Bárbola de Jesús and María de Jesús in AMS, Sección Especial, Papeles del Señor Conde de Aguila, Tomo 20 en folio, addendum to 1624; and the description of Catalina de Jesús in Tomo 4 en fol., Número 47. The term "spiritual arrogance" is discussed in Pérez de Valdivia, *Aviso*, pp. 475–85.

[67] Márquez, *Alumbrados*, p. 62.

[68] For a more detailed discussion of alumbrados, see Márquez, *Alumbrados*, and Selke, *Santo Oficio*. The heresy of the Free Spirit is discussed in Cohn, *Pursuit of the Millennium*, pp. 170 and 186–87; and in McDonnell, *Beguines*, pp. 496–98.

[69] AHN, Inquisición, Legajos 107 and 3716; Libro 1299. Isabel de la Cruz is also discussed in Guilhem, "L'Inquisition et la dévaluation," pp. 196–239.

[70] AHN, Inquisición, Legajo 107, Número 10; Legajo 3716, Número 14; and Libro 1299, which contains the alumbrado heresies that had been identified in 1525. AHN, Inquisición, Legajo 2962, and AMS, Sección Especial, Papeles del Señor Conde de Aguila, Tomo 4 en folio, Número 47, contain the most complete charges against Catalina de Jesús and Juan de Villapando.

[71] AHN, Inquisición, Legajo 2962, Cartas. Henningsen, *The Witches' Advocate*, pp. 20–22, helps to explain how people find themselves making false confessions.

[72] See the edict and instructions for issuing it in AMS, Sección Especial, Papeles del Señor Conde de Aguila, Tomo 4 en folio, Números 43 and 44.

not yet beatified or canonized was undoubtedly a response to the cult developing around madre Catalina, and it may have stimulated more witnesses to testify to the specific errors that ecclesiastical leaders identified.[73]

Official response to madre Catalina and other beatas took place within a complex power struggle in the religious establishment. Dominicans, who had earlier led the Inquisition, opposed doctrinal positions of the Jesuits and criticized them for so often being chosen as confessors by women. Neither side could afford to associate with women who moved on the margins of respectability, and Jesuits in particular took pains to distinguish themselves from alumbrados.[74] Leaders of reform for religious orders also hesitated to associate with beatas, concerned that the independence of these women and the hints of eroticism in their visions could discredit the reform movement.[75]

The power of beatas crumbled as the Inquisition completely deprived them of their means of self-presentation. Confiscating their writings, inquisitors kept beatas in isolation and subjected them to interrogation. They recorded testimony that presented beatas as weak women with erroneous beliefs, far more vulnerable to temptations of the devil because they lacked a good male director.[76] Determining that these women had merely been misled by their own delusions and heretical clerics, inquisitors avoided portraying them with the special powers that diabolical possession was believed to give to witches and sorcerers.[77]

Sex became an effective weapon to discredit beatas. Inquisitors ridiculed madre Catalina's assertion that she had such purity in body and soul that she could "deal with all the world" and still remain as pure as an "angel

[73] This prohibition was printed and appears in AHN, Inquisición, Legajo 2962.

[74] Pedro de León, *Compendio*, pt. 3, entitled "De los confesores de mujeres." For Jesuits, see Antonio Astrain, *Historia de la Compañía de Jesús en la asistencia de España* (Madrid: Administración de Razon y Fe, 1912); and see Hugo Rahner, S. J., *Saint Ignatius Loyola Letters to Women* (Edinburgh and London: Nelson, 1960), pp. 12–14, for Loyola's concerns with women's confessions. A broader discussion of heresy and religious dissension is in Russell, *Dissent*, and in Derek Baker, ed., *Schism, Heresy, and Religious Protest*, vol. 9 of *Studies in Church History* (Cambridge: Cambridge University Press, 1972).

[75] See Pinero Ramírez, *Sevilla imposible*, pp. 70–78, for concerns that the reform effort within the Carmelite Order would suffer from the enthusiasms of female religious; and see Rahner, *Letters*, pp. 12, 255, and 257, for Ignatius's fear that such women could discredit and distract his newly founded Society of Jesus.

[76] Pérez de Valdivia, *Aviso*, pp. 146, 350–58, esp. Gaspar Navarro, quoted in Deleito y Piñuela, *La vida religiosa*, pp. 244–45. See also the quotation of Navarro in Bennassar, *L'Inquisition espagnole*, pp. 221–22. Pitt-Rivers, *Fate of Shechem*, p. 44, esp., has found a similar belief in twentieth-century Andalusia, although it does not necessarily require belief in the devil.

[77] AHN, Inquisición, Legajo 2962, Tomos 6–13; Menéndez y Pelayo, *Heterodoxos*, 2: 195; Guilhem, "L'Inquisition et la dévaluation," pp. 221–25, esp.

incarnate."[78] Even beatas' vows of chastity, which had sought to minimize sexuality by strictly forbidding it, became transformed into danger as priests warned that the devil ranges his "major artillery" against those who have vowed chastity.[79] They said that beatas should sleep fully dressed, never with a living creature in the bed, not even a kitten or puppy. To control carnal temptations, they advised beatas to think of their own bodies as corpses, stinking and "full of worms."

From ecstatic personal experiences of the divine, beatas' visions became transformed through clerics' interpretations into the troubling apparition of Satan in the form of a writhing snake or a toad or a youth dressed in crimson silk, exposing his private parts.[80] It is impossible to know whether these women would have recognized without inquisitorial prompting that their visions had more to do with Satan than with God, and we shall never know which interpretation afforded them more satisfaction. In either case, inquisitors were as concerned with their mental activity as with their physical behavior; and they used skillful questioning to make these women agree to an official version of their visions.

Inquisitors further discredited beatas such as madre Catalina by attributing any charisma to manipulative self-indulgence. They repeatedly described her visions as "pretended" in order to win some favor, and they wrote that she faked reluctance to accept the gifts pressed on her while she actually ate very well and lived with many luxuries.[81] They reported her "illness for the love of God" to be mere lazy indulgence, and they accused her of sexual license. She had given a key to a cleric so that he could visit her at all times of the night and in the very early morning, they declared, insinuating that she had had carnal relations with Juan de Villapando.[82]

The Inquisition constructed cases against beatas on the testimony of

[78] AMS, Sección Especial, Papeles del Señor Conde de Aguila, Tomo 4 en folio, Número 47. This is not to deny that sex was also used to discredit male alumbrados; see Caro Baroja, *Formas complejas*, p. 470, for a sixteenth-century writer who associated alumbrados with sodomy.

[79] For example, see Pérez de Valdivia, *Aviso*; the quotations in this paragraph appear on pp. 633, 747, 752, and 812.

[80] See the reports of the visions of Juana de la Cruz and Ana de los Santos, in AHN, Inquisición, Legajo 2075, Expedientes 22 and 31.

[81] AHN, Inquisición, Legajo 2962, Tomo 4.

[82] AMS, Sección Especial, Papeles del Señor Conde de Aguila, Tomo 4 en folio, Número 47; AHN, Inquisición, Legajo 2075, Expediente 31. I do not mean to imply that all sexual activity attributed to beatas was fabricated by the Inquisition to discredit them. Sánchez Ortega, "Flagelantes," pp. 37–54, discusses sexual activity of beatas and other female penitents in the eighteenth century. Russell, *Dissent*, pp. 35, 39, and 205, esp., suggests that the accusation of licentiousness against dissenters was a "cliche" in orthodox writings, but he acknowledges that occasionally dissenters' behavior provided a factual base for the accusation. Pitt-Rivers, *Fate of Shechem*, pp. 81–82, describes a traditional belief that older widows or single women are sexually ravenous.

hundreds of witnesses. Some witnesses must have cooperated with the Inquisition in order to save themselves, their friends, and family members from torture, imprisonment, and confiscation of property. However, some of them may have believed that beatas such as madre Catalina had forfeited any claim to holiness when they became too powerful in directing male followers, dictating which confessors the faithful could see, excusing wives from obedience to their husbands, and children from obedience to their parents. Some people may have felt offended when madre Catalina presumed to know who was predestined for salvation, particularly when she did not name her listeners. The woman who madre Catalina had said was doomed by her fine dress must have welcomed an opportunity to testify against her. In the same sense, it is easy to understand the testimony of those for whom she had had revelations promising punishment after they had doubted her holiness or neglected to give her alms. Members of the religious orders may have perceived as very threatening her criticism that more sinners thrived among them than in the secular clergy, and they may have testified against her in self-defense. The same could be said of the learned men of the city, whom she reportedly had belittled and ridiculed.[83] What should be noted is that the power of the Inquisition came not simply from its institutional privileges, but also from discontents and hostilities already present among the people.

Confronted by the powerful Inquisition and the testimony of more than two hundred witnesses against her, madre Catalina defended herself more vigorously than any other prosecuted beata. In 1612 she had successfully countercharged a witness who had denounced her to the Inquisition. After her release, she had continued to build up her following, undoubtedly aware that her "sect" alarmed ecclesiastical authorities. When the Holy Office once again imprisoned her ten years later, this woman who was called madre by so many challenged the image of mother as passive and self-sacrificing. She argued that inquisitors had fabricated both her confession and testimony against her, so disconcerting two inquisitors that they recommended dropping all charges in order to quiet the uproar. Others, however, urged that she be penanced, implying that clandestine communication between madre Catalina and other prisoners had promoted their resistance to charges against them.[84]

The Inquisition punished beatas in rituals that sharply enforced their isolation from the people. Avoiding the bonfire that would exalt them to

[83] All of these charges are contained in the 1625 memorial in AHN, Inquisición, Legajo 2962. See Bennassar, *L'Inquisition espagnole*, pp. 123–40, for a discussion of the factors that resulted in fear of the Inquisition.

[84] See especially the letter dated January 28, 1625, in AHN, Inquisición, Legajo 2962. Also, see Bernardino Llorca, "Documentos inéditos interesantes sobre los alumbrados de Sevilla de 1623–1628," *Estudios Ecclesiásticos* 11 (1932): 414.

martyrdom, the Holy Office sentenced most to be penanced in an auto de fe. Further public degradation could follow, such as requiring the beata to wear a sanbenito, the characteristic penitential costume, and process through the city streets, or march into exile from the city.[85] These punishments effectively demonstrated that beatas had no special power or independence and, like all ordinary people, had to accept the direction of an official church. In these public rituals, the people acted as a collective of silent witnesses, carefully distinguished from the guilty beatas.

Following public degradation, the Holy Office sentenced most beatas to reclusion in an enclosed house where they were to work for their food and shelter. Under the direction of an appointed confessor, they lived strictly confined from public contact, no longer permitted to report prophesies or visions or ecstasies. The example of these women made an impact, and most beatas disappeared from the public life of the city. Whether in reclusion under sentence or accepted into a convent of tertiaries, they faded into invisibility. Madre Catalina also disappeared from view, her voice silenced with a six-year sentence of reclusion.

In contrast to the silence imposed on madre Catalina, the Inquisition required her first disciple, Juan de Villapando, to speak publicly "in a high voice" from the pulpit and retract twenty-two erroneous propositions.[86] Inquisitors considered his public retraction essential to preserve the orthodox faith, but they dismissed into reclusion madre Catalina, who had taught the same propositions. They encouraged the people of Seville to attend and hear the recantation of the erring priest; but they cut off public concern with the false beata by collecting and destroying all her relics, portraits, and writings. Traditional gender roles thus imposed, the Holy Office appeared to restore order.

Yet the transformation of these once powerful religious symbols would take some time. Madre María de Jesús carried on a long correspondence with Philip IV, becoming a "power in the state," in the words of one historian.[87] A few beatas continued to prophesy, stirring up enough notice that the Holy Office called them for questioning.[88] Legends of holiness preserved the visibility of other beatas, such as another madre María de Jesús, a Franciscan beata who founded a hospital for the poor in Seville. In 1669, the stories say, her body remained soft and pliable after she died, giving off a "sweet fragrance," rather than an "intolerable stink," amazing

[85] Kamen, *Inquisition and Society*, pp. 186–88, esp.

[86] AMS, Sección Especial, Papeles del Señor Conde de Aguila, Tomo 4 en folio, Número 47.

[87] Lea, *Chapters*, p. 322.

[88] See, for example, AHN, Inquisición, Legajo 2061, Número 12, for the case against María de la Concepción in 1645.

the entire city population that had come to view her body at the funeral.[89] Some thirty years later another beata, Isabel de la Cruz, entered legend as a wealthy widow who gave all that she had to the poor and developed a special devotion to the Child Jesus. Known for her prophecies and ecstasies inspired by this image, she was called upon by a woman long childless. Through the intercession of this beata, the story says, the woman had a child and named her Isabel.[90]

Safely confined in legend, convent, or reclusion, beatas had to develop less public forms of power, for they never again assumed the leadership role that madre Catalina had attained. The people who waited on that February day in 1627 for one more glimpse of madre Catalina must have known that they would never see her again. Now flanked by bigamists and blasphemers, Judaizers and heretics, this once powerful woman had been humbled by authorities who appealed to a "natural" gender order, a horror of the body, and a conviction that women's inner world must be as closely controlled as their outer behavior. They had effectively reduced her to silence, to invisibility, to nothing.

[89] The most complete story of this madre María de Jesús appears to be in AMS, Sección Especial, Papeles del Señor Conde de Aguila, Tomo 32 en folio, Número 2. Warner, *Alone of all Her Sex*, pp. 99–102, discusses the association of sweet fragrance after death with holiness.

[90] AMS, Efemérides, Cuaderno 4.

Chapter 6

SEXUAL REBELS

ECCLESIASTICAL and secular authorities cooperated to define a gendered moral order as they worked to defend religious orthodoxy and the developing state during the Counter-Reformation. After the 1570s, churchmen and secular officials in Seville increasingly prosecuted people accused of adultery, bigamy, fornication, love magic, sodomy, and soliciting sexual acts on the streets and in the confessional. These acts, they believed, not only violated secular laws and official standards of decency; they also offended the gender prescriptions of God's holy order in the nature that he had created.

As a challenge to official order, sexual deviance became the focus of a theater of power. It brought together actors who represented rich and poor, young and old, male and female, secular and ecclesiastical, official and nonofficial, local and imperial. Within a setting of rapid population growth and commercial expansion unequaled in any other city of the time, these actors moved through rituals of defining, performing, prosecuting, and punishing sexual deviance. Their drama included many different strata of power in scenes both public and private. As carefully staged spectacle, this theater reflected and acted upon power relationships developing in the early modern period that provided a basis for subsequent state building.[1]

Historical sources describe sexual rebels, but with certain limitations. The permanent tribunal of the Inquisition in Seville left written records of 1,678 cases between 1559 and 1648.[2] Charges of bigamy account for 10 percent of these cases, those of fornication account for 11 percent, 3 percent of them concerned clerics soliciting sexual acts in the confessional, and a handful involved accusations of blasphemy and conjuring devils while working love magic. During this same period, city chronicles and Pedro de León, a Jesuit who attended prisoners in the Royal Prison of Seville, report

[1] Useful theories of state building are in Perry Anderson, *Lineages of the Absolutist State* (New York: Schocken, 1979); Antonio Gramsci, *Selections from the Prison Notebooks of Antonio Gramsci*, trans. and ed. Quentin Hoare and Geoffrey Nowell Smith (New York: International Publishers, 1972); and in Charles Tilly, ed., *The Formation of National States in Western Europe* (Princeton: Princeton University Press, 1975). Patricia Labalme, "Sodomy and Venetian Justice in the Renaissance," *The Legal History Review* 52 (1984): 217–54, also recognizes the significance of sexual deviance in building state power, but she has focused on legal institutions within Venice rather than social relationships, which I see as a basis for state building.

[2] Records for the tribunal in Seville are in AHN, Inquisición, Legajos 2061, 2067, 2072, 2074, 2075, 2962, and 3742.

that secular courts prosecuted seventy-one cases of sodomy.[3] Most records of criminal cases in Seville have disappeared, some lost to the bonfires that periodically broke out around the city hall during rebellions such as that of 1652.[4] Moreover, the records that do exist represent an official rather than popular version of sexual deviance, and they describe only a small number of those people who actually engaged in sexual deviance, as well as some who were innocent. Despite these limitations, however, available sources say enough about sexual deviance to show how it was defined, who was prosecuted, and how they were punished.

Because Inquisition documents were written by male officials, they present a particular perspective on the conjunction of popular and official cultures and the conjunction of male discourse and female experience.[5] Even the testimony of women was recorded by men in response to questions posed by men. The rhetoric in these records became a discourse, that is, according to the theory of Michel Foucault, an expression of a power relationship between language and the object to which it referred, in this case, sexual deviants. Although Foucault's theory of discourse has recognized the power functions of language, it has ignored the significance of gender in the development of power, the role of gender in extending power to some and restricting it from others.[6]

An analysis of Inquisition records demonstrates the complexity of this discourse. Although inquisitors used their discourse to impose order on women who had defied the limitations of their gender, their efforts did not by any means focus exclusively on deviant women. In fact, women accounted for fewer than one-quarter of all people prosecuted by the tribunal of the Inquisition in Seville during the sixteenth and seventeenth centuries. Not merely a catalog of misogynist attitudes in male inquisitors, Inquisition records also show that women played more than the passive roles of

[3] Pedro de León, *Compendio*, appendix 1 to pt. 2.

[4] For example, see Perry, *Crime and Society*, chap. 11, pp. 246–62, esp.

[5] Other works that note these conjunctions include Guilhem, "L'Inquisition et la dévaluation"; Carlo Ginzburg, *The Cheese and the Worms: The Cosmos of a Sixteenth-Century Miller*, trans. John and Anne Tedeschi (New York: Penguin, 1980); idem, *Nightbattles: Witchcraft and Agrarian Cults in the Sixteenth and Seventeenth Centuries*, trans. John and Anne Tedeschi (New York: Penguin, 1985); E. W. Monter, "Women and the Italian Inquisitions," in Rose, *Women in the Middle Ages and the Renaissance*, pp. 78–87; and Mary R. O'Neil, "Sacerdote ovvero Strione: Ecclesiastical and Superstitious Remedies in Sixteenth Century Italy," in *Understanding Popular Culture: Europe from the Middle Ages to the Nineteenth Century*, ed. Steve Kaplan (New York and Berlin: Mouton, 1984), pp. 53–84.

[6] Michel Foucault, "What Is an Author?" in his *Language, Counter-Memory, Practice*, ed. Donald F. Bouchard (Ithaca: Cornell University Press, 1980), pp. 113–38; see the discussion in Janet E. Halley and Sheila Fisher, "The Lady Vanishes: The Problem of Women's Absence in Medieval and Renaissance Texts," in *Seeking the Woman in Late Medieval and Renaissance Writings: Essays in Feminist Contextual Criticism*, ed. Sheila Fisher and Janet E. Halley (Knoxville: University of Tennessee Press, 1989), p. 14.

victims. Indeed, women participated in the inquisitors' discourse, giving testimony as both witnesses and the accused. Most of them tried to say what they believed inquisitors wanted them to say, but they also sought influence through denouncing themselves and others, making confessions, and answering questions.

Inquisitors who wrote reports of their activities for their superiors followed a particular form. After a salutation, they listed by categories of offense or punishment the names of prisoners and those people whose cases had been judged. Women's names usually followed those of men. With few exceptions, women's cases were strictly distinguished from those of men. The report identified each male by name, origin, and residence and often added an occupation or social status. The first identifying words following the name of a woman, however, gave her position as a wife, widow, daughter, nun, or slave. In the few cases in which a woman fit into none of these categories, she was described as an "honest woman" or a "public woman."[7] The form thus emphasized that a woman should be identified through a man or her sexual status, major concerns of male discourse.

Between 1559 and 1648, the Inquisition prosecuted 174 people for "simple fornication," or heterosexual relations between unmarried people. Testimony in these cases shows that fornication was punished not because a person engaged in sex, but because that person insisted that simple fornication was not a mortal sin. Inquisitors attempted to defend an official ecclesiastical view that sexuality, which was a basic quality of human nature, was too dangerous to be left unregulated. Ideally, it should be kept within marriage, restricted to heterosexual relations for procreation. Prosecution of fornication aimed to eliminate both casual sex and concubinage, or living together without benefit of marriage.

Inquisitors viewed fornication as very gender-specific, bringing 87 percent of the fornication cases against men. Those women who were prosecuted for fornication were widows or single, sometimes described as prostitutes. The Inquisition brought very few cases against female prostitutes, however, leaving this to secular officials who enforced laws that restricted prostitutes to licensed brothels and required them to keep a specific dress code.[8] Married women who engaged in extramarital sexual activity were prosecuted for adultery under secular law, which provided that the wronged husband could execute his wife and her lover in a public square.[9] Married men were not prosecuted for extramarital sex unless they could be accused of saying it was not a mortal sin.

Concerned with the lack of orthodox Christian indoctrination in the vil-

---

[7] AHN, Inquisición, Legajo 2075, Número 4. Note that the term "morisca" may precede other identifying words.

[8] For more on prostitutes, see chap. 7, below; and Perry, "Deviant Insiders," pp. 138–58.

[9] Two such cases are discussed in Perry, *Crime and Society*, pp. 140–42.

lages surrounding Seville, the Inquisition most commonly prosecuted for fornication young males who were rural laborers. Although their ages ranged from seventeen to sixty-two years, most of them appeared to be in their twenties. Accused fornicators included day laborers, artisans, and sailors, as well as farm workers and shepherds. They also included two Frenchmen. The absence of nobles or men of wealth is explained by an economic double standard that enabled these men to buy the silence of sexual partners or victims and to keep concubines because they could afford them.

Witnesses listed in these cases were usually adult males. Many said they were working with the accused or simply talking with him about women when he made the incriminating statement. Francisco de Guillan, however, was denounced by four witnesses, three of whom were women with whom he had had sex.[10] And Elvira López attempted to discredit the two witnesses against her, saying that they were a married couple who were her neighbors.[11] Motivations for these witnesses undoubtedly included the desire to gain an edge in ongoing disputes or to even up old scores, an attempt to relieve social tensions, which was a more significant function of the Inquisition than its attempts to defend the faith.[12]

Once they were imprisoned by the Inquisition and subject to questioning, most of the accused confessed to having made the offensive statement. Many, however, insisted they had only said that simple fornication was not a mortal sin; they did recognize it was a venial one. Others tried to defend themselves by claiming they had only meant that going to a prostitute was not a mortal sin. Money given to the woman, in this argument, prevented sexual relations with her from being a mortal sin. As seventeen-year-old Juan Godo said, the money that the woman received could be considered "alms" given by the man in expiation for his sin, a revealing insight into the commercialization of female sexuality and the perceived need for prostitutes.[13]

Most explanations by the accused declared that simple fornication was the lesser of evil options. Some of the accused argued that going to a prostitute was not a mortal sin, while having sex with a married woman or a *doncella*, an unmarried virgin, was. Others defended simple fornication as a form of concubinage, which they said was better than casual and promiscuous sex. According to five witnesses, Augustina de la Sierra had declared that to be the concubine of a white man was better than to marry a mu-

[10] AHN, Inquisición, Legajo 2075, Número 16.

[11] Ibid., Número 12.

[12] Recent scholarship exploring this social function of the Inquisition includes Contreras, *Santo Oficio*; Gustav Henningsen and John Tedeschi, eds., *The Inquisition in Early Modern Europe: Studies in Sources and Methods* (DeKalb: Northern Illinois University Press, 1984); and Pérez Villanueva, *La inquisición española*.

[13] AHN, Inquisición, Legajo 2075, Número 17.

latto.[14] Francisco de Guillan, in trying to convince a woman to live with him, told her that it would be better to live with him as a concubine than to marry "poorly."[15] Two men testified that it was better to have sex with a single woman than with a female burro.[16]

Several of the accused threw themselves on the mercy of the inquisitors, saying that they were such "simple" men that they did not understand what it was that they had said. In the case of seventeen-year-old Juan Godo, the appeal worked. Inquisitors agreed that because of his youth, he should simply be reprimanded and then attend religious instruction for two months.[17]

Most of the convicted received far more severe penalties, at least a sentence to participate in an auto at which their sentences were read publicly and they recanted their offense formally as an abjuration de levi. In addition, many received a whipping or sentence of exile. A few also had to pay a fine, and one man was forbidden to ever again live with a concubine. The accused who made better defenses received only a reprimand and had to hear mass as a penitent in the Chapel of San Jorge in the little castle of the Inquisition.

Officials punished far fewer women for fornication because gender beliefs discussed in previous chapters provided much more effective means for discouraging women from sexual promiscuity, or at least from talking so much about their exploits. Women were socialized from a very young age by parents who were exhorted to guard their daughters' chastity, their greatest treasure, "as a dragon."[18] When they married, they were expected to grant to their husbands a monopoly on their sexuality. Women who entered a convent heard from confessors that erotic or sensual thoughts separated them from God as surely as the grille was to separate nuns from their male admirers. Women who became beatas were advised to protect themselves from "unclean thoughts" by thinking of their bodies as corpses, full of worms.[19]

Gender worked so effectively in imposing sexual control over women in this city because women imposed it on themselves. Vergüenza, the Mediterranean consciousness of shame, motivated them far more to internalize gender restrictions than honor motivated men to restrain themselves sexually. In fact, male pride may have encouraged some men to brag about their sexual adventures. Female subcultures seemed to remind women to be discreet, even when they engaged in extramarital sex or in love magic,

[14] Ibid., Número 13.
[15] Ibid., Número 16.
[16] Ibid., Números 13 and 15.
[17] Ibid., Número 17.
[18] Juan de la Cerda, *Vida política*, p. 14. Also, see Pérez, "La femme," p. 21.
[19] Pérez de Valdivia, *Aviso*, p. 812.

preparing charms made from the hair of a desired man or slipping into his food a concoction believed to make him crazy with desire. Those who talked too much appear in Inquisition records as "lewd sorceresses" and in the Royal Prison as "lost women" whom beatas and priests advised to ask for confinement in local Magdalen houses for contrite women so they could escape more severe punishment.

Many churchmen regarded seductive women as the cause of all sins of fornication. Francisco Farfan, a canon at Salamanca, wrote two books in the late sixteenth century about the problems of maintaining chastity in the face of carnal temptations.[20] He quoted Saint Augustine: "It is evil to look at the woman; it is worse to speak to her; and it is worst of all to touch her."[21] Describing men who engaged in fornication as not defending themselves from seductive women, Farfan presented female fornicators as victims of themselves.[22] This cleric and many others refuted beliefs that coitus promoted the health of men and concluded that only "rustics" and those very poorly instructed by the Church would make a statement of such "crass ignorance" as that of fornicators who said theirs was not a mortal sin.[23]

Officials reserved their most severe condemnations for sodomites. *Las Siete Partidas* required the death penalty for sins "against nature," except for those people forced against their will or for children younger than fourteen years.[24] The possibility of lesbianism evidently did not preoccupy these officials, who saw women as sexually dependent on men, for few commented on sexual activity between women.[25] In contrast, male homosexuality appeared so dangerous that men accused of homosexual behavior were isolated from others in the Royal Prison of Seville, their deviance regarded as a contagion that could easily infect others.[26] Preachers and

---

[20] Farfan, *Tres libros* and *Regimiento*.

[21] Farfan, *Tres libros*, p. 426.

[22] Farfan, *Regimiento*, pp. 24–47ᵛ.

[23] Farfan, *Tres libros*, pp. 758 and 860–68.

[24] *Las Siete Partidas*, Partida 7, Title 21, Laws 1 and 2; LaBalme, "Sodomy and Venetian Justice," p. 230, discusses a belief, presented in his *Confessions* by Saint Augustine, that sodomy violates the relationship between God and human because it pollutes human nature with a perverted lust.

[25] One source that reports homosexual activity between women is a manuscript by Cristóbal de Chaves entitled "Relación de las cosas de la cárcel de Sevilla y su trato," Tomo B-C in AMS, Sección Especial, Papeles del Señor Conde de Aguila. The second source is an addendum to the report for 1624, in AMS, Sección Especial, Tomo 20. Gregorio López, who wrote the gloss for the edition of *Las Siete Partidas* that was widely accepted in the sixteenth century, declared that sodomy was a crime possible between women, as well as between men or between men and women (see the 1884 edition, 4: 330–31).

[26] Chaves refers to segregation within the prison in both pt. 1 and pt. 2 of his "Relación." Pedro de León refers to homosexuality as a contagion in case 129 of appendix 1 to pt. 2 of his *Compendio*. All subsequent references to his report will be from this appendix unless oth-

moralizers warned of the wickedness of sodomy, the temptations of allowing men to share a bed, and the danger implicit in those men who let their hair grow long and dressed in extravagant fashion.[27]

Both secular and ecclesiastical authorities prosecuted cases of sodomy in Habsburg Spain. The Inquisition had jurisdiction over these cases in Aragon and punished offenders with appearance at an auto, then a whipping and exile.[28] In Castile, however, secular authorities rather than the Inquisition had jurisdiction over sodomy. Moreover, those convicted of this offense received the most severe punishment: they were burned alive. Seventy-one men convicted of sodomy suffered this fate in Seville between 1567 and 1616.[29]

With one exception, all of the reports of sodomy in this city involved males only. In 1612 a forty-year-old cleric, Joan de Buendía, confessed to inquisitors that he had committed sodomy three times with a woman who was his "friend."[30] Penanced as a "solicitante" guilty of sexual misbehavior in the confessional, he escaped with a reprimand, exile, one-year reclusion in a monastery, and loss of the privilege to hear confession. Because no other case involved females, it seems likely that heterosexual sodomy was not considered such a serious crime against nature as homosexual inter-

---

erwise stated. See also the discussion in Pedro Herrera Puga, *Sociedad y delincuencia en el Siglo de Oro* (Madrid: Biblioteca de Autores Cristianos, 1974), p. 262.

[27] Pedro de León, *Compendio*, especially cases 7, 8, and 122; and fray Francisco de León, quoted in Carmelo Viñas Mey, *El problema de la tierra en la España de los siglos XVI y XVII* (Madrid: Consejo Superior de Investigaciones Científicas, 1941), p. 47.

[28] Historical studies of the Aragonese records have found that during the period 1540–1700 inquisitors prosecuted 379 for this offense in Valencia, 453 in Barcelona, and 791 in Zaragoza. See Ricardo García Cárcel, *Herejía y sociedad en el siglo XVI: La inquisición en Valencia 1530–1609* (Barcelona: Ediciones Península, 1980), p. 288; it should be noted that not all those prosecuted were executed. E. W. Monter has found that between 1560 and 1640 the Inquisition prosecuted 477 people in Zaragoza for *pecado nefando* (heinous sin), but executed only 95; 248 in Valencia, where they executed only 50; and 189 in Barcelona, where only five were executed. See his *Frontiers of Heresy: The Spanish Inquisition from the Basque Lands to Sicily* (Cambridge and New York: Cambridge University Press, 1990) pp. 276–302.

[29] Pedro de León listed 54 men burned for sodomy in his *Compendio*, appendix 1 to pt. 2; the Efemérides in the AMS, Sección Especial, Papeles del Señor Conde de Aguila, states that 15 men were burned as sodomites in April 1600 (a period of time when Pedro de León was absent from Seville); the Efemérides also recorded that Alonso Henríques de Guzmán was condemned in 1567 for pecado nefando, and it recorded the burning of a deaf and blind old man for pecado nefando in July 1604; Francisco de Ariño, *Sucesos de Sevilla de 1592 á 1604 recojidos de Francisco de Ariño, vecino de la ciudad en el barrio de Triana* (Seville: Rafael Tarascó y Lassa, 1873), p. 43, describes the arrest of don Alonso Girón, alguacil mayor of Seville, for sodomy and other crimes; because he was a noble, he was garroted before his body was burned in a public execution in 1597. Note that the cases of Francisco Iniesta (1603) and Joan de Buendía (1612) disclosed accusations of sodomy, but these men were penanced by the Inquisition as *solicitantes* (clerics accused of soliciting sex in the confessional), as recorded in AHN, Inquisición, Legajo 2075, Números 13 and 22.

[30] AHN, Inquisición, Legajo 2075, Número 22.

course. This implies that the real crime of sodomy was not in ejaculating nonprocreatively, nor in the use of the anus, but in requiring a male to play the passive "female" role and in violating the physical integrity of a male recipient's body. In this view, females only could be receptacles for semen, their biological integrity "naturally" inviting this invasion of their inner physical space.

A commonly accepted sixteenth-century commentary on the law against "unnatural crime" acknowledged that it prohibited sexual activity between women as well as between men. However, one interpretation of this law called for a lighter punishment when sexual activity between women did not involve an instrument for penetration, implying that the more serious crime was not sex between women, but impersonation of a male.[31] This focus on the artificial phallus expresses a concern with bodily integrity and with the danger of venturing into forbidden passages by "unnatural" means. Using an artificial appendage for sexual purposes may have been seen as unnatural just as tree-branch "horns" tied to a man's head signified the unnatural state of the cuckold. It seems significant that the only two reports on female homosexual activity mentioned the use of false genitalia. However, the women in the first report were not burned, but whipped and exiled. In the second report, a woman who had used a false penis with other women was hanged in 1624 for "robberies, murders, and audacity."[32]

Men accused of sodomy often used popular beliefs and social status to defend themselves. They stated that they were first seduced into committing sodomy by a foreigner, especially an Italian. Many said that they had first committed sodomy during military service. Some, such as Francisco de Iniesta, who was penanced by the Inquisition in 1603, asserted that sodomy was not a sin because he had paid for it.[33] Iniesta also said that another man had told him that his remedy for hemorrhoids was to be sodomized by a male, but under questioning Iniesta confessed that the devil had made him say these things. His confession and clerical status saved him from punishment more severe than a reprimand and sentence to hear mass as a penitent.

Iniesta's is not the only case in which male prostitution appeared. Mayuca, a black sentenced in 1585, apparently acted as a procurer in finding

[31] Antonio Gómez, who wrote *Variae resolutiones, juriscivilis, communis et regii* in the sixteenth century, quoted in Louis Crompton, "The Myth of Lesbian Impunity: Capital Laws from 1270 to 1791," in *Historical Perspectives on Homosexuality*, ed. Salvatore J. Licata and Robert P. Petersen, vol. 2 of themonograph series, *Research on Homosexuality* (New York: Haworth Press; Stein and Day, 1981), p. 19.

[32] AMS, Sección Especial, Tomo 20; Chaves, "Relación," pt. 1.

[33] AHN, Inquisición, Legajo 2075, Número 13.

male clients for his "handsome, painted young gallants."[34] Moreover, the sheriff who kept boys in his gambling house may have regarded them as a commercial enterprise as well as a diversion for his own pleasure.[35] Hamete, the black Turk sentenced in 1616, had boasted that he was paid eight ducats each time he agreed to engage in sodomy, and an actor who was condemned for sodomy told the judge that he was given one hundred reales each time he took the active role in sodomy.[36] None of these cases referred directly to male prostitution, but this is not surprising in a city in which prostitution was believed to be a female service for male clients.[37] The sexual double standard in Seville barred males from selling sex while permitting females to do so, but male officials tried to carefully control female prostitutes.

Information from several of the cases implies the existence of a male homosexual subculture. Pedro de León described a "quadrilla," or little squad of sodomites led by Diego Maldonado, who was punished in 1585.[38] Eight men burned in that year were reported to meet in an area just outside the city walls called the Huerta del Rey, where fig trees helped to conceal their illicit activity.[39] It is also likely that men met male sexual partners in gambling houses, such as that owned by the sheriff punished in 1590.[40] The fact that fifteen men were burned together for sodomy in 1600 suggests the existence of a group of sodomites, although records report nothing more about them.[41]

Descriptions of the physical appearance of those condemned for sodomy may also indicate that they were perceived as a male homosexual subculture. Francisco Galindo, for example, "walked with such charm and appeared more woman than man" in his dress and demeanor.[42] The boys kept in the sheriff's gambling house were described as "painted" and "handsome."[43] Pedro de León described Mayuca as wearing a wig, a large lace

[34] Pedro de León, *Compendio*, case 122.

[35] Ibid., cases 180 and 181.

[36] Ibid., case 308; and Pedro de León, *Compendio*, pt. 2, chap. 26. A ducat was worth about thirteen reales.

[37] The legal concept of male prostitution was undoubtedly poorly developed here as it was in nineteenth-century England. See Jeffrey Weeks, "Inverts, Perverts, and Mary-Annes: Male Prostitution and the Regulation of Homosexuality in England in the Nineteenth and Early Twentieth Centuries," in Licata and Petersen, *Historical Perspectives*, pp. 115–17; note, however, that Labalme found complaints about male prostitutes from female prostitutes in sixteenth-century Venice, "Sodomy and Venetian Justice," pp. 247–48.

[38] Pedro de León, *Compendio*, cases 127 and 128.

[39] Ibid., cases 107, 120, 121, 122, 124, 127, 128, and 129.

[40] Efemérides, Noticias y casos, Número 1.

[41] Ibid., case 180. See also the discussion in Herrera Puga, *Sociedad y delincuencia*, pp. 257–58.

[42] Pedro de León, *Compendio*, case 129, also described in Cases 120 and 121.

[43] Ibid., cases 180 and 181.

ruff, and facial cosmetics, although this may have been how he was sentenced to appear at the bonfire rather than how he usually adorned himself.[44] It seems likely that criminal justice officials deliberately caricatured his appearance in order to humiliate him and better impress the public with his crimes. Pedro de León noted the assertions of many "honorable gentlemen" who attended his burning that wigs, hairpieces, and lace collars should also go into the fire. Not all men who wore these things were considered homosexuals, but moralists such as Francisco de León preached with vigor against "men converted into women" and "effeminate soldiers, full of airs, long locks, and plumes."[45] His description contrasts with the sodomite whom Quevedo described in *La vida del Buscón* as "a mean-looking fellow" with one eye, "a moustache, and broad shoulders covered with whip scars."[46] León's ridicule of men dressed as women also contrasts with the condemnation of masculine-dressed women who were considered to be lewd.[47] Evidently homophobia had gender-specific forms in Counter-Reformation Spain.

A major exception to the vilification of women who dressed as men appeared in 1630 in Seville when Catalina de Erauso, "the nun-ensign," created a sensation as she entered the cathedral, for she wore men's apparel and had a royal license to do so. Much earlier in the seventeenth century she had run away from a convent in northern Spain where she was a novitiate. Dressed as a boy, she had made her way to Seville and the New World, where she worked for merchants and then joined the Spanish army, successfully disguising herself for many years. Convicted in 1620 of killing another soldier in a tavern brawl in Guamanga, Peru, she revealed her identity as a woman and a nun. The bishop called in three matrons to examine the felon, and then he stayed the execution, declaring that the viceregal court could not execute this person because she was a nun, subject first to ecclesiastical law.[48]

[44] Ibid., case 122.

[45] From a sermon in 1635, quoted in Viñas Mey, *El problema*, p. 47.

[46] Francisco de Quevedo Villegas, *Historia de la vida del Buscón* (Zaragoza, 1626), reprinted in *Novela picaresca: Textos escogidos* (Madrid: Taurus, 1962), p. 531; and translated by Michael Alpert as *The Swindler* in *Two Spanish Picaresque Novels* (Harmondsworth, Middlesex: Penguin, 1981), p. 172. I am indebted to Professor Anne J. Cruz for suggesting literary descriptions of male homosexuality.

[47] Juan de la Cerda, *Vida política*, Tomo 5, Capitulo 16, describes women who disguise themselves as men. Professor Richard Kagan has found records of several other women who disguised themselves as men in this period, and he also presented a paper, "Eleno/Elena: Annals of Androgyny in Sixteenth-Century New Castile," to the Society for Spanish and Portuguese Historical Studies at the University of Minnesota in April 1986. For Valencia, see Vicente Graullera, "Mujer, amor y moralidad en la Valencia de los siglos XVI y XVII," in Redondo, *Amours légitimes*, pp. 114–15.

[48] Notarized documents by and about Catalina de Erauso are in AGI, Documentos escogidos, Sección 5, Legajo 1, Número 87, año 1626–1630. See also AMS, Sección Especial,

Catalina de Erauso subsequently escaped discipline by either secular or ecclesiastical law, and she became a legend in her own lifetime. Philip IV rewarded her with a pension and the license to dress as a man, a privilege quickly confirmed by the pope. Crowds followed her wherever she went, curious to see this woman who dressed and lived as a man, who had fought as a soldier in the New World, and who appeared remarkable even in a period noted, as we shall see, for real and fictional manly women. Like other women in male disguise, she captured the popular imagination. She became the subject of a play and three autobiographies, which may or may not be genuine.[49] In contrast with other manly heroines of this period, Catalina de Erauso made a complete and total renunciation of her femaleness. It is this quality, and not the fact that she was a woman and a nun, which set her above the law and accounts for her reprieve.[50] It is also this quality that made her into a legendary sexual rebel.

Historical evidence reveals a factual basis for the legends that developed around Catalina de Erauso. Baptismal records for the village of San Sebastián in the northern province of Guipúzcoa indicate that she was baptized on February 10, 1592, the legitimate daughter of Miguel de Erauso and María Pérez de Galarraga.[51] Books for the Dominican convent of San Sebastián, called el Antiguo, show that Miguel de Erauso and his wife paid the convent in 1603 for keeping three of their daughters, Mari Juan, Isabel, and Catalina. Both Mari Juan and Isabel professed and subsequently died in this convent, but Catalina disappeared from the books in 1607.

Some eighteen years later Catalina de Erauso resurfaced in notarized documents filed in 1625.[52] Now in the Archivo de las Indias, these docu-

---

Papeles del Señor Conde de Aguila, Efemérides, "Noticias y casos," número 1; and Joaquin María de Ferrer, *Historia de la monja alférez, doña Catalina de Erauso, escrita por ella misma* (1625) (Paris: Julio Didot, 1829). There are discrepancies between the archival and autobiographical versions of her life. They should be read as the stories that Catalina de Erauso and others told as they transformed her life into legend.

[49] Many scholars question the authenticity of her published autobiographies. See, e.g., the "Prologo" in Ferrer, *Historia*, and *Autobiografías y memoriales*, vol. 2 of *Nueva Biblioteca de Autores Españoles* (Madrid: Librería Editorial de Bailly, 1905), ser. 2, chap. 9. Luis de Castresana, *Catalina de Erauso: La monja alférez* (Madrid: Afrodisio Aguado, 1968), p. 12, believes they are genuine and points out that other statements verify Catalina de Erauso's claim to heroic military service in the New World. See also Rima-Gretchen Rothe Vallbona, "Historic Reality and Fiction in *Vida y sucesos de la monja alférez*" (Ph.D. diss., Middlebury College, 1981).

[50] Frances E. Olsen, "From False Paternalism to False Equality" (Paper presented to the National Women's Studies Association, University of Illinois School of Law, Champaign-Urbana, Illinois, June 1986); Christine A. Littleton, "Debating the Legal Meaning of Sexual Equality" (Paper presented to the UCLA Faculty Seminar on Women, Culture, and Theory, November 1986), pp. 17–18.

[51] This baptismal record and all documents from her life are reprinted as appendixes in Ferrer, *Historia*, pp. 129–67.

[52] AGI, Documentos escogidos, Sección 5, Legajo 1, Número 87.

ments include a petition of "alférez doña Catalina de Erauso," which described her service of fifteen years to the king in Chile and Peru and requested that the king reward "her services, long pilgrimages, and brave deeds." Another, a petition of "ensign Antonio de Erauso," requested that the king receive information supporting her story of being attacked and detained as a "spy of the king of Spain" while making a pilgrimage to Rome in the same year. Notarized statements accompanied and verified both petitions.

In Rome Catalina told her story to a sympathetic cleric, Pedro de Valle Peregrino, who wrote her account in a letter dated July 11, 1626.[53] Obviously concerned to win his approval, she explained that she had run away from the convent because she was "displeased with that enclosed life" and wanted to live as a man. She became a soldier in the Indies, she said, because she was "inclined naturally to arms and to seeing the world." Defending herself against accusations that she had killed many people in brawls, she told him that she had killed men in battle and had won a reputation for bravery as well as the commission of ensign. She had preserved the secret of her female identity because others, accepting the common assumption of the period, believed sex and gender were the same. Since she dressed and acted as a man, they simply concluded she was male; when a beard did not appear even as she grew older, they assumed she was a eunuch. She assured this cleric, just as she had told the bishop in Guamanga, that she had assumed male identity not "for an evil purpose, but only through her natural inclination for military service."

Accepting Catalina's explanations, Pedro de Valle Peregrino described her physical appearance in an attempt to resolve the puzzle of sex and gender, that is, how a biological woman could have lived as a man. He said that she was of "large stature and bulky for a woman, although she does not appear to be a man." Commenting on her flat chest, he said that she told him she had used a remedy from a young age to dry up her breasts. Her face, he found, was "not ugly, but not beautiful, and it is recognized to be somewhat badly treated, but not of much age." Catalina dressed as a man, revealing that she was a woman only in how she moved her hands. During one of her several visits to Seville, Francisco Pacheco painted a portrait of her, which is dated 1630 and inscribed, "the ensign Miss Catalina de Erauso, native of San Sebastián." Figure 13 presents an etching made from this portrait.

Later in the seventeenth century the Capuchin Nicolás de Rentería dictated a testimony about the soldier-nun in which he remembered seeing her in 1645 in Veracruz.[54] At that time, he said, she was known as Antonio de Erauso. With a string of mules and some blacks she transported mer-

---

[53] Reprinted as "Notas finales" in Ferrer, *Historia*, pp. 122–27.
[54] Ibid., pp. 119–22.

FIGURE 13. *Catalina de Erauso*, engraving from the portrait by Francisco Pacheco

chandise between ships and other parts of Mexico. She wore men's clothing and carried a sword and dagger with silver trimming. He said that she appeared to be about fifty years old then, of good body size, olive-skinned, and "with some little hairs as a moustache."

This memory of Catalina de Erauso as a middle-aged, wispy-moustached teamster contrasts sharply with her depiction in the play *La monja alférez, comedia famosa* by Juan Pérez de Montalván.[55] Written at the same time as the first alleged autobiography, the play emphasizes her attraction for women and her proclivity for gambling and fighting. None of the historical documents evidence these qualities, but they do appear in the three "autobiographies," which describe at least fifteen murders that she committed and several women who fell in love with her. If these were, indeed, facts in her life, Catalina de Erauso may not have acknowledged them in her petitions and accounts because they would have shown her to be less chaste and sober than the persona that won approval from clerics, the pope, and Philip IV. Facts alone, then, cannot explain the historical significance of Catalina de Erauso. Like so many women noted in historical documents, she can be analyzed more effectively as a symbol than as a person.

Catalina and other manly women in the seventeenth century won approval not for dressing as men, but for thinking like men, acting like men, and speaking like men.[56] Giovanni Boccaccio had already established a tradition of using *manly* as an adjective of the highest praise for women in his fourteenth-century book *Concerning Famous Women*.[57] Summarizing the life of Artemesia, queen of ancient Casia, he conceded admiration for her deeds; yet he asked what one could think except that it was an error of Nature to give female sex to a body which had been endowed by God with a magnificent and virile spirit. Writers such as Thomas Heywood continued this tradition in the seventeenth century, praising women, in Heywood's words, "of masculine and heroicke spirits."[58]

---

[55] The play is reprinted in Ferrer, *Historia*, pp. 169–311. Note that there is some question about the authorship of *La monja alférez*. Jack H. Parker, *Juan Pérez de Montalván* (Boston: Twayne, 1975), p. 69, suggests that the real author may be Luis Belmonte Bermúdez and quotes a complaint by Montalván that some publishers attributed to him work which was not his.

[56] Melveena McKendrick, *Woman and Society in the Spanish Drama of the Golden Age: A Study of the Mujer Varonil* (London: Cambridge University Press, 1974), p. x.

[57] Giovanni Boccaccio, *Concerning Famous Women* (London: George Allen and Unwin, 1964), introduction by Guido A. Guarino, pp. xxvii, 127.

[58] Thomas Heywood, *Exemplary Lives and Memorable Acts of Nine the Most Worthy Women of the World: Three Jewes, Three Gentiles, Three Christian* (London: Richard Royston, 1640), p. 92. In this and all quotations, I have preserved the spelling and punctuation of sixteenth- and seventeenth-century writers. For more on praise of manly women, see Shepherd, *Amazons*, p. 133. Two Spanish writers who praised manly women include fray Luis de León, *La perfecta casada*, p. 215; and Pérez de Valdivia, *Aviso*, p. 258.

Catalina was able to use for her own defense this tradition of the praise-worthy manly woman, but she did so differently from other women noted for their "masculine and heroicke spirits" in the seventeenth century. In contrast with other women praised for bravery in battle, Catalina went to war for her own "inclination," and not for the time-honored motive of joining a husband or lover. Moreover, she did not later voluntarily resume female identity, as does the heroine Leonor in *Comedia famosa de valor, agravio y mujer*, a play written about the same time by Ana Caro Mallén y Soto. Abandoned by her lover, Leonor assumes male dress in order "to cover my lost honor."[59] She finds the culprit on whom she has sworn re-venge, but by the play's end she has forgiven him, resumed her female identity, and promised to marry him.

In another legend of the woman disguised as a man, an account of Feli-ciana Enríquez de Guzmán asserts that this writer from Seville fell in love with a young man who went off to the university at Salamanca. She dis-guised herself as a man and followed him there, where she studied litera-ture and even won academic prizes before she revealed her female identity. She won praise not for her combat bravery, but for her "manly mind," which enabled her to succeed in scholarly pursuits believed appropriate only for men.[60]

Some scholarly women in seventeenth-century Spain, however, won rid-icule rather than praise for their academic interests. Quevedo wrote a dev-astating satire of women who knew Latin, and Calderon lampooned pre-tentious learned women in one of his plays about women, men, and love.[61] Feliciana Enríquez may have been applauded for her manly intellect be-cause she abandoned her male disguise, resumed her female identity, and married the man she loved. She thus represented the woman in love who dressed as a man in order to follow her love, rather than the woman pre-tending out of pride to be a man. Note that "manly intellect" was com-mended in the woman who accepted her female subjection to men and thus lacked the status to really compete with them.

Transvestism clearly involved serious risk in seventeenth-century Spain. Men who dressed or appeared too much like women were likely to be sus-pected of homosexual sodomy, a crime legally punishable by burning alive, and women who dressed as men were believed to be "past both honesty

[59] This play is reprinted in Serrano y Sanz, *Apuntes*, 268: 179–212; the quotation appears on p. 185.

[60] McKendrick, *Woman and Society*, p. 19. Her poetry is reprinted in *Biblioteca de Autores Españoles* (Madrid: M. Rivadeneyra, 1857), 42: 544–45. This story may be less accurate as a historical description of her life than as a commentary on the making of women into patriar-chal mythic figures who sacrificed their lives out of love for men.

[61] McKendrick, *Woman and Society*, p. 219; María del Pilar Oñate, *El feminismo en la liter-atura española* (Madrid: Espasa-Calpe, 1938), pp. 125–31.

and shame," as Vives warned.[62] Citing the injunction against cross-dressing in Deuteronomy, chapter 22, philosophers and moralists warned that transvestism leads to lasciviousness. They condemned in particular the actresses who dressed as men both on and off the stage. In contrast to the English stage where young boys played female roles, women appeared in the theater of Golden Age Spain in both male and female roles.[63] Ana Muñoz, for example, was famous as the beautiful first lady of the acting company of Andrés de Claramonte. She often appeared dressed as a man, either to portray a man or to portray a female in disguise. In one scene she appeared as an Amazon astride a horse. When the audience cheered, the horse bolted and tossed her to the ground, causing the premature birth of her daughter.[64] Moralists saw this as divine punishment for "unnatural" women. One cleric denounced male dress that exposed the contours of a woman's body, for which nature required more effective concealment; another simply concluded that women in male costume presented "a major perversity."[65]

Fictional characters, as long as they are distinguished from actual historical women, can provide more information about the symbolic meaning of the manly woman. Catalina de Erauso can be compared with these fictional characters, even though she was an actual historical person, because she was also fictionalized as the hero of a play written during her own lifetime and as the hero of a legend that continued to grow after her death. These fictional accounts of manly women do not directly reflect actual women's lives, but they do indicate attitudes about them.[66] In a sense, seventeenth-century drama can be considered prescriptive literature because it portrayed idealizations of women, both good and evil.

The manly woman functioned as a gender symbol, evoking normative prescriptions that developed out of and functioned within specific historical contexts. The political significance of this symbol becomes very clear when we ask why the manly woman appears in seventeenth-century Spain. The New World provided a frontier in which women might more easily lose their past identities and preserve a male disguise. Furthermore, the woman who chose to live as a man served to glorify traditional knightly values and thus to support attempts by the nobility to regain supremacy over a central monarch. The manly woman's adventures distracted atten-

---

[62] Vives, *A Very Frvtfvl and pleasant boke*, p. 28ʳ.

[63] Lorraine Helms, "The Martial Art of Captain Moll: From Elizabethan Cross-Dressing to Jacobean Androgyny" (Unpublished MS, 1986), p. 5; Carmen Bravo-Villasante, *La mujer vestida de hombre en el teatro español (siglos XVI–XVII)* (Madrid: Sociedad General Española de Librería, 1976), pp. 149–66.

[64] Bravo-Villasante, *La mujer*, p. 151.

[65] Ibid., pp. 155–59.

[66] McKendrick, *Woman and Society*, pp. 3–4, discusses this issue.

tion from economic decline and political unrest in the Habsburg Spanish empire. They also reassured people concerned about the numbers of men who left Spain for the New World, allowing them to believe that the country had not "feminized" and consequently gone to the dogs.

Catalina, in fact, refused feminization and embraced only masculine qualities. In the play based on her life, she says she would rather die than let others know she was a woman. She fought as a man to preserve her honor as a man.[67] Aware of the restrictions that gender imposed on her life, she did not try to change the inequity between the sexes. Instead, she chose to change herself, to deny her body, to repudiate the convent, habit, and submission expected of her as a woman, and to construct for herself a male persona that would completely obliterate her identity as a woman.

Unique among manly women who lived both actual and dramatized lives in the seventeenth century, Catalina de Erauso defied the law. As a woman with the audacity to wear masculine attire and, even worse, kill men, she should have been subject to the full punishment of the law. After all, other women had suffered capital punishment in seventeenth-century Spain; and the royal government must have felt a great concern to maintain order in its colonies where Catalina lived so much of her life as an outlaw before 1620. Moreover, authorities should have been especially intent upon enforcing a gender order in this period of considerable instability.

The soldier-nun used two strategies to save herself from legal punishment. First, she won the protection of ecclesiastical law by telling the bishop in Guamanga that she was a virgin. She urged him to have some matrons examine her, and their report that she was a "virgin intact as the day [she] was born" convinced the bishop that she could indeed be a nun and that, in any case, she was a virtuous woman, although she repudiated female roles.[68] Second, she accommodated herself to the legal system, meekly agreeing to await proof from her convent that she had not professed before her flight, and energetically preparing notarized petitions and testimonies to present to the king of Spain. Catalina may have broken every rule for women, but she preserved the most important one—virginity. And she may have broken the law against murder, but she demonstrated her respect for the legal system.

Authorities considered the case of Catalina de Erauso within the framework of a sexist legal system. At this time, there was not even a pretense of

---

[67] Helms, "The Martial Art," p. 10. See also the discussion of male and female honor in Lerner, *Patriarchy*, p. 80.

[68] See her "Historia," in Ferrer, *Historia*, p. 99. In the celebrated case of Eleno/Elena Céspedes, a hermaphrodite prosecuted by the Inquisition in Toledo in 1587, lack of virginity may have been a major factor leading to official condemnation. See Michèle Escamilla, "A propos d'un dossier inquisitorial des environs de 1590: Les étranges amours d'un hermaphrodite," in Redondo, *Amours légitimes*, pp. 167–82; and also Kagan, "Eleno-Elena."

juridical equality in the Spanish empire. A combination of ecclesiastical and secular rules and a hodgepodge of local ordinances, the system provided special protection for women, requiring a man to provide for a woman he had impregnated, for example. However, law justified this special protection because it considered her weak, vulnerable, irrational, and emotional. These qualities contrasted with law itself, which was believed to represent reason and strength, qualities considered to be male and also regarded as the highest level of human culture.[69] This legal system allowed husbands and fathers to collect damages from men who raped their women; and it seldom punished women who were chaste and respectful. However, it required the death penalty for women who carried out abortion, and it also allowed wronged husbands to publicly execute wives and their lovers.[70]

Inextricably bound up with a gender system, the law was deeply obsessed with female sexuality; and it is this relationship that explains the transformation of Catalina de Erauso from outlaw to hero. As a person born female who refused to accept her sex, who even tried to dry up her breasts to make her body conform to maleness, Catalina de Erauso symbolized male superiority. Her life suggested that anyone with a choice would choose the adventure, the freedom, the exhilaration of being a man. At the same time, Catalina was not biologically a male. Thus, she could not fit into the legal system that organized all human beings into two categories: men and women. As a man or as a woman, she should have been hanged for murder; as neither, and as both, she could be legally processed only with difficulty.

The solution was to transform Catalina into a hero "protected" by the law, but not as a woman, although legal tradition excused some female outlaws, such as women who stole in order to feed their children. Catalina won reprieve as a woman who fought as a man, who killed others to defend her honor as a man, who represented the supremacy of male honor and the preeminence of man's right to defend his honor. The law in this case functioned to maintain order not by punishing a person who murdered others, but by making a hero of a woman who chose to be a man. Transformed from outlaw to hero, the manly woman participated in the making of her own myth. She reinforced the values of patriarchal society and justified sexism in the implementation of law.

As transvestites, fornicators, and sodomites, women appeared in the formal courts that prosecuted sexual deviance, but they were only a minority. This is not to say that females were the virtuous sex, nor does it mean that

[69] Frances Olsen, "The Sex of Law" (Paper presented to the UCLA Faculty Seminar on Women, Culture, and Theory, March 1985), develops this argument in looking at law at the present time.

[70] Perry, *Crime and Society*, pp. 67 and 140.

they were the inconsequential sex, too passively acquiescent to even provoke denuncation. Not all cases of crime are reported, and gender plays a role here: women are usually not perceived to be as criminal as men, nor in the same ways. Still more important, women do not appear in great numbers in the formal courts of Seville because gender provided such effective control on their sexuality through the home, the convent, the brothel, the confessional, and a system of charity.

Chapter 7

PROSTITUTES, PENITENTS, AND
BROTHEL PADRES

A SYPHILIS EPIDEMIC hit Seville in 1568, leaving in its wake a group of city officials even more determined to enclose all prostitutes in the legal brothel.[1] In the hospitals just outside the city walls, treatments, which varied from a water solution of bark to mercury salves, could not cure the disease.[2] Attempting to protect the city from such a terrible affliction, officials agreed to inspect more frequently the women of the brothel and to confine infected prostitutes in hospitals. New brothel ordinances sent by the royal government to Seville in 1570 stipulated that medical doctors should visit the brothels every eight days and notify the city officials of any ailing prostitutes.[3] For the first time, ordinances provided that brothel padres who failed to carry out these medical measures would be penalized through fines and short periods of incarceration. Disease now added urgency to the traditional moral argument for regulated brothels.

Legal prostitutes had been tolerated for centuries as deviant insiders essential to the moral order of the city. They clearly strayed from the moral restrictions on female sexual activity, but they were believed to divert males from more serious sins of homosexuality, incest, adultery, and propositioning honest women. The careful regulations imposed on them in the legal brothel defused their potential for disorder. Rather than barring them from the community, legalized prostitution provided a label for these women that functioned not to exclude them, but to integrate them into society under specific regulated conditions.[4]

---

[1] Velásquez y Sánchez, *Anales epidémicos*, p. 67.

[2] Ibid., p. 67. Prostitutes were reputed to have remedies for treating venereal diseases, but those remedies kept in brothels were not very effective, as reported in AMS, Sección 3, Siglo XVI,Escribanías de Cabildo, Tomo 11, Número 69, which warned of the poor condition of *endibia* (endive) and *lengua cervina* (probably the plant called deer's tongue) sold as remedies in the brothel in Seville.

[3] The 1570 brothel ordinances are in BM, Egerton 1873, "Tractatus varii, et collectanea," fols. 155–56.

[4] For sociological theories of labeling, see Kai T. Erikson, *Wayward Puritans: A Study of the Sociology of Deviance* (New York: John Wiley & Sons, 1966); and his "Notes on the Sociology of Deviance," *Social Problems* 9 (Spring 1962): 303–14; Howard S. Becker, *Outsiders: Studies in the Sociology of Deviance* (New York and London, 1963); Harold Garfinkel, *Studies in Ethnomethodology* (Englewood Cliffs, N.J.: Prentice-Hall, 1967); and the same author's "Conditions of Successful Degradation Ceremonies," *American Journal of Sociology* 61 (March 1956):

This perception of prostitution provides insights into a consciousness of gender and deviance that extended far beyond brothel walls and, in fact, symbolized a much broader ambiguity of attitudes about sin, sex, and power. Prostitution, or promiscuous and nonaffective sexual barter, was usually carried out by men who bought sex and women who sold it.[5] A livelihood for women, prostitution in this patriarchal society represented an expression of power for men, permitting those with wealth to buy the sexual use of women and to regulate this commerce. Other men were also provided the opportunity to buy the sexual services of women, so that their sense of privilege prevented them from raising questions about the greater power and wealth of the first group. The man who purchased the services of a prostitute freed himself from bothersome entanglements and a guilty conscience. His purchase also reduced a woman to nothing more than her sexuality.

The potential power of the seller in this transaction was rarely realized because it took place within a gender system that offered fewer economic options for women and condemned female promiscuity. Theoretically, the prostitute owned her sexuality and made money from selling what other women had to give away. In practice, however, prostitutes worked from a position of vulnerability. Not only did the prostitute have to sell if she was to survive in this system; she had to carry out her work under conditions that stigmatized it and increased her physical and emotional vulnerability. In the male-dominated society of Counter-Reformation Spain, prostitution was a sexual transaction so deeply embedded within a power system that it became a relationship at least as concerned with power as with sex or sin.

Legalized prostitution assumed that unregulated prostitutes posed a grave danger of social disorder. Free from compulsory medical inspections, these women were believed to pass on infectious diseases, especially syphilis. Unsupervised by a brothel padre, they were sometimes blamed for fomenting bloody quarrels in the streets and plazas and inns of the city. Able

---

420–24; Walter R. Gove, ed., *The Labelling of Deviance: Evaluating a Perspective* (Beverly Hills: Sage, 1980); J. I. Kitsuse, "Societal Reaction to Deviant Behavior: Problems of Theory and Method," *Social Problems* 9 (Winter 1962): 247–57; Edwin M. Lemert, *Human Deviance, Social Problems and Social Control* (Englewood Cliffs, N.J.: Prentice-Hall, 1967); and James Orcutt, "Societal Reaction and the Response to Deviation in Small Groups," *Social Forces* 52 (December 1973): 259–67. Orcutt's theory appears particularly appropriate for legalized prostitution in Seville because he has proposed that social response to individuals who break rules does not always exclude them and may, in fact, hold them within society.

[5] This definition of prostitution is derived especially from Kingsley Davis, "The Sociology of Prostitution," *American Sociological Review* 2 (1937): 744–55; but also see Jennifer James et al., *The Politics of Prostitution* (Seattle: Social Research Associates, 1977), pp. 37–38. Although male prostitution and clandestine prostitution existed in Seville and in other towns and villages of Spain, this chapter will focus on legalized prostitution and female prostitutes.

to escape legal restrictions on their dress, they could present themselves as respectable women, confusing the distinction between good women and bad.

With the ordinances of 1570, the city government adopted a set of regulations that more clearly established the brothel as the only acceptable place for women to work as prostitutes. In response to urban growth and to increased incidence of disease, the formal institutionalization of prostitution imposed greater control over prostitutes and transformed the position of brothel padre from a feudal privilege to a bureaucratic office. The 1570 ordinances provided that anyone serving as brothel padre had to be named by the city government, and they attempted to limit his economic power. He could not rent clothing to women in the brothel, nor could he loan them money. He could rent a room, furniture, and other necessities to each woman for no more than one real per day.

Enclosure became more rigorous in the 1570 regulations, which required any woman who wanted to sell her sexual services to work within the brothel, not only to reduce "disorders" resulting from men fighting over women, but also to lessen the threat of disease. However, the surgeon nominated by the city council to register and inspect women in the brothel warned in 1572 that infected prostitutes discharged from the brothel simply continued their trade from the streets and taverns of Seville, causing "much damage" to public health. Control over these women had to be increased, he urged, and diseased prostitutes should be transported from enclosure in the brothel to enclosure in a hospital.[6]

Even as legalized prostitution emphasized the danger of unregulated women, it also viewed women as weak and vulnerable victims requiring special care through formal protective measures. The ordinances of 1570 in Seville prohibited the brothel administrator from accepting women who had been pawned into the brothel for a sum of money. A priest who worked with people in the city's brothel wrote of "ruffians" who pawned their women for ten or twenty ducats or more.[7] Regulations forbade brothel administrators to accept a pawned woman, even if she agreed to the arrangement, or a woman already in debt, and they forbade brothel administrators to keep a woman in the brothel against her will even if she owed money. This policy clearly assumed that women were so commonly exploited economically and were so easily duped into exploitative situations that the city government had to protect them from themselves and their men.

Since the late fifteenth century, laws had required legal prostitutes to

[6] AMS, Sección 3, Siglo XVI, Escribanías de Cabildo, Tomo 11, Número 62.

[7] Antonio Domínguez Ortiz, "Vida y obras del Padre Pedro de León," *Archivo Hispalense*, ser. 2, 26–27 (1957): 167. The account of his ministry to people of Seville's brothel is in pt. 1, chaps. 4–6 of Pedro de León's *Compendio*.

attend mass and rest from work on Sundays and feast days. Imposing some discipline on the lives of prostitutes, these regulations also imposed some control on the activities of men. A desire to contain prostitution within a socioreligious order may have motivated these regulations as much as a wish to protect the souls of prostitutes and provide them some days of rest. Whether motivated by fear or compassion, the requirements implied that prostitutes would not decide independently to attend mass or to refrain from work on Sundays. They assumed that prostitutes could be best protected and integrated into the social order by requirements to observe certain religious customs.

The laws of the kingdom that prohibited anyone from living off the earnings of a prostitute implied that women who sold their sexual services did so because they were made to work, usually by a male pimp.[8] According to a seventeenth-century commentary, the Nueva Recopilación of the laws made under Philip II defined five categories of pimps, which began with "bad rascals" who kept women in the public brothel. A second group acted as brokers in selling the sexual services of women in their homes, and a third group sold those of slaves or servant women in their homes. The fourth type of pimping occurred when a man was "so vile that he pimps his own wife," and the fifth type involved a man's receiving some payment for allowing a married woman to commit adultery in his home. Proponents of the legal brothel argued that it would help to prevent such evil exploitation of women.

The paternalism of this system of legalized prostitution served important social functions. It reinforced the power position of officials and clerics who could play the role of authority in rituals that portrayed their power as acceptable because it was compassionate. In addition, creating rules to protect legal prostitutes neutralized their danger. If they were portrayed as weak and vulnerable, their deviance seemed less threatening. Their vulnerability also helped to provide an explanation for why these women would become prostitutes. Finally, protective rules for prostitutes established boundaries for the deviance that could be tolerated in this city. Women could sell themselves to men, but men could not sell them into the brothel; and prostitutes could violate sexual codes for respectable women, but they must attend church. Although such attitudes seem contradictory, they clearly illustrate how this society set limits on deviance.[9]

Protection and punishment, in fact, mingled in some confusion in pro-

---

[8] Ioannis Gutiérrez, *Praxis criminalis civilis et canonica in librum octanum nouae Recopilationis Regiae* (Lyons: Sumptibus Lavrentii Anisson, 1660), pp. 336–38.

[9] Mary Douglas discusses the danger of anomalous people and the necessity of giving them definable boundaries in *Purity and Danger*, pp. 95–102, esp. Also see Erving Goffman, *Interaction Ritual: Essays on Face-to-Face Behavior* (Garden City, N.Y.: Doubleday, 1967), pp. 47–49.

nouncements about unenclosed women. Prostitutes who observed regulations would be protected, but those who did not forfeited all social protection; and women unrestrained by enclosure in the home, the brothel, or the convent deserved not only what violence they received at the hands of men, but also special punitive measures. Traditionally, clandestine prostitutes were subject to public humiliation, whippings, having the nostrils slit, and exile. Forms of punishment changed, however, so that by 1596 the royal council declared that the many "lost" and vagabond women who wandered about Seville should be gathered together in a house where they could be confined to support themselves by the work of their hands.[10]

Strict discipline within the enclosure of a convent was prescribed for women who wanted to convert from their sinful lives as prostitutes. The Convent of the Most Sweet Name of Jesus, which had been established in the mid-sixteenth century for penitent prostitutes, instituted a severe regimen to protect these women from their "sinful natures."[11] They were to carry out a program of prayer and work for the rest of their lives in order to do penance for past sins. However, these penitent women had to be separated from "honest" novices who entered the convent and nuns who taught and supervised them, presumably to protect these less worldly women from the contagion of both venereal diseases and sinful knowledge.

Some churchmen and officials in the seventeenth century recognized that the severe discipline of a convent could deter many women who would otherwise leave prostitution. The Jesuits founded a *casa pía* in Seville, which functioned as a transition home for women leaving prostitution. One cleric in particular became noted for his compassionate treatment of these women and his attempts to make the Magdalen house less forbidding. Before he began work here, the casa pía contained only one or two converted women, but he soon had forty or more converted women in the shelter.[12] Pedro de León wrote that these women usually stayed in the shelter only two or three days. He had convinced a wealthy woman of the city to provide dowries of forty ducats for each young woman that he could convert from the brothel into matrimony.[13]

These Magdalen houses could function effectively for former prostitutes who voluntarily entered them, but they could do nothing about the problem of women who refused to stay in either the legal brothel or a convent for converted women. Madre Magdalena de San Jerónimo had worked many years in a convent for converted prostitutes in Valladolid when

---

[10] AMS, Papeles Importantes, Siglo XVI, Tomo 9, Número 1.

[11] Morgado, *Historia*, pp. 465–66; Llorden, *Apuntes históricos*, pp. 7–15, esp.

[12] Pedro de León, *Compendio*, pt. 1, chap. 5, fols. 14–15.

[13] Ibid., pt. 1, chap. 4, fols. 10–14; chap. 5, fols. 14–15. Cf. the account of Ignatius Loyola and the founding of the House of Saint Martha in Rome in Rahner, *Letters*, pp. 15–19.

Philip II called her to direct the Galera de Santa Isabel, a prison for women in Madrid.[14] In 1608 she wrote a memorial to the king proposing a special prison for recalcitrant women. Long before the penitentiaries that developed in the modern period, madre Magdalena's proposal influenced penal policies and promoted a sex-specific transition from corporal public punishments into private reformatory incarceration.[15]

Madre Magdalena's proposal should also be noted as a clear example that women could assume masculine roles of enforcing male domination.[16] As a patriarchal woman, this nun did not sympathize with prostitutes who refused conversion, nor did she identify them as belonging to her own sex. Accepting the dichotomization of good and evil women, she proposed a harsh discipline of work, silence, and shaven heads for those evil women who refused to become good. She noted with pride that her plan had won considerable attention for its severity, "particularly being invented by a woman against women." She carefully stated, however, that her treatise was not intended to impugn the honor of virtuous women, only "the lost and evil ones, who insult the honesty and virtue of the good ones with their corruption and evil."[17]

From twenty years of working with such evil women in Valladolid, madre Magdalena had concluded that they were not simply a nuisance, but a true threat to the kingdom. At night, she wrote, they emerge as "wild beasts who leave their caves to look for prey," spreading disease among men, "family dishonor, and scandal among all the people." Moreover, their

[14] Madre Magdalena de San Jerónimo, *Razón, y forma de la galera y casa Real, que el Rey nuestro señor manda hazer en estos Reynos, para castigo de las mugeres vagrantes, ladronas, alcahuetas y otras semejantes* (Valladolid: Francisco Fernández de Córdova, 1608), reprinted in Serrano y Sanz, *Apuntes*, 270: 304–16. It should be noted that Serrano y Sanz compares madre Magdalena's proposal with the later writings of Concepción Arenal and finds that both call for love rather than vengeance in the treatment of criminals. However, he may have overlooked the harsh quality of madre Magdalena's prison because his own gender consciousness identified her as one of the tender, loving sex; see his discussion, pp. 304–5. My references are to the text in Serrano y Sanz, but also see María Dolores Pérez Baltasar, *Mujeres marginadas: Las casas de recogidas en Madrid* (Madrid: Gráficas Lormo, 1984), who places this woman's proposal in a larger context.

[15] This, of course, is the theme of Michel Foucault, *Discipline and Punish: The Birth of the Prison*, trans. Alan Sheridan (New York: Pantheon, 1977). But several scholars have criticized his argument that public bodily punishments changed so quickly into private, discipline-imposing incarceration; see, e.g., Pieter Spierenburg, ed., *The Emergence of Carceral Institutions: Prisons, Galleys and Lunatic Asylums, 1550–1900* (Rotterdam: Erasmus University, 1984). Inquisition punishments, which included both public chastisement and private imprisonment, may also be seen as bridging the gap that Foucault considered a leap into modernism.

[16] Nicole Dufresne discusses the powerful woman as an agent of patriarchy in " 'I Wish I Were a Man': The Gender Role Transgressions of Lorca's Tragic Heroines," (Paper delivered to Themes in Drama Conference, North American Session, University of California at Riverside, February 1986).

[17] Madre Magdalena de San Jerónimo, *Razón*, pp. 307, 308.

evil example infected many respectable women "who fall into similar evil." She indicted women younger than sixteen who solicited customers in the streets, as well as older women who literally sold girls of ten years and less and pretended to place other young girls in positions as domestic servants. "I know them well," she added; "the demon has taken possession of them and is so angry . . . that he will induce them to many evil things."[18]

To reinstill the fear of God in such women, madre Magdalena proposed a prison "strong and well enclosed," with the royal arms and an unsheathed sword of justice over the door. The prison should include a dormitory, workroom, and also a "secret prison where in particular the rebellious incorrigible ones will be punished." The inmates would have their heads shaven and would wear only burlap or rough clothing; they were forbidden to speak together or to have visitors from outside. The five people in charge of the inmates were to guard them vigilantly with courage and "a hundred eyes." Inmates who talked would be gagged, and those who tried to run away were to be chained or pilloried. To ensure that this discipline would bring about their conversion to better ways, she recommended that they be held for one or two years and that they be branded when they left the prison so that they could be identified as deserving even more severe punishment if they should be returned to prison. "This prison will be a warning," wrote the nun, "for many lost women to collect themselves and live well, through the fear and horror of this punishment and pain."[19]

The doctor Cristóbal Pérez de Herrera, medical inspector for the king's galleys, wrote a similar treatise at the same time, proposing a workhouse for delinquent women, but without the severity of the nun's. In contrast to madre Magdalena, he noted that even though they were bad women, "they will be treated in everything as women, who are of a more delicate nature."[20] They must work, he believed, not only as punishment or to earn their keep in the workhouse, but to learn a livelihood to support themselves after their release. This kind of punishment was better than public humiliation, which only served to confirm them as bad women. In fact, he said, women in Madrid had been given as many as fifteen hundred lashes without any effect in changing their lives, except that they might die from the whippings.

Power, sin, and sex underlay the euphemisms of the continuing dialogue about prostitution. On a symbolic level, this dialogue developed through a ritualized confrontation of money and morals, purity and evil, rich and

[18] Ibid., pp. 309, 313.

[19] Ibid., pp. 310, 311, 314.

[20] Cristóbal Pérez de Herrera, *Discurso de la reclusión y castigo de las mugeres vagabundas y delinquentes destos reynos* (Madrid: Luis Sánchez, 1608), reprinted in Serrano y Sanz, *Apuntes,* 270: 319–24; the quotation appears on 322.

poor, Church and state.[21] On a more visible socioeconomic level, the dialogue led to an evolution from toleration of sexual commerce to institutionalization and then on to intensification of control. By the end of the sixteenth century, the dialogue had become a debate between those who wanted to retain legalized prostitution as a necessary evil and those who believed that it must be abolished as an offense to God. The longtime alliance of pragmatists and moralists crumbled as each side presented its position with increasing passion.

Clerics such as Juan de Mariana had already begun to question more vigorously the traditional wisdom that prostitution was a necessary evil. Mariana argued that prostitution was a serious social evil which multiplied in growing cities. Far more destructive than merely corruptive of women, prostitution, Mariana declared, had produced a generation of worthless men. "Many youths we have seen who, coming from places where there are no prostitutes, were very modest and sober," he wrote, "and later in the larger cities they found a liberty to sin, [and] suddenly changed into shameless and dishonest [men], losing estate, youth, health, and counsel, and ending up completely without any value." Moreover, the brothel did not serve as a remedy for lust, he argued, but actually encouraged it. Women, who are much weaker than men, did not have brothels, he observed; and if prostitution were really necessary, then women would have to have "houses of boys."[22]

Pedro de León, the Jesuit who left a record of his ministry in Seville at the turn of the seventeenth century, wrote of the men and boys who frequented the legal brothel, damaging property and harassing priests who came to preach to the prostitutes.[23] He urged these men and boys, as well as the prostitutes, to leave their lives of sin. Some of the boys were as young as fourteen and already infected with venereal disease. The priest identified these males as "petty officials, workers, and apprentices of the field." In the previous century it had been easier to see the brothel as a service for transients, soldiers, and sailors; now it was apparent that the clientele of the brothel included many city residents, including young boys who could be corrupted by the prostitutes.

Disease threatened not only prostitutes and their clients who were sin-

---

[21] I am relying here on Clifford Geertz's theory that ideology can be analyzed as a cultural system, and that ritualized events can hold a much deeper symbolic meaning; see his *Interpretation*, chaps. 8 and 15, esp.

[22] Padre Juan de Mariana, "Tratado contra los juegos publicos," in his *Obras*, in *Biblioteca de Autores Españoles* (Madrid: M. Rivadeneyra, 1855), 30: 446, 447.

[23] Pedro de León, *Compendio*, pt. 1, chap. 4, fols. 10–14, and chap. 6, fol. 16; see also AMS, Sección 3, Siglo XVI, Escribanías de Cabildo, Tomo 11, Número 63, and Tomo 12, Número 44; and AMS, Sección Especial, Papeles del Señor Conde de Aguila, Tomo 7 en folio, Número 20.

gle. It threatened the entire society because, as madre Magdalena de San Jerónimo noted, prostitutes infected married men with "a thousand disgusting and contagious diseases," and these men passed them on to their wives.[24] Although congenital syphilis had not yet been identified, reformers such as madre Magdalena called for stringent measures to "remedy such great evil, devastation, and corruption of the republic."[25] She defended the severity of her proposal, pointing out that in times of epidemics, infected people were walled up within their houses to keep them away from others whom they might infect.

Syphilis seemed an especially terrifying threat because no one had yet found an effective cure. Cures used by prostitutes and surgeons merely treated the symptoms of the disease and could not prevent its return after a period of latency.[26] Some hospitals specialized in treating patients with syphilis, usually with a cure of *agua del palo*, a solution of bark in water. A sixteenth-century writer praised this cure in the Hospital de San Cosme y San Damian in Seville, asserting that it was effective in thirty days.[27] Reports from the seventeenth century, however, implied that patients could require repeated thirty-day treatments that were given each spring and fall.[28] Mercury treatments appeared to be more immediately effective, but they were also blamed for causing deaths. As one physician of the period stated, the mercury cures were more "damaging" than the disease.[29]

Many people in this period regarded syphilis not simply as a very virulent disease, but as a "divine illness" imposed by God as punishment for lust and other moral offenses. Mixing beliefs about sin with contemporary medical wisdom, Francisco Farfan wrote that syphilis originated not in the New World, as others had declared, but as God's punishment on the army of Charles VIII of France, which had so brutally destroyed Naples in 1494. He warned that this "pestilence of Venus, and Heaven's lash" was very contagious because its humor was very penetrating. The "carnal act" alters and warms the parts of the body that become penetrated, opening the pores to its venom so that it can damage the liver, which "is the source and root of this evil." The disease did not spread through the sexual act alone, however, for Farfan declared that people became infected by eating or

---

[24] Serrano y Sanz, *Apuntes*, 270: 309; also quoted in Pérez Baltasar, *Mujeres marginadas*, p. 31.

[25] Serrano y Sanz, *Apuntes*, 270: 315.

[26] Granjel, *Renacentista*, p. 140.

[27] Morgado, *Historia*, p. 365.

[28] AMS, Sección Especial, Papeles del Señor Conde de Aguila, Tomo 32 en folio, Número 1.

[29] Carlos Rico-Avello, *Vida y milagros de un pícaro médico del siglo XVI: Biografía del bachiller Juan Méndez Nieto* (Madrid: Cultura Hispánica, 1974), pp. 85–86; also see Fielding H. Garrison, "An Epitome of the History of Spanish Medicine," *Bulletin of the New York Academy of Medicine*, 2d ser., 7, no. 8 (1928): 589–634.

drinking from utensils used by those already infected or by wearing the clothing or using the same cloth that an infected person had used. Describing remedies such as diet, agua del palo, sarsaparilla, purges, potions, and sweatings, he said these were rarely effective. Even worse, he wrote, was the "vulgar practice" of trying to cure oneself of syphilis by expelling the venom when having sexual relations with a healthy person.[30]

Declining fortunes in the seventeenth century combined with repeated epidemics to increase alarm about the state of public morals, particularly the moral frailty of girls and women. Pedro de León wrote of women who went to the orphanage, pretending to want to serve God by indoctrinating the young girls there in Christian virtue, but actually intending to teach them to be prostitutes. Seeing one "infernal stepmother" selling a young girl in the street, he intervened and rescued the girl.[31] The sinfulness of these women seemed less threatening when depicted behind the bars of a window or prison, as in the painting reproduced in figure 14; and Pedro de León attributed it not to their evil natures, but to their poverty and inability to marry. Later in the century economic essayists warned that failure to marry had resulted in many impoverished women, and charitable appeals emphasized the need to protect poor women as victims of circumstances, exceptionally vulnerable to exploitation and the loss of virtue.[32]

Prostitutes, too, could be perceived as victims of circumstances, their vulnerability to sin increasing with poverty. Clerics now more often portrayed them as sinners to redeem, rather than necessary evils. In them they saw examples of Mary Magdalen, the woman portrayed as a prostitute converted by the love of Christ. A traditional ritual developed for the feast day of Mary Magdalen as churchmen assembled the prostitutes of the brothel and preached earnestly to them of God's love and the wages of sin. The sermon would end with an invitation for those who repented to come forward and seek a new life. Then the penitents were taken in a procession to the cathedral or another prominent church where they would be publicly received as converts.[33] A woman could thus exchange her formal label of prostitute for that of penitent. Although historical records do not include numbers of converted prostitutes, one account describes a monk who preached so eloquently to a group of prostitutes on this feast day that he converted twenty-seven of them.[34]

Official policy approved the female penitent more than the prostitute, but the new label did not erase all the stigma of the old. Most people as-

---

[30] Farfan, *Regimiento*, pp. 278, 279–279ʳ, 280ʳ, 289ʳ.

[31] Pedro de León, *Compendio*, pt. 2, chap. 25, fols. 191–92.

[32] See chap. 8, below.

[33] Pacheco, *Libro de descripción*, n.p. See Goffman, *Interaction Ritual*, pp. 21–22, for a broader discussion of rituals of penitence.

[34] Pacheco, *Libro de descripción*, n.p.

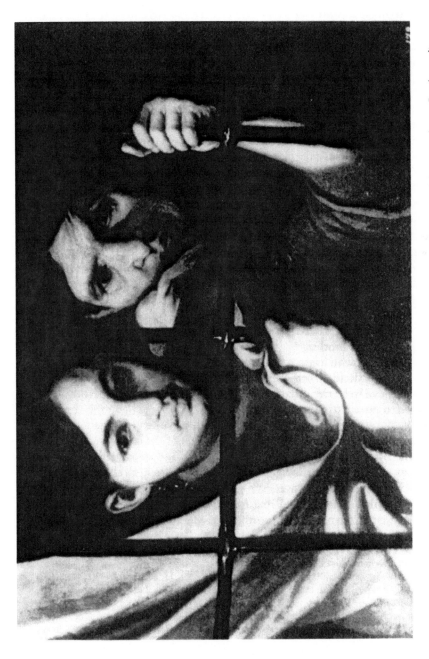

FIGURE 14. *Celestina and Her Daughter*, attributed to the School of Murillo (Museum of the Hermitage, Leningrad).

sumed that prostitutes who converted would have to enter a convent established exclusively for reformed prostitutes, where strict religious discipline could continue to protect them from the weakness of the flesh. The Convent of the Most Sweet Name of Jesus maintained three separate spaces for converted prostitutes, novitiates, and professed nuns, but professed nuns did not always succeed in teaching and disciplining the former prostitutes, and it took considerable effort to dissuade those who wanted to leave the convent.[35] Confession with contrition did not itself simply reintegrate these women into the social order; instead, it served to adjust or redefine their stigmatization as deviant insiders who were carefully integrated into society under specific regulating conditions.[36]

Growing concern about the sin of prostitution led to a zealous movement in Seville during the early seventeenth century to convert all prostitutes and close the brothel. Preachers went to the brothel on Sundays and feast days, presenting prayers and sermons in rituals intended to convince prostitutes to convert, even as "scandalous men" shouted catcalls and faked conversions.[37] Conversion sermons also reached men, such as the brothel padre who asked if salvation were possible for him in his "evil profession." A Jesuit, perhaps caught off guard or continuing to believe that prostitution was a necessary evil, did not urge him to leave his office but assured him that he could, indeed, be saved if he preserved "the just and holy ordinances" of the brothel.[38]

City officials who inspected the legal brothel of Seville on July 22, 1620, did not try to decide whether prostitutes were sinners to be converted or a necessary evil to be regulated.[39] They brought a clergyman with them who wanted to preach to the prostitutes to try to convert them on this the feast day of Mary Magdalen. They ordered the three supervising padres to assemble their prostitutes and then directed each of the eighteen women to give her name. Dutifully noting that others had also assembled to hear the sermon, the officials proceeded with their inspection, carefully balancing their pragmatism with a moralist's care for the souls of the "lost women" in the brothel. They realized that moral critics were making increasingly vigorous attacks on legalized prostitution, and they sought to maintain it

[35] Morgado, *Historia*, pp. 465–66; also Llorden, *Apuntes históricos*, pp. 7–12.

[36] Mike Hepworth and Bryan S. Turner, *Confession: Studies of Deviance and Religion* (London: Routledge & Kegan Paul, 1982), p. 37, esp.

[37] AMS, Sección Especial, Papeles del Señor Conde de Aguila, Libros en folio, Tomo 7, Número 20.

[38] Pedro de León, *Compendio*, pt. 1, chap. 6.

[39] AMS, Sección Especial, Papeles del Señor Conde de Aguila, Tomo 7, Letra A, Número 73. This document has been published in "Documentos relativos a la mancebía," *Archivo Hispalense*, 1st ser., 3 (1887): 16–18. Unfortunately, the voices of prostitutes appear in none of the available records, which present only male and official views of prostitution. Despite these limitations, the historical sources offer remarkable insights into power, gender, and deviance.

within a moral and Catholic context as they briskly reported the details of their inspection.

The report of this visit provides little information about the lives of the women who worked in the city brothel, for the officials who wrote it had a much greater interest in the city's system of legalized prostitution. They imposed a fine on one padre who had accepted an unlicensed prostitute into the brothel, and they threatened her with one hundred lashes if she did not leave at once. They ordered Angela del Castillo to leave "because of her age" and the length of her employment in the brothel. They also banished Ana María from the brothel because she appeared ill and infectious to others. The three officials agreed to notify a city resident who had been nominated to accompany a doctor in examining the prostitutes. Finally, they forbade padres to give help or shelter to any woman who had been ordered to leave the brothel. Violations of these orders, they warned, would be punished "with all severity."

By the end of 1620, preachers and pious laymen had effectively closed the city brothel. One of the padres complained to the city council that the brothel had been closed for ten months because the preachers had driven the prostitutes away, and he noted that this was injurious to the city.[40] Closing the brothels did not prevent prostitution; it simply meant that prostitutes now spread disease and disorder throughout the city. Moreover, the chapels, hospitals, churches, and other religious foundations that had been given the income from the brothel property were losing support on which they depended. He urged the city government to approve new prostitution ordinances that had arrived from Madrid and to forbid further "meddling" by preachers trying to convert prostitutes. The administrator of the girls' orphanage joined the padre's protest, complaining that preachers who converted prostitutes on Mary Magdalen's day then placed these women in his orphanage, where there was neither room nor clothing nor sufficient discipline for them, and where they provided a bad example for his young girls.[41]

Finally in 1621 the city government decided to support the brothel padres against the reforming preachers and approved new regulations. While placing the usual restrictions on the brothel padres, the 1621 ordinances protected their privilege by reducing their number to two and doubling to two reales per day the amount they could charge each prostitute.[42] Moreover, the ordinances repeated the prohibition of any other person's profit-

---

[40] AMS, Siglo XVII, Sección 4, Escribanías de Cabildo, Tomo 22, Números 9–11. Evidence that religious groups benefited from the income of the brothels is in ADPS, Libros de Protocolos del Hospital del Amor de Dios, Legajo 49, Expediente 2; see the discussion in Perry, "Deviant Insiders," p. 145.

[41] AMS, Sección 4, Siglo XVII, Escribanías de Cabildo, Tomo 22, Número 12.

[42] The 1621 ordinances are in AMS, Sección 4, Siglo XVII, Escribanías de Cabildo, Tomo 22, Número 14.

ing from prostitution and explicitly prohibited servants of authorities from pimping "since for the most part those who have the said women in the said house of the brothel are servants of authorities, and it is not possible that their masters know of this" (article 11). These regulations again required regular medical inspections and added that the doctor should give each prostitute a certificate that she had been examined and found free from disease, but the great emphasis in these ordinances was on enclosing prostitutes in the brothel as a means to enforce order. Article 17 described "scandal" and "turbulence," and "great inconveniences that result from the many women who pursue their evil profession night and day." Figuratively placing above the brothel door an unsheathed sword, the actual insignia that madre Magdalena had proposed for her prison, the new ordinances of 1621 made it clear that padres who enclosed wandering women preserved their own honor, and that of all men, by ensuring social order.

The debate over legalized prostitution in Seville revealed some basic assumptions about women and men. On the one hand, pragmatists argued that prostitutes were an essential part of the moral order because men were so lusty that they would commit worse sins without brothels. On the other, moralists argued that women should not be made to serve in this way the sinful desires of men. Both agreed that unenclosed women posed a very real danger; but pragmatists believed that the brothel provided an acceptable form of enclosure, while the moralists did not. Significantly, brothels continued to have male administrators in Spain, although women supervised legal houses of prostitution in other parts of Europe at this time.[43] Evidently, both moralists and pragmatists believed that social order required women enclosed under male supervision.

And yet ensuring social order is not so simple as merely passing new ordinances. In fact, repeated legislation to regulate prostitution demonstrates that laws in themselves were not sufficient to establish social order, and neither were punishments. In 1623 Philip IV formally prohibited brothels in all of his kingdom.[44] Prostitutes did not disappear, of course, and neither did concern about unenclosed women. In fact, the distinction between wandering women and those of virtue continued to defy definition despite repeated attempts through legislation. In 1639, for example, the city council approved for the fourth time regulations prohibiting women from going about with their faces covered.[45] In language similar to a proverb that warns against masked women, the 1639 law noted the danger of anonymous females and required all women, regardless of class or status, to allow their faces to be seen and recognized, under penalty of a

[43] For an example in southern France, see Rossiaud, "Prostitution," p. 290.

[44] *Novísima Recopilación*, Ley 7, Título 26, Libro 12, quoted in Pérez Baltasar, *Mujeres marginadas*, p. 14.

[45] AMS, Sección 4, Siglo XVII, Escribanías de Cabildo, Tomo 29, Número 18.

fine of ten thousand maravedís for a first offense and twenty thousand plus exile for a second. The law also warned that no one could use the privilege or status of her husband to circumvent its requirements. All women were thus seen as dangerous, not simply those required to identify themselves as prostitutes.[46]

Women kept slipping through these regulations, however, and countless complaints about their wandering reached the city council. A decade after passing the 1621 prostitution ordinances, city officials wrote to the king of their alarm about the multiplication of prostitutes outside the brothel, a "bad example," they wrote, for "the daughters of the city."[47] Seven years later the administrator of the girls' orphanage complained that "many women of bad life who are called prostitutes" were using young girls, whom they called their daughters or nieces, to run after people for "their evil business."[48] Finally, in 1675, Carlos Ramírez de Arellano, the asistente of Seville, wrote to the queen regent of the city's need for a prison for "lost and scandalous women."[49] The queen regent agreed with his plan to use for the prison the royal mint in Seville that had fallen into disuse.

It seems very likely that the women selling themselves on the streets of Seville chose to do so not out of female perversity, but out of necessity. The economic decline that struck this city in the seventeenth century directly hit abandoned wives and daughters and single mothers. Caught in a context in which street hawking came under regulation and French competition undersold local silk weavers, in which Cadiz replaced Seville as primary port for transatlantic shipping and prices rose while real wages fell, women found in prostitution one of the few ways that they could earn money. To enter the brothel meant leaving behind one's children and pretensions of respectability, and accepting as a pimp the padre who had to be paid. To solicit in the streets, on the other hand, might bring enough money to feed the children, maintain a relationship with some man, and even preserve the family unit and survive with hope. These women transformed their governing ethos from male honor to human survival, and they broadened the sexual economy from brothel to streets.

More than dangerous female sexuality, then, the wandering woman could also represent female determination to survive and female resistance to a brothel system enforced for the interests of men. This voice must also

---

[46] Anne J. Cruz discusses the dangers perceived in all women, prostitutes and nonprostitutes alike, in "Sexual Enclosure, Textual Escape: The Pícara as Prostitute in the Spanish Picaresque Novel," in Fisher and Halley, *Seeking the Woman*, pp. 135–59.

[47] AMS, Papeles Importantes, Siglo XVII, Tomo 5, Número 21.

[48] AMS, Sección 4, Siglo XVII, Escribanías de Cabildo, Tomo 24, Número 26. For concerns in Valencia about procuresses who recruited girls and women into prostitution, see Graullera, "Mujer, amor," in Redondo, *Amours légitimes*, p. 116.

[49] AHN, Consejos, Legajo 7185.

be heard in the dialogue about prostitution, although it is barely audible in the polyphony that so often seemed limited to men speaking about women. Some female voices, such as that of madre Magdalena, served to support male domination; but others, closer to the margins of society, transposed the question from "What is woman?" to "How does one survive?" Prostitution provided the answer for many women who lived out their lives in this time of brothel padres and converting preachers.

Chapter 8

MOTHERS OF THE POOR

DESCRIBING SEVILLE as "unique and singular" in his *Teatro eclesiástico de las iglesias metropolitanas, y catedrales de los reynos de los dos Castillas* (1647), Gil González Dávila wrote that it was "composed of the opulence and riches of two Worlds, Old and New, that come together in its plazas to confer and discuss all their commerce" and carry out a "multitude of pious works to benefit the needy and the poor."[1] He might have added that demands for charity had increased markedly over the past century and that the aims of giving to the poor had also changed. Charity had long been carried out by the residents of Seville who were anxious to save their own souls. "Good works" did not diminish in importance during the Counter-Reformation, but charity also came to be seen as a means to strengthen the moral order.

Gender ideology permeated the moral charity that developed in Seville during the sixteenth and seventeenth centuries. It affected very directly the ways that women and men became poor, asked for charity, received it, and gave it. Usually women appeared as "mothers of the poor," but this category included two very different groups: those with some property or access to it, who symbolized the high moral calling of women to care for the poor as a mother cares for her children; and those who lacked the material resources to raise their own children without help, symbolizing the terrible moral vulnerability of impoverished females. After the middle of the sixteenth century, women appeared increasingly in this second group, as recipients rather than providers of charity. Not surprisingly, men built the largest hospitals constructed in Seville, and the major hospital of the seventeenth century resulted from the charity of a man. However, the great hospital of the sixteenth century was meant to carry on the charitable work of a woman.

Seville's most famous mother of the poor lived as a woman of wealth at the beginning of the sixteenth century. Catalina de Ribera converted a house that she owned into a hospital to shelter and treat poor women who were ill or injured. She obtained a papal bull for the institution, endowed it generously, and served in it personally to care for the inmates, inspiring Queen Isabel to join her in ministering to the ill during her visits to Seville. Doña Catalina requested in her will that the hospital continue "in praise

[1] González Dávila, *Teatro eclesiástico*, 2: 1–2.

and service of God, Our Savior, and the Blessed Virgin Mary in remission for all my sins."[2] Regarded by the poor as their "protective angel," this "most pious and illustrious matron" also earned the epithet "true mother of the poor."[3]

Hospitals had been known from the medieval period as "houses of God" that provided shelter and hospitality for pilgrims and travelers, the poor and the ill. In 1248 Ferdinand III had decreed that each of the parishes in Seville should establish a hospital and confraternity to provide supportive care. Royal patronage helped to establish the Hospital Real, which cared for twelve former soldiers, and the Hospital de San Lázaro, which sheltered lepers from Seville and Cadiz. In the middle of the fifteenth century, a wealthy couple founded the Hospital de los Inocentes to shelter the mentally ill. At about the same time the city council became principal patron for the Hospital de los Niños de la Doctrina, a school and shelter for poor and orphan children. Supported by both secular and religious patrons, these small buildings usually sheltered very few. Invariably, they contained an altar.[4]

By the sixteenth century, hospitals had proliferated in Seville. They symbolized a pious desire not only to provide physical and spiritual care for God's less fortunate children, but also, and perhaps more importantly, to provide a means for those with some wealth to save their souls. Charity in this city seemed to function as the primitive and reciprocal exchange described by anthropologist Marcel Mauss.[5] The hospital represented a gift from a donor who could expect in return heavenly credit toward eternal

[2] The will of Catalina de Ribera is in ADPS, Libro 8 of the Inventario del Hospital de las Cinco Llagas, and is also reprinted in Francisco Collantes de Teran, "Testamento de la muy ilustre señora doña Catalina de Ribera, fundadora del Hospital de Las Cinco Llagas, vulgo de la Sangre, de Sevilla," *Archivo Hispalense* 3 (1887): 51–66. Her hospital is discussed in Morgado, *Historia*, p. 364; Carmona García, *El sistema*, pp. 54–59; José de Sigüenza, *Historia de la órden*, p. 307; Gestoso y Pérez, *Sevilla monumental*, 3: 107–10. For the story of Queen Isabel coming to serve in this hospital, see chap. 1, above, and Ortiz de Zuñiga, *Anales*, 3: 178–79.

[3] Vicente Alvarez Miranda, *Glorias de Sevilla: En armas, letras, ciencias, artes, tradiciones, monumentos, edificios, carácteres, costumbres, estilos, fiestas y espectáculos* (Seville: Carlos Santigosa, 1849), pp. 76–77. Tiles decorating a bench near the Paseo de Catalina de Ribera in Seville still identify her as the mother of the poor.

[4] The hospital of Christian tradition is discussed in Dankwart Leistikow, *Ten Centuries of European Hospital Architecture* (Ingelheim am Rhein: C. H. Boehringer Sohn, 1967), p. 9. For Seville, see Carmona García, *El sistema*, pp. 18–27; Morgado, *Historia*, pp. 356–62; and J. B. Ullersperger, *La historia de la psicología y de la psiquiatría en España: Desde los más remotos tiempos hasta la actualidad* (Madrid: Editorial Alhambra, 1954), pp. 118–19. Ortiz de Zuñiga, *Anales*, 4: 137, discusses the hospital for orphans and poor children.

[5] Marcel Mauss, *The Gift: Forms and Functions of Exchange in Archaic Societies*, trans. I. Cunnison (London: Cohen and West, 1966). I am indebted to Natalie Zemon Davis for bringing this anthropologist to my attention. Please see her essay, "Beyond the Market: Books as Gifts in Sixteenth-Century France," *Transactions of the Royal Historical Society*, 5th ser., 33 (1983): 69–88.

salvation. Even those of modest means could act as donors through larger organizations such as guilds. The silk-weavers' guild, for example, maintained the Hospital de San Onofre to shelter female members and widows of male members who could not support themselves with their own work.[6] Providing mutual benefit, this gift system affirmed the solidarity of the community even as it helped to preserve a social hierarchy.

Donors contributed property, yearly income, large and small money gifts, and personal labor to serve the sick and the poor. Mendicants and lay brothers also humbled themselves to beg alms for the inmates, seeking redemption through their humility as well as the good work of their charity. Nuns and beatas usually did not beg publicly, but they accepted alms on behalf of hospitals and contributed their labor in receiving and caring for the inmates. Some hospitals cared for only a few paupers, and some provided no shelter at all, simply giving charitable dowries or providing Christian burials.[7]

Ironically, the hospital came to symbolize pride as well as humility during the sixteenth century. The son of Catalina de Ribera, don Fadrique Enríquez de Ribera, endowed in his will a new building in order to carry on the work of his mother. He asked that following his death the patronage of this hospital should be held by the priors of the Carthusian monastery of San Jerónimo and the Jeronimite monastery of San Isidro del Campo. Stipulating that the building should be "simple and without gilding or decoration," he may not have foreseen that the inevitably grand proportions of a building to shelter three hundred people would imply power and wealth.[8] He may not have recognized that his gift to the poor could become a monument of civic pride.

The priors took seriously their charge to erect a new building for the Hospital de las Cinco Llagas, or "Sangre," as doña Catalina's hospital was commonly called. Following the death of her son in 1539, they selected a site in a large field just outside the Gate of the Macarena in the city's walls. Here, they believed, the new hospital would have space, comfort, health, independence, and ventilation.[9] From plans submitted by many architects, they selected that of Martín Gainza, which called for a large freestanding church and patients' rooms that opened out onto spacious courtyards. The completed building would be a huge rectangle, two stories high, measuring 600 feet from east to west and 550 feet from north to south.

One sixteenth-century observer noted that the "magnificent and impres-

[6] Carmona García, El sistema, p. 41.

[7] For beatas, see Pedro de León, Compendio, pt. 1, chap. 4, and pt. 2, chap. 25. Also see chap. 5, above. Benefactors for many of the hospitals are listed in ADPS, Libros de Protocolos del Hospital del Amor de Dios and del Hospital del Espíritu Santo.

[8] The will is discussed in Manuel Justiniano y Martínez, El Hospital de las Cinco Llagas (Central) de Sevilla (Seville: Crónica Oficial de la Provincia, 1963), pp. 8–9.

[9] See especially Alvarez Miranda, Glorias de Sevilla, pp. 76–77.

sive buildings" of the hospital resembled "more the palaces of kings than a hospital of the poor."[10] Tile-covered towers reared twenty feet above the building at its corners. Over the main entrance appeared the figures of Faith, Hope, and Charity, and the coats of arms of the Enríquez and Ribera families. Just inside the main entrance, an entry hall of ninety feet in width and fifteen feet in length featured two-storied galleries. This led to a patio surrounded by columned galleries adjoining the patients' quarters. Straight ahead through the patio stood the hospital's church, freestanding and much larger than the usual hospital chapel.[11]

The church of the hospital became noted as "one of the most precious and beautiful temples of the Christian world."[12] Designed in the form of a Latin cross, its vaulted nave with a dome over the crossing contrasted with the usual Andalusian architecture. A large altar made from a single piece of alabaster stood in front of life-sized portraits of Christ and his saints. Jerónimo Ramírez, a follower of Roelas, painted a large canvas that was placed behind the lectern for the Epistle. It depicted Saint Gregory as pope, seated in a circle of cardinals and clerics. A painting hanging on the opposite side, which has been attributed to an Italian school, shows two angels crowning the Virgin. Later eight paintings by Zurbarán were placed in the church, each showing the Virgin with magnificent draped clothing. The design and decor of this church may have been intended to glorify God and the charity of Jesus Christ, but they also bore witness to a very human ambition to overcome mortality through a magnificent building.

Even in its splendor, however, the church did not ignore suffering. Crucifixes and paintings emphasized the martyrdom of saints and the Passion of Christ. The central painting at the main altar presented a life-size portrait of Christ showing his wounds to the doubting apostle Thomas. Artists from the *escuela sevillana* presented suffering as holy in these paintings, awesome reminders of Christ's sacrifice and the courage of his followers. The suffering depicted did not imply injustice in the world, but rather the opportunity to emulate Christ in the Way of the Cross, winning salvation through martyrdom.[13]

---

[10] Morgado, *Historia*, p. 364.

[11] Juan Colon y Colom, *Sevilla artística* (Seville: Francisco Alvarez y Compañía, 1841), pp. 92–95. In sixteenth-century Spain the only other hospital with a large separate church building rather than a chapel was the Hospital de San Juan Bautista in Toledo. See Catherine Wilkinson, *The Hospital of Cardinal Tavera in Toledo: A Documentary and Stylistic Study of Spanish Architecture in the Mid-Sixteenth Century* (New York: Garland Publishing, 1977), p. 215.

[12] Alvarez Miranda, *Glorias de Sevilla*, p. 79. See also Morgado, *Historia*, pp. 364–65; and Ortiz de Zuñiga, *Anales*, 4: 13–14.

[13] Suffering and martyrdom were exalted in many other baroque paintings and were not unique to paintings in Spain. Stanley Payne, *Spanish Catholicism: An Historical Overview* (Madison: University of Wisconsin Press, 1984), pp. 49–50, esp., discusses this aspect of

This hospital became a major institution that cared for sick females of all ages. The admissions book for 1605, for example, listed two girls who were eight years old, one who was nine, and another who was ten years old.[14] Although ages were not recorded for adult women, the book listing deaths recorded individuals such as Luisa, "an old woman and stupefied from paralysis," adding that "nothing more can be understood."[15]

With few exceptions, most of the people cared for in the Hospital de las Cinco Llagas came as unfortunates who had no other options. Presumably, twelve-year-old Catalina, "maidservant of Pedro de Valdes," came in January of 1605 because she lacked a family to care for her and could not be kept in the home of her employer. Several, such as Polonia de la Cruz and María de los Angeles, came as "daughters of the Church," a term used for illegitimate girls or abandoned women.[16] Most of the women listed in the admissions books were widows or unmarried women, but married women represented a significant proportion of the admissions, evidently because some wives did not receive the care that they needed from husbands or other family members. In 1605, for example, 44 percent of the women admitted to the hospital said they were married; in 1655, 36 percent were recorded as married. Contrast this with the men who entered the Hospital del Amor de Dios, the major hospital for men, whose records indicate that less than 25 percent were married in 1600 and 1655.[17] One explanation for the difference is that wives were better able to care for ill spouses at home, but a more probable explanation is that sick wives were often abandoned by husbands who could neither feed nor care for them.

Throughout the sixteenth century the disturbing certainty grew that poverty breeds disease, disorder, and immorality. In his treatise *Del socorro de los pobres*, Juan Luis Vives warned that poverty could lead to crime, dishonor, epidemics, and even civil war. Noting that charity was not only a

---

Spanish religiosity. See also Christian, *Local Religion*, pp. 142–43; and Caro Baroja, *Formas complejas*. But note that some people in this period believed that the suffering of the poor was not necessarily an emulation of Christ, and they proposed that it ought to be relieved by changing external conditions. See, e.g., the discussion of Vives and Juan de Medina (or Robles) in Linda Martz, *Poverty and Welfare in Habsburg Spain: The Example of Toledo* (Cambridge: Cambridge University Press, 1983), pp. 7–44; and the debates in the Cortes of Castile discussed in Cristóbal Espejo, "La carestía de la vida en el siglo XVI y medios de abaratarla," *Revista de Archivos, Bibliotecas y Museos*, ser. 3, 41 (1920): 159–204 and 329–54; and 42 (1921): 1–18 and 199–225.

[14] ADPS, Hospital de las Cinco Llagas, Legajo 242, Libros de entrada y salida de enfermos, fols. 48–51.

[15] ADPS, Hospital de las Cinco Llagas, Legajo 250.

[16] ADPS, Hospital de las Cinco Llagas, Legajo 243.

[17] ADPS, Hospital del Amor de Dios, Libros 22 and 46. After the hospital consolidation carried out under the direction of Cardinal Archbishop Rodrigo de Castro in 1587, Sangre became the principal hospital for women, and Amor de Dios became the major hospital for men.

Christian obligation, but also a practical concern, he urged governing officials to care for the poor "because those who look only at the rich, scorning the poor, do the same as a doctor who does not oblige himself to care much for the hands and feet with medicine, because they are a distance from the heart; and as one would not do this to harm so gravely a person, so in the republic the most weak and poor are not scorned without danger for the powerful." He advocated that the poor should be supported in hospitals where the able-bodied could work, and he argued that even the ill, the blind, and the aged should be given some kind of work to prevent the "bad inclinations" that result from idleness.[18]

In contrast with Vives's proposal to put the poor to work, some argued that paupers should be allowed to beg, although with limitations. Fray Domingo de Soto, for example, wrote in 1545 in his *Deliberación en la causa de los pobres* that those allowed to beg should be examined so that only those who were truly poor, natives of the area, and good Christians would be given a certificate permitting them to ask alms.[19] Fears continued, however, that good Christians would not be able to distinguish between the deserving poor and vagabonds who only pretended to be poor so they would not have to work. Some of them, it was said, were even spies for the Turks.[20] Giving alms to them would conduce more to disorder than to salvation for the donor's soul.

Increased xenophobia undoubtedly affected city residents' perceptions of paupers. After an uprising of moriscos in the mountains near Granada in 1568, Philip II ordered the resettlement of more than four thousand of these people in Seville. Commonly suspected of sustaining Muslim practices and loyalties, most moriscos found only menial occupations open to them in Seville. They could not depend upon charitable help because some hospitals aided only Old Christians.[21] Despite restrictions on who could receive charity, a belief persisted that many who got shelter and aid from the city's hospitals were outsiders. The *arbitrista* Francisco Martínez de Mata argued in the mid-seventeenth century that two-thirds of those sup-

[18] Vives, *Pobres*, pp. 279–80, 283.

[19] AMS, Sección Especial, Papeles del Señor Conde de Aguila, Libros en folio, Tomo 30, Número 1.

[20] See the *Discurso* of Cristóbal Pérez de Herrera in AMS, Sección Especial, Papeles del Señor Conde de Aguila, Libros en folio, Tomo 30, Número 2.

[21] For example, see Francisco Collantes de Teran, *Los establecimientos de caridad de Sevilla, que se consideran como particulares: Apuntes y memorias para su historia* (Seville: El Orden, 1886), p. 212. Ruth Pike discusses the resettlement of moriscos in *Aristocrats and Traders: Sevillian Society in the Sixteenth Century* (Ithaca: Cornell University Press, 1972), pp. 154–55, esp. See also her "Sevillian Society in the Sixteenth Century: Slaves and Freedmen," *Hispanic American Historical Review* 47 (1967): 344–51; and Celestino López Martínez, *Mudéjares y moriscos sevillanos* (Seville: Tipografía Rodriguez, Giménez y Compañía, 1935).

ported in Spanish hospitals were foreigners who did not want to spend the money they had made in Spain.[22]

As paupers multiplied, authorities often assumed that the problem to be solved was not poverty, but the disorder of paupers. In 1597 the Royal Council of Philip II sent instructions to the city of Seville to regulate beggars.[23] City officials were directed to examine every beggar and give a license to beg only to those found to be truly poor. The license would be given for one year, beginning at Easter, and it would have written on it the name, origin, age, physical characteristics, and marital status of the beggar. The insignia for the beggars' license would be "more honorable and devout," the council advised, if it were made as a rosary on a chain of strong iron bearing an image of Our Lady on one side and the arms of the city of Seville on the other.

The city government quickly complied with the instructions, and on April 29, 1597, it rounded up some two thousand poor people in the field of the Hospital de la Sangre. According to one contemporary, the crowd contained "some healthy and others old, and others crippled and with sores, and infinite women, who covered all the field and the patios of the hospital."[24] City officials and doctors in the hospital directed the women to enter a large room. They warned those who were able to work that if they were caught begging, they would be given one hundred lashes. They gave the old women little tablets on which "license to ask" was written, and white ribbons to hang them around their necks.

The doctors and officials also examined the poor men. Doctors undoubtedly knew how to identify the "false beggars" who pretended to have only one leg or who knew how to make simple scratches appear to be chronic running sores. Those whom they found to be incurably ill they ordered to hospitals, but they gave licenses to beg to the truly handicapped and elderly men. Others were warned to find work within the next three days. If they were found begging after that time, they were told, they would receive a whipping.[25]

Official recognition that the beggar represented disorder did not completely replace the traditional belief that beggars symbolized holiness. City officials did not try to enclose all of them in hospitals, nor did they discount

[22] See seventh discourse in his *Memoriales y discursos*.

[23] AMS, Sección Especial, Papeles del Señor Conde de Aguila, Libros en folio, Tomo 30, Número 3.

[24] Ariño, *Sucesos de Sevilla*, p. 45.

[25] Ibid., p. 47. The phrase used was "limosna en las espaldas" (alms on the back). Note that Ariño's account does not say whether the doctors were simply educated men or trained physicians who could distinguish malingerers from paupers who were genuinely ill or disabled. For more information about ruses that false beggars practiced in this period, see Vives, *Pobres*, p. 267; Davis, *Society and Culture*, p. 25; and Olwen Hufton, *The Poor of Eighteenth-Century France, 1750–1789* (Oxford: Oxford University Press, 1974), pp. 210–11.

all of them as idle fakes. In fact, they had prepared four thousand licenses in 1597, believing, evidently, that many of the beggars of the city were truly needy.[26] Through licensing, the city government attempted to systematize this form of charity so that it could distinguish those deserving charity and also provide Christians with an opportunity to perform the good works required for salvation.

Counter-Reformation programs to support the poor no longer considered every pauper worthy of aid, nor did they leave the poor free to beg. Religious ideas may not have been as responsible for these changes as humanist thinking and the practicalities of providing charity for greater numbers of people; however, religion continued to provide the rationale for charity and its evolving forms.[27] The "secularization" of charity in this period was less a matter of state replacing Church than the success of both Protestant and Catholic leaders in enlisting lay people to carry out charitable programs through guilds and confraternities.[28] Religious institutions, Protestant and Catholic alike, had the task of promoting a supportive mentality for the charitable programs that sought to combine social discipline with economic gains.[29]

In the towns and cities of early modern Spain, Church and secular authorities worked together to reform poor relief, developing a unique partnership and forms of charity that both resembled and differed from those in other parts of Europe. Churchmen who debated the godliness of begging indicated that they knew of attempts to reform charity elsewhere, but no Spanish town attempted to completely confine the poor in a general hospital on the French model or put them to work, as the English did, in workhouses.[30] Limited fiscal resources of the Spanish state and the weakness of the economy prevented the establishment of a widespread organized system of regulating beggars through such means.[31]

Yet charity in Spain did not simply stagnate, nor did the Church play

[26] Ariño, *Sucesos de Sevilla*, pp. 45–47.

[27] Davis, "Poor Relief, Humanism, and Heresy," in her *Society and Culture*, pp. 17–64. See also Vives, *Pobres*; and Cristóbal Pérez de Herrera, *Amparo de pobres* (1598) (Madrid: Espasa-Calpe, 1975).

[28] For the importance of religious lay organizations for charity in France and Italy, see Emanuel Chill, "Religion and Mendicity in Seventeenth-Century France," *International Review of Social History* 7 (1962): 400–425; and Brian Pullen, "Catholics and the Poor in Early Modern Europe," *Transactions of the Royal Historical Society*, 5th ser., 26 (1976): 21. See also his very fine study, *Rich and Poor in Renaissance Venice: The Social Institutions of a Catholic State, to 1620* (Cambridge: Harvard University Press, 1971).

[29] Robert Jutte, "Poor Relief and Social Discipline in Sixteenth-Century Europe," *European Studies Review* 11 (1981): 42.

[30] Martz, *Poverty and Welfare*, pp. 157–58.

[31] William J. Callahan, *La Santa y Real Hermandad del Refugio y Piedad de Madrid, 1618–1832* (Madrid: Consejo Superior de Investigaciones Científicas, 1980), p. 21.

merely a reactionary role in conserving the traditional forms of charity. In Seville, support for the poor seemed to follow a pattern of indiscriminate individual giving in the early sixteenth century, but it had become far more organized and discriminating by the end of that century. In addition, the secular government played an increasingly active role in both organizing and supporting the major forms of poor relief in Seville.

Nevertheless, the Church continued to be a major benefactor, and it encouraged private citizens to give to the poor. The people who administered and carried out charitable programs often came from religious communities or the clergy. Even more important, people debated the issues of poor relief through the rhetoric of religion. They perceived poverty through a consciousness of a "just order," which included a conception of "God's poor," as well as a "moral economy."[32] In this just order, religion acted as a set of symbols that promoted and explained action and also changed in meaning.

Recurring crises, in fact, required changes; and they also frustrated attempts at systematization. Seville began the seventeenth century with a severe epidemic of the plague that increased the number of orphans, homeless, and destitute.[33] Major crises struck again in 1626 and 1649, with both epidemics and severe dearth. Antonio Domínguez Ortiz has estimated that the epidemic of 1649 cost Seville 60,000 lives, far fewer than the 300,000 reported by Ignacio Góngora, but still amounting to about half the city's population.[34] Accustomed to care for 30 or 40 infants a year, the city's foundling hospital reported in 1659 that it was caring for 340.[35] Death

[32] E. P. Thompson, "The Moral Economy of the English Crowd in the Eighteenth Century," *Past and Present* 50 (1971): 76–136, offers an impressive study of the lag between traditional attitudes and economic changes but does not explore the significance of religion or gender in those attitudes. A broader study of economic thought is Marjorie Grice-Hutchinson, *Early Economic Thought in Spain, 1177–1740* (London: Allen and Unwin, 1978). Gertrude Himmelfarb, *The Idea of Poverty: England in the Early Industrial Age* (New York: Alfred A. Knopf, 1984), p. 8, esp., discusses the significance of collective mentalities in affecting perceptions of poverty in times past. A primary source for studying a "just economy" is Thomas de Mercado, *Summa de tratos y contratos* (Seville: Hernando Diaz, 1571). For an expanded perspective on the continuing role of religion in Spanish history, see Payne, *Spanish Catholicism*. A more specialized study of wills in the APS is by Morell Peguero, *Contribución etnográfica*, pp. 151–58, esp., which shows how religious conceptions motivated charity.

[33] Velázquez y Sánchez, *Anales epidémicos*, pp. 76–87. Note, however, that symptoms of swellings and carbuncles that were reported could indicate venereal disease, as well as bubonic plague.

[34] Domínguez Ortiz, *Orto y ocaso*, p. 86. See also AMS, Sección Especial, Papeles del Señor Conde de Aguila, Efemérides, Cuadro 2, and Tomo 36 en folio, Número following 27; and Diego Ignacio Góngora, "Relación del contagio que padeció esta ciudad de Sevilla el año de 1649," in *Memoria de diferentes cosas*, BC, 84-7-21.

[35] Antonio Domínguez Ortiz, *El Barroco y la Ilustración*, vol. 4 of *Historia de Sevilla* (Seville: Diputación Provincial de Sevilla, 1976), p. 54.

filled the streets of Seville, and clerics and lay people who worked in the hospitals seemed helpless.

The growing numbers of babies abandoned in Seville resulted from several interrelated factors. Comparing records of foundling hospital admissions to the price of wheat, a recent study shows a correlation that is particularly striking in the last three decades of the seventeenth century.[36] Attitudes about acceptable sexual behavior compounded the effect of economic developments that made it more difficult for mothers to keep their children. Although the gender belief persisted that condemned extramarital sexual activity much more stringently for women than for men, the fluctuating rigor of its enforcement may account for periodical increases in the number of mothers who abandoned their newborn infants.[37] In addition, these increases undoubtedly resulted from the growth of a population of young transient males and the rising number of single young women who left their birth homes to work as domestic servants.[38]

Officials of the foundling hospital attempted to provide mothers for abandoned babies. They hired lactating women who were willing to nurse foundlings as well as their own babies. Paid only twenty vellón reales per month, these women were usually so poor that they welcomed any small additional income.[39] Since the city paid them to provide care for only the first two years of a child's life, the foundlings' future then depended upon whether these mothers were willing or able to continue caring for them "out of Christian charity," or whether others would come forward to adopt them. Widows sometimes adopted young orphans for companionship, but most of the adoptive parents came from artisan groups who were probably more interested in the potential value of a child's labor.[40] Most babies admitted to the foundling hospital, of course, did not survive for adoption: mortality rates rose to more than 93 percent, with most deaths occurring in the first few months of life.[41]

[36] León Carlos Alvarez Santaló, *Marginación social y mentalidad en Andalucía occidental: Expósitos en Sevilla (1613–1910)* (Seville: Consejería de Cultura de la Junta de Andalucía, 1980), pp. 57–58. See also idem, "La Casa de Expósitos de Sevilla en el Siglo XVII," *Cuadernos de Historia* 7 (1977): 491–532.

[37] Alvarez Santaló, *Marginación*, pp. 49–50. See also Davis, *Fiction*, p. 86, for a discussion of infanticide in early modern France in which she notes changes in sexual values that accompanied both religious reform and family strategy.

[38] Ibid., pp. 65–66; for more on the vulnerabilities of domestic servants, see Cissie Fairchilds, *Domestic Enemies: Servants and Their Masters in Old Regime France* (Baltimore: Johns Hopkins University Press, 1984); and Jesús Bravo Lozano, "Fuentes para el estudio del trabajo femenino en la edad moderna: El caso de Madrid a fines del siglo XVII," in Matilla and Ortega, *El trabajo de las mujeres*, pp. 22–24.

[39] Alvarez Santaló, *Marginación*, p. 121.

[40] Ibid., pp. 101–17.

[41] Ibid., Cuadros 21–22.

In this context of death and disaster, one of the city's wealthiest residents experienced a personal tragedy that apparently led to his religious conversion. Miguel de Mañara, heir to a commercial fortune, decided to devote his life and income to the poor of Seville just after the death of his wife in 1661.[42] He entered the Brotherhood of Holy Charity, a confraternity that had been founded in the mid-fifteenth century to bury executed felons and those people found drowned in the river. Quickly elected *hermano mayor*, don Miguel revitalized the brotherhood with a new set of regulations that emphasized the spiritual purpose of its charity. The regulations also implied a concern that the brotherhood not deteriorate into a group of poor mendicants. Declaring that all brothers must be "Old Christians, of pure and honorable generation, without morisco, mulatto, or Jewish blood," they required that members of the brotherhood have "sufficient wealth to keep themselves according to the quality of their persons."[43]

Seeing the genuine need for charity in his city, don Miguel led his brotherhood to expand the scope of their charitable activities. In 1664 the brothers agreed to Mañara's proposal to found a small hospice alongside the chapel that they had maintained near the river. They established a dispensary in the hospice to provide some medical treatment for the poor, but they resisted making it into a true hospital. The hospice, they stipulated, should provide only matting and benches rather than beds.[44] Even so, Mañara insisted that the brothers' charity must be personal. "And if they bring some poor, sick man from the city," he instructed them, "go to meet him with love and lower him in your arms from the conveyance and carry him to the infirmary. And before putting him to bed, wash his feet and kiss them."[45] Seeking salvation through humiliation, the brothers of this confraternity humbled themselves to perform "women's work"—work that in the Hospital de la Sangre was indeed carried out by "a numerous family of women" and directed by a *madre mayor*, who was praised for being of good birth and well suited "for such an important ministry."[46]

Mañara provided the funds and energy in the 1670s to transform the modest chapel of the brotherhood into an impressive church, and the small

[42] Juan de Cardenas, *Breve relación de la muerte, vida, y virtudes del venerable caballero Don Miguel Mañara Vicentelo de Leca, Caballero del Orden de Calatrava, Hermano Mayor de la Santa Caridad* (1679) (Seville: E. Rasco, 1903); P. Jesús María Granero, *Don Miguel Mañara* (Seville: Artes Gráficas Salesianas, 1963); Francisco Martin Hernández, *Miguel Mañara* (Seville: Universidad de Sevilla, 1981); Miguel de Mañara, *Discurso de la verdad* (1671), discussed in E. Valdevieso and J. M. Serrera, *El Hospital de la Caridad de Sevilla* (Seville: Editorial Sever-Cuesta, 1980).

[43] Valdivieso and Serrera, *El Hospital*, p. 64.

[44] Ibid., p. 24.

[45] Quoted in Jonathan Brown, *Images and Ideas in Seventeenth-Century Spanish Painting* (Princeton: Princeton University Press, 1978), p. 143.

[46] Ortiz de Zuñiga, *Anales*, 4: 136–37.

hospice into a hospital that soon eclipsed the earlier hospital built to continue the work of doña Catalina. Designed and built by Bernardo Simon
de Pineda, Mañara's church became a primary example of Spanish baroque
architecture.[47] Just outside the entry to the single nave, four tiles attributed
to the artist Bartolomé Murillo depicted Charity, Hope, San Jorge, and
Santiago. The inscription over the entry identified the church as "the house
of the poor and stairway to heaven." Ornamentation virtually covered the
church within, with decoration overflowing the main niches to flood onto
adjacent vaults and walls.

The richly ornamented altarpieces would later be identified with the
style named for José Churriguera, a well-known Spanish architect who
lived from 1650 until 1723. The main altarpiece, in particular, caught the
eye with its domed canopy supported by four richly carved columns and
four larger spiral columns carved with vine leaves. Above a curling cornice
appeared carvings of the virtues, with seated angels, candelabra, and other
decoration in a swirling pattern. Beneath the canopy Pedro Roldan had
sculpted *The Burial of Christ*. Painted and gilded by Juan Valdés Leal, the
sculpted figures presented profiles against a deeply recessed landscape relief
of Calvary in the distance. The figures' expressive faces and graceful movement denoted a tender grief that focused on the naked body of the dead
Christ.

Death provided the theme, as well, for two striking paintings by Valdés
Leal and one by Pedro Camprobin. *Vanitás*, the painting by Camprobin,
depicts a young man tipping his hat to a skeleton, veiled and with one eye
showing, accompanied by a guitar, money, books, a pistol, and playing
cards, all symbols of vanity. Valdés Leal's *Finis Gloriae Mundi* (fig. 15)
shows a stigmatized hand holding a weighing balance above cadavers being eaten by insects. The plate on the left side of the balance contains ani-
mal symbols of the seven deadly sins; that on the right side holds symbols
of prayer, penitence, and charity. *In Ictu Oculi* (fig. 16), by the same artist,
presents death as a skeleton standing over symbols of wealth and power
and extinguishing a candle that symbolizes life. Both artists translated into
paintings Mañara's personal feelings about death, which he expressed in a
proposal for a sermon: "Ponder the brevity of life and the certainty of
death, and that it ends everything; paint the rigorous agony of death and
how the greatest grandeur ends in worms."[48]

Mañara also commissioned for his church eleven paintings by Bartolomé
Murillo. Most of these paintings represent the miraculous quality of charity and thus soften the theme of death. Christ heals a paralytic at the pool

---

[47] George Kubler and Martin Soria, *Art and Architecture in Spain and Portugal and Their
American Dominions 1500–1800* (Harmondsworth, Middlesex: Penguin, 1959), p. 162. Note
that the architect has been referred to as Pereda rather than Pineda, p. 50.

[48] Valdivieso and Serrera, *El Hospital*, pp. 10–47; Brown, *Images and Ideas*, pp. 138–40.

FIGURE 15. *Finis Gloriae Mundi*, by Juan de Valdés Leal (Hospital de la Santa Caridad, Seville).

FIGURE 16. *In Ictu Oculi*, by Juan de Valdés Leal (Hospital de la Santa Caridad, Seville).

of Bethesda in one painting, and another depicts him feeding the multitude. The *Miracle of Moses Striking the Rock* (fig. 17) includes a small scene off to the side that shows a woman giving water to some children. Other paintings, such as *Saint John of God Carrying an Invalid* and *Saint Elizabeth of Hungary Healing the Sick* (see fig. 19 below), show that the miraculous power of charity can infuse humans as well as the divinity. Human need cries out from the beggar boy in the latter painting, but the tender care of Saint Elizabeth as she washes his scabbed head reassures the viewer of her healing power. Murillo's paintings seem to reaffirm Mañara's faith that "holy alms" and charity could "achieve a happy death."[49]

Mañara's church became the focal point for three large wings subsequently erected next to it as wards to shelter and treat the ill. He directed the building of a "gran enfermería" in the name of Jesus Christ in 1673, another in the name of the Virgin in 1677, and a third in the following year. By 1678, the small hospice of the Brotherhood of Holy Charity had been transformed into the Hospital de la Santa Caridad. Marble columns and spacious galleries had replaced the crumbling buildings of a boatworks dating from the thirteenth century. Constructed around a central courtyard that featured marble figures of Charity and Faith, this hospital seemed to look inward. The Hospital de la Sangre had also been built around a courtyard, but no marble figures drew the eye to it. Sixteenth-century commentators emphasized, instead, the main facade and entry door of this hospital. Outward appearance seemed to be paramount in the sixteenth-century hospital, while a turning inward marked the Caridad of the seventeenth century.

Sites for the two hospitals provide another point of contrast. Mañara chose as site for his building the chapel that his brotherhood had maintained since the fifteenth century. Warehouses and shipyards had fallen into decay in this area near the river where the gallows had stood above a walled cemetery that received the bodies of executed felons.[50] No spacious field surrounded the Hospital de la Santa Caridad to separate it from the rest of the city. Unlike the Hospital de la Sangre, Mañara's hospital stood within the walls of the city, hemmed in by other buildings in various states of decay. The new hospital associated charity with urban blight. Although the sixteenth-century hospital might imply a wish to use charity for separating the poor from the life of the city, Mañara built his hospital where he found the poor within the city. It is true that residential areas for the poor grew up outside the city walls in the sixteenth century, and it is true that property within the walls of the city could have been purchased at a lower price in the seventeenth century. Nevertheless, the selection of these sites pro-

---

[49] Quoted in Brown, *Images and Ideas*, p. 140.
[50] Ortiz de Zuñiga, *Anales*, 4: 85–86.

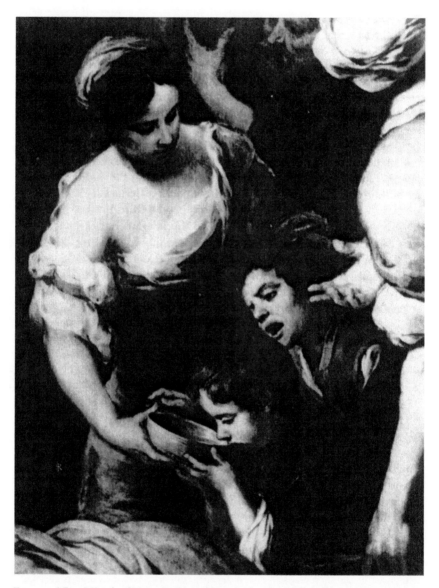

FIGURE 17. *Miracle of Moses Striking the Rock* (detail), by Bartolomé Murillo (Hospital de la Santa Caridad, Seville).

moted different views of charity even though the hospital in both cases continued to be a symbol of Christian salvation as well as a shelter for the poor.

A church provided the focal point for each hospital, but the two churches' main altars differed remarkably. Viewers in the church of Sangre saw a large table carved from a single piece of alabaster, impressive for its natural beauty and rarity. Presumably only a wealthy person could locate, buy, transport and donate such a marvelous altar. The pride of the donor might be seen in this altar, as well as in the family coats of arms that flanked the main entry. In contrast, the Caridad's altarpiece appeared marvelous because of its workmanship. Representing the finest work of an architect-designer, a sculptor, and a painter, the altarpiece drew the viewer into the tender feelings of grief expressed by the sculpted figures. The three-dimensional scene probably appeared more immediate to the viewer than a two-dimensional painting. Swirls and spirals in the sculpture further enveloped the viewer in feelings of piety and compassion.

Paintings used to adorn the church of each hospital cannot be used conclusively to show a change in attitude about charity between the sixteenth and seventeenth centuries because many of the paintings in Sangre were not added until the seventeenth century. Nevertheless, a comparison of the paintings suggests some diversity in perceptions of poverty and charity that should be acknowledged. Paintings in the Hospital de la Sangre emphasized the suffering of Christ and his martyrs, the perfect beauty of the Virgin, and the holy authority of Saint Gregory as pope. In contrast, those in the Hospital de la Santa Caridad depicted the vanity of life and the miraculous ability of charity to defeat death. Paintings in both hospitals associated charity with death. In the paintings of Sangre, however, the depiction of death emphasized suffering as an experience shared by humanity and divinity. The paintings of the Hospital de la Santa Caridad portrayed death as a reminder of the vanity of life. Charity in the artistic decoration of this church represented a primary way to defeat death through winning eternal glory.[51] Charitable deeds were thus represented as having less to do with the suffering of others than with the donor's quest for salvation.

Both hospitals depicted charity as a female figure, but they differed in other representations of women. Paintings in Sangre presented Mary, the mother of Jesus, as human perfection. Zurbarán portrayed her as pious and compassionate, beautifully draped in richly colored clothing, as in figure 18. For the Caridad, Murillo depicted Saint Elizabeth, seen here in figure 19, as pious and compassionate, as well; but this holy woman leans into

[51] Valdiviesa and Serrera, El Hospital, p. 10; Carmona García, El sistema, pp. 116–19. To consider these paintings in the larger context of Spanish painting in the sixteenth and seventeenth centuries, see Kubler and Soria, Art and Architecture, pp. 199–302.

FIGURE 18. *The Immaculate Conception*, by Francisco Zurbarán (Szépmüvészeti Múzeum, Budapest).

FIGURE 19. *Saint Elizabeth of Hungary Healing the Sick*, by Bartolomé Murillo (Hospital de la Santa Caridad, Seville).

her task of washing a diseased beggar boy. His sores attract attention before any detail about her figure. It is not her clothing that strikes the eye, but the radiance and serenity of her face. Here is a true "mother of the poor" whose help is immediate and material.

In the actual landscape of poverty and charity in seventeenth-century Seville, females appeared less frequently as benefactors than as recipients of charity. City chronicles describe no seventeenth-century successor to doña Catalina as the "Mother of the Poor," although wealthy women provided dowries for young women and girls that Jesuits found on the streets, in the brothel, and in the prison.[52] Beatas had provided supervision for children and young women who were brought to them by Jesuits, and they also had worked in the hospitals and prisons of the city.[53] A few years before Mañara built the Caridad, a beata named madre María de Jesús founded the Hospital de Santo Cristo de los Dolores to shelter and care for poor women.[54] However, beatas had fallen into disfavor with the Inquisition during the seventeenth century, and they appeared to require more charitable services in this period than they provided.[55]

Miguel de Mañara directed a survey of the poor in Seville in 1667; and its results suggest that poverty, at least in its respectable form, had become almost exclusively a problem of women and children.[56] In the parish of the cathedral, for example, 297 women were listed, but only twenty-three adult males. In all cases, the males were crippled, blind, ill, or very old.

Mañara's survey describes a subculture of poor women in Seville. Hundreds of women lived together, most with children and few with men. Of the 297 women listed in the parish of the cathedral, for example, only twelve lived with husbands or fathers. More typical was the group of five widows who shared living space in the Casa del Alféres in this parish, or the three women who lived together in the Corral de Antonio with their

[52] Pedro de León, *Compendio*, pt. 1, chap. 4, names doña Brigida Corzo as one who promised to provide a dowry of forty ducats for each woman he converted from the city's brothel.

[53] Ibid., and also pt. 2, chaps. 12 and 25. Charitable work of beatas is also described in AMS, Archivo General, Sección 2, Archivo de Contaduría, Carpeta 13, Número 148, and Carpeta 16, Números 142 and 206; and in AMS, Sección 4, Siglo XVII, Escribanías de Cabildo, Tomo 10, Números 26 and 27.

[54] AMS, Sección Especial, Papeles del Señor Conde de Aguila, Tomo 32 en folio, Números 2 and 3.

[55] AMS, Sección 4, Siglo XVII, Escribanías de Cabildo, Tomo 24, Número 41.

[56] Mañara's survey is in the archive of the Hospital de la Santa Caridad (HSC), Estante 4, Legajo 18, entitled *Memoria de todas las parroquias de Sevilla y de las necesidades y pobres que había en ellas; que pedía, el Ves D. Miguel Mañara para tener cuidado de socorrer las como lo hijo, y mientras ricibo los remedios como por estas memorias parece* (1667); see especially the listing for the parish of the Sagrario and Santa Iglesia. Cf. the poor that Olwen Hufton has described in early modern France. She quotes a cleric who recognized that women were frequently at the bottom of a "hierarchy of hunger," in "Women in Revolution, 1789–1796," *Past and Present* 53 (1971): 93.

twelve children. Almost half of the adult women listed lived with children. Twenty-six lived with sisters, and fifty-five were recorded as widows. Figure 20 shows a portrait by Murillo in which he depicts an old beggar woman whose benign smile softens the realities of chronic poverty.

Two and three generations of the poor lived together in the rooms and hovels visited by the cleric who counted the poor in the parish of the cathedral. Several women lived with adult daughters and grandchildren. Isabel Hernándes and María Lópes each cared for their grandchildren whose parents had died. Even those women who were not related lived in households of old and young. In the Corral de Valdesuvia, for example, lived Francisca Ruiz and her son, Beatriz Jiménes, who was a "very old woman," Inés Romero, and Sebastiana de los Reyes.

Unfortunately, the census does not tell how these people decided to live with one another. Some large households contained members of the same family and nonrelated people as well. In the Corral de Segovia in the parish of the cathedral lived seven adults and four children: Madalena de Ayala, Isabel Rodríguez with an infant and two small children, Juana Rodríguez, Catalina Rodríguez with daughters of five and six years, Isabel González, María de Galves, and Catalina García, who had to sleep on the floor. The largest household listed in this parish contained ten adults and five children. A smaller group that lived in the Casa de la Concepción included Florencia Beatriz with a four-year-old son and a husband who had been sick in bed for eight months. Living with them were María de Figueroa and Luisana de Toro, and the four sons and one daughter of Luisana. Both María and Luisana were pregnant. Poverty may explain why the husbands or lovers of these and other women of the parish had abandoned them. But if poverty acts as an acid in corroding human relationships, as Olwen Hufton has documented among the poor of eighteenth-century France, it may also act as a catalyst in forming new relationships that become essential for survival.[57]

Pregnancy and dependent children appeared to be the most common attributes of the people identified as "deserving poor" in the 1667 survey. In only a few cases was the name of a husband included with that of a pregnant woman. More often the woman was identified by her own name only, the month of her pregnancy, and whether she had other children. Too often a phrase followed the name stating that the woman did not even have a bed on which to bear her child. The men who took the survey could include expectant unmarried mothers among the "deserving poor" not because they were respectable, but because they were especially vulnerable.

Age and illness also contributed to this vulnerability. Among the 297 adult women listed in the parish of the cathedral, seventeen were described

[57] Hufton, *The Poor*, p. 114.

FIGURE 20. *Old Woman Asking for Alms*, by Bartolomé Murillo (Museo de Bellas Artes, Cordoba).

as "ancient" or over sixty years old. One was eighty years old. Another, Isabel María, deeply distressed the recording cleric. He wrote that she was a poor beggar who was ill and "very naked" and appeared to have no dwelling of her own. She was listed in a household living near the knife maker on the Calle de la Mar, but it appeared that she would have to move. The cleric recorded this, he said, because the Brotherhood of Holy Charity might have to decide what to do with her.

Compassion mingled with practicalities in the survey of 1667. For the large household in a house near the Calle de la Mar, the priest carefully recorded the names of ten adults and the ages of five children. For each his notes called for a mattress, bedding, or clothing that he believed most necessary. María Josepha, for example, was to receive a mattress because she had only a straw mat for a bed. A mattress was also to be given to María Ramírez, who "sleeps on a little straw." María de Rivera was to have petticoats and her six-year-old daughter a jacket. Numbers written in the margins of the survey may indicate money that was either given in addition or would be necessary in order to provide those practical items that the cleric recorded. He did not include any information about food, perhaps because the poor could usually find food in monasteries, churches, at the back doors of private homes, and as leftovers from inns, taverns, and the marketplaces.[58]

The cleric who took the survey for the parish of the cathedral included a separate list of fifty-one people whom he described as "pobres vergonzantes," or the shamefaced poor. These were people who had once enjoyed a respectable social status that now entitled them to be treated differently from the other poor. They should not be subjected to the humiliation of public begging, it was believed, nor to public knowledge of their poverty.[59] So that lack of money would not completely destroy their status, clerics and lay brothers provided charity for them very discreetly. The cleric who recorded the forty-seven women and four men on the list of shamefaced poor for the parish of the cathedral noted that many had been wealthy at one time. Some had been nobles, and some of the men had held prestigious military and civic offices. Doña Escolestia de Montesonos, the widow of a member of the Brotherhood of Holy Charity, had been reduced to living on alms in the house of a man who had once been apprenticed to her husband.

Mañara's census indicates a desire to limit charity to the "deserving poor" and to provide practical relief, in the form of money, clothing, or bedding, that could help to sustain these people outside hospitals. Practicalities, however, did not eclipse religious motivations for charity, and Seville's poor did not simply become a secular issue. It is true that the city

[58] Ibid., pp. 101 and 109, for some of the ways that the poor found food.
[59] Martz, *Poverty and Welfare*, p. 9, esp. discusses the shamefaced poor.

government was increasingly asked to provide money for hospitals, and it is true that secular officials voiced concern about the inadequacy of charitable programs.[60] However, most of the money for charity continued to come from individuals who gave alms for the good of their own souls. Some of these contributions went through religious corporations or brotherhoods, but initially they represented a preoccupation with the salvation of individual souls.[61] Donors gave so that they might receive.

Licensed begging continued in seventeenth-century Seville, and individual donors sustained it with their alms. In 1675 the city licensed 231 people for begging.[62] Unlike the Elizabethan poor law that restricted charity to the parish of birth, Seville's system included outsiders: two-thirds of the licensed beggars in Seville were listed as natives of another place. Many suffered chronic illness or physical disability. Their ages ranged from 16 to 104 years, with 84 percent 50 years old or older.

In contrast to the census directed by Mañara, nearly two-thirds of those licensed to beg were males. Begging appeared to be unacceptable for women, especially those who were young. Of the seventy-nine women licensed to beg in 1675, only five were younger than fifty years. Presumably, those women requiring charity would be given it by clerics and lay brothers who received alms for them. Because Mañara's census had identified them as deserving charity in their own homes, they did not have to beg, nor leave their children at the foundling hospital, nor did they have to be confined in hospitals. Seville did not have to confine its poor in hospitals because its charity converted so many paupers, especially women and children, into "envergonzantes," who would not beg—the shamefaced poor who would voluntarily avoid public view. Charity thus became another form of enclosure for the women of this city.

Those paupers who most successfully survived conformed to expectations of respectability required by the donors. Women in particular learned to use the paternalism of a social order that considered them most needful of protection. Realizing that survival required at least the appearance of obedient submission, mothers of the poor quietly raised their children and lived out their lives, while male officials ignored their strength as survivors and forgot the power of those other women who provided charity as mothers of the poor.

[60] AMS, Sección 3, Siglo XVI, Escribanías de Cabildo, Tomo 10, Números 11, 12, and 14; AMS, Papeles Importantes, Siglo XVI, Tomo 9, Número 6; AMS, Sección 4, Siglo XVII, Escribanías de Cabildo, Tomo 24, Número 1; Perry, *Crime and Society*, pp. 177–78. Carmona García, *El sistema*, pp. 202–7, esp., goes so far as to say that the secular state displaced the Church in providing charity.

[61] See ADPS, Libros de Protocolos del Hospital del Amor de Dios y del Espíritu Santo, for a collection of testaments granting goods and money to charitable hospitals. Also, note the wills and charitable bequests discussed in Morell Peguero, *Contribución etnográfica*, pp. 151–58.

[62] AMS, Sección 4, Siglo XVII, Escribanías de Cabildo, Tomo 29, Número 9.

SURVIVORS AND SUBVERSIVES

THROUGH the magnifying lens of early modern Seville, the order-restoring function of gender becomes especially visible. Secular and ecclesiastical officials increased their powers of social control in this city as they responded to religious schisms, developing capitalism, dramatic demographic changes, urbanization, the growth of a central state, and increasing imperial rivalries. In this process women lost both autonomy and influence.

Attempts to restore and preserve order persisted in Seville despite economic and political decline that sapped their energy. Assumptions about order and survival proved particularly long-lasting, based upon a belief that the only order worth restoring was the "natural order" of God, Man, and Woman, arranged in a hierarchy with women at the bottom. Prescribed roles for women and men were thus biologically determined, according to this ideology, and divinely ordained.

During the period of the Counter-Reformation, people formulated their questions about women and men according to this view of God's order. Those two young men in Espinosa's *Diálogo* spoke for many as they focused on the distinction between good and evil women.[1] Far more than mere idle chatter about women, their conversation epitomized the significance of gender for this period. They never doubted that the evil woman could undermine an entire social order, God willing or not.

A theology of purity developed to establish the values and enforce the positions in this gendered "natural" order. It equated the good and the true with conformity to gender expectations, and it included a double standard for judging women and men that extended far beyond sexual behavior. The tremendous concern with morality that marks the Counter-Reformation sparked an outpouring of prescriptive literature as well as countless laws and regulations, and disciplinary institutions such as Magdalen houses and women's prisons. People who lived in this period could not plead ignorance of the gender-specific values of this theology of purity, for they learned of them through religious symbols as powerful as the Virgin, the Holy Martyrs, and the Penitent Magdalen.

Counter-Reformation attempts to restore order required a separation of the sacred from the profane. This meant not simply the exclusion of certain

[1] Juan de Espinosa, *Diálogo*, p. 258.

dramas and dances from religious festivals; it also meant a careful distinction of good women from evil, a closer regulation of the brothel, cloisters to protect nuns from the secular world, and charity for those who lived as the "respectable poor" in hovels crowded with women and children.

To protect the pure from the profane, order depended upon a program of enclosure that went far beyond cloistered convents or the prohibition against study abroad. This defensive posture was nowhere more evident than in the lives of women. Needing protection not only from outside influences, but also from their own weaknesses, women were told to stay in the "natural" confinement of convent, home, or brothel. Such enclosure protected men, as well. The wandering woman, after all, brought with her the broken sword of male dishonor.

Surely women were victimized in this gendered view of God's order, for the enclosure that protects also imprisons, discrediting those who are enclosed and depriving them of autonomy and opportunity. Victimization is only one part of the story, however, which is really about survival. Women survived the programs of the Counter-Reformation in many ways, some by conforming to gender prescriptions, internalizing the lessons of dutiful daughters. Some governed themselves in convents and beaterios, establishing female communities and preserving a sense of freedom even within enclosure. Others accepted their subservient roles as daughters, wives, nuns, beatas, prostitutes, or the deserving poor. And a few women enforced discipline themselves in women's prisons and Magdalen houses.

But even in conformity, women found ways to push against gender restrictions. Daughters of the poor learned out of necessity to break the prescription of enclosure, for they had to work in order to survive. While conforming to definitions for work appropriate to women, they often had to go outside the home and sometimes they went with little expectation of ever acquiring the means to marry or enter a convent.

Women such as María de San José and Catalina de Erauso simply defied gender restrictions. Teresa's first abbess of the Reformed Carmelite convent in Seville had to pay the price of many months in solitary confinement for defying authorities, but in the end she regained her position and even more confidence in her freedom within the cloister. The nun-lieutenant, on the other hand, ran away from the convent, and she was able to preserve both her life and her privilege to live as a man. Others, such as madre Catalina de Jesús, challenged the gender order in presuming to direct men as their "spiritual mother." In only a few cases were these female religious leaders able to preserve voice and position against ecclesiastical authorities.

It is difficult to know how many women were able to develop their own personal power within the gender restrictions of the sixteenth and seventeenth centuries. A few, such as Catalina de Ribera and madre María de Jesús, converted enclosures into lasting ministries to the poor and ill. Others found in education a means to more than the gendered virtue that Juan Vives described.[2] They used their knowledge of language to enlarge the boundaries of their world and increase their influence through writing. Oliva Sabuco even dared to use her writing to present a theory of anatomy very different from that accepted by most medical authorities of the period, and María de Zayas wrote "love stories" that directly challenged gender assumptions. Luisa Roldán had the advantage of learning about sculpture in her famous father's workshop; but she also learned to use her artistic gifts in her own name, creating statues of saints, angels, and Mother and Child that suggest the sensibilities of a working mother.

The work of these women shows that neither the eloquence of preachers nor the numbers of books published by writers could bridge the gap between the order they idealized and the disorder of their society. This gap produced a tension that invigorated much of the moral exhortation of the Counter-Reformation. It also caused some to despair of ever attaining a real reform, and it led others to question the validity of ideals that seemed so out of tune with practicality. The tension increased concern with people who did not conform, so that orthodoxy became more than religion and the efforts to impose a parochial homogeneity among all Catholics expanded to include attempts to impose a social conformity according to class and gender. Despite valiant efforts, these attempts did not fully succeed. The tension between ideal and real led finally to the redefinitions and adjustments of historical change.

The crisis of patriarchy in the sixteenth and seventeenth centuries would be repeated in countless cities as they entered the modern period. Seville's response to this crisis produced a pattern for gender and order that persisted in both Catholic and Protestant countries. Even in our own "secularized" period, gender is often regarded as fixed, based entirely on "nature" or biology. Counter-Reformation enclosure may seem quaint to modern minds, but it led directly to the doctrine of "separate spheres" for women and men. In our own time, women still live within prescriptive enclosures; like the women of Seville some three centuries ago, they are still questioning, ignoring, resisting, and using them for their own needs.

The partnership of secular and ecclesiastical authorities that was so apparent in early modern Seville had a lasting impact on gender. Its answer to the question of what is Woman transformed all women into daughters of perfidious Susana. Defining women as ideally pure, it also emphasized their dangerous sexuality, their weakness and propensity for disorder that require special protection. With hands and feet and mind and voices, the

---

[2] Vives, *Libro llamado instrucción*; also see the discussion of education as a means to virtue in José Antonio Maravall, *Estudios de historia del pensamiento español* (Madrid: Cultura Hispánica, 1983), 2: 18–19.

women of Seville confronted this paradigm: conforming, questioning, defying, refining. The stories of some demonstrate how authority reasserts itself by convincing the oppressed to participate in their own oppression. Other women turned from the self-accusation, penitence, and despair of Susana. They developed new ways to assert their autonomy and exert an influence, so quietly effective in hiding themselves that few have noticed their subversion.

GLOSSARY

abjuration de levi — a formal oath renouncing errors and professing a return to the faith, often required of those found guilty by the Inquisition; abjuration de vehementi was required for more serious offenses

alumbrado — an illuminist heresy identified by the Inquisition in the sixteenth and seventeenth centuries that emphasized personal and internal religious experience

amiga — a female friend, but a term also used to describe a female lover

aojamiento — the state of being bewitched or under the spell of a curse

aojar — to cause illness, death, or damage by cursing, especially by giving the evil eye

arbitrista — an essayist in seventeenth-century Spain particularly concerned with economic problems

asistente — a city official, usually a noble appointed by the Crown to head the city council

auto de fe — a public or private ceremony of penitence and reaffirmation of faith prescribed for those found guilty by the Inquisition

beata — a woman who dedicated her life to God and took a vow of chastity, but not of poverty or obedience to any particular religious order; she often wore a religious habit, but usually lived outside a convent

beaterio — a dwelling in which two or more beatas lived together

cantiga — a poem or ballad

Casa de Contratación — the royal agency established in Seville in the sixteenth century to regulate trade with and colonization in the New World; see *Lonja*

cofradía — confraternity, or lay association, usually dedicated to a particular religious observance, and often carrying out charitable work

converso — technically, any person who converted to Christianity in early modern Spain, but usually a former Jew and New Christian suspected of apostasy

corral — courtyard often lacking trees and shared by adjoining buildings

cortes — an assembly of representatives from the Church, aristocracy, and major towns and cities, who met at the Crown's invitation to consider taxes, other grievances, and succession to the throne

devoto — a person dedicated to a specific religious devotion, but more particularly a man, usually young and single, who designated a young comely nun or beata as the object of his devotion

doncella — a maiden, usually a young woman past the age of puberty who is an unmarried virgin

ducat — a gold coin worth 440 maravedís at the beginning of the seventeenth century

emparedamiento — a walled-up house that provided absolute seclusion for nuns and other women who dedicated their lives to God

enfermería — a room or building to treat the ill

envergonzante — a poor individual who had once enjoyed a respectable social position and was too ashamed to beg or be seen publicly in a state of want; see *pobre vergonzante*

escuela sevillana — a painting style developed by artists in late sixteenth- and seventeenth-century Seville that emphasized piety and suffering

fray — brother, a title given to friars of certain mendicant religious orders, such as Augustinians, Carmelites, Dominicans, and Franciscans

limpieza de sangre — genetic purity resulting from the absence of inbreeding with religious groups other than Christian; it became a legal requirement for most offices and privileges in the sixteenth and seventeenth centuries.

Lonja — a building near the cathedral in Seville, designed by Juan de Herrera and built in the late sixteenth century to house the royal agency that regulated trade and colonization of the New World; see *Casa de Contratación*

mal de madre — an illness associated with female organs

mal de ojo — illness of the eyes, but also the act of cursing

maravedí — a gold coin in ancient times, but reduced to vellón, a mixture of silver and copper, by the sixteenth century, so that 34 maravedís equaled a real, and 440 equaled a ducat

ministra — a beata who directed the work and care of lay women in a convent

mora — a female Muslim not converted to Christianity

morisca(o) — a former Muslim who had converted to Christianity and, in the sixteenth and seventeenth centuries, was commonly suspected of apostasy and disloyalty to the Spanish Crown

muezzin — the person who calls Islamic faithful to prayer, often from a tower such as the Giralda in Seville

pobre vergonzante — a person reduced to poverty from a former position of respectability; see *envergonzante*

protomédico — a principal physician directed by the Crown to examine and license those who practiced medicine, including empirics, physicians, and surgeons

quadrilla — a small group of at least four people who undertook activities together

real — a silver coin, usually worth 34 maravedís

recogimiento — a religious practice of withdrawing from the world and seeking God within the self

sanbenito — also *sambenito*; the sacklike penitential garment that the Inquisition could require penitents to wear, often bearing the insignia of the Holy Office, the crimes the penitent had committed, and the family name of the penitent

sor — sister, a title commonly given to a nun

Torre de Oro — a medieval tower on the bank of the Guadalquivir River that emblematized the inland seaport of Seville

vecino pechero — a taxable citizen or commoner

vellón — a copper and silver alloy used for coins

vergüenza — a sense of shame or modesty expected of respectable individuals

BIBLIOGRAPHY

Archival Manuscripts

ADPS, Hospital del Amor de Dios, Libros 22 and 46

ADPS, Hospital de las Cinco Llagas, Legajos 242, 243, 250

ADPS, Inventario del Hospital de las Cinco Llagas, Libro 8

ADPS, Libros de Protocolos del Hospital del Amor de Dios, Legajo 49

ADPS, Libros de Protocolos del Hospital del Espíritu Santo

AGI, Documentos escogidos, Sección 5, Legajo 1

AHN, Clero, Legajo 6246

AHN, Consejos, Legajos 4415, 7185

AHN, Inquisición, Legajos 107, 2056, 2061, 2067, 2072, 2074, 2075, 2962, 3716, 3742, 4520

AMS, Archivo General, Sección 2, Archivo de Contadura

AMS, *Ordenanzas de Sevilla.* Seville: Diego Hurtado de Mondoca, 1631

AMS, Papeles Importantes, Siglo XVI, Tomo 9, Número 1

AMS, Papeles Importantes, Siglo XVII

AMS, Sección Especial, Papeles del Señor Conde de Aguila

    Libros en folio

    Efemérides

    Cristóbal Chaves, "Relación de las cosas de la cárcel de Sevilla y su trato"

AMS, Sección 3, Siglo XVI, Escribanías de Cabildo

AMS, Sección 4, Siglo XVII, Escribanías de Cabildo

APS, 1550, Oficio 1, Libro 1

BC, 74-7-118, "Relación de un auto de fee que se celebró en el Oficio de la Inquisición de la Ciudad de Sevilla en el Conv^{to} de S^n Pablo . . . el último día del mes Febreo del año de 1627"

BC, 83-7-6, Luis de Peraza, *Vida de Santa Justa y Santa Rufina, virgenes y mártires de Sevilla*

BC, 83-7-14, *Papeles varios*, "Consulta theológica, en que se pregunta si será justo y conveniente que se apliquen las obras pías de esta ciudad al remedio de la necesidad pública que al presente ay en esta ciudad de Sevilla"

BC, 84-7-19, "Memorias eclesiástics y seculares de la muy noble y muy leal ciudad de Sevilla"

BC, 84-7-21, Diego Ignacio Góngora, "Relación del contagio que padeció esta ciudad de Sevilla el año de 1649," in *Memoria de diferentes cosas*

BM, Egerton 1873, "Tractatus varii, et collectanea"

BN, MS 2176, María de San José, *Ramilleta de Mirra*

BN, MS 3537, María de San José, "Carta que escribe una pobre, y presa descalça consolándose, y consolando a sus Hermanas, y hijas que por berla asi estaban afligidas, del año 1593"

BN, MS 13493, Ana de Jesús, *Vida de la Venerable Ana de Jesús escrita por ella misma*

HSC, Estante 4, Legajo 18, *Memoria de todas las parroquias de Sevilla y de las necesidades y pobres que había en ellas; que pedía, el Ves D. Miguel Mañara para tener cuidado de socorrer las como lo hijo, y mientras ricibo los remedios como por estas memorias parece* (1667)

WRITINGS OF THE PERIOD AND PUBLISHED PRIMARY SOURCES

Alfonso X. *El 'códice rico' de las Cantigas de Alfonso X el Sabio.* Madrid: Edilan, 1979.

Alonso y de los Ruizes de Fontecha, Juan. *Diez previlegios de preñadas.* Valladolid: n.p., 1606.

Ariño, Francisco de. *Sucesos de Seville de 1592 á 1604 recojidos de Francisco de Ariño, vecino de la ciudad en el barrio de Triana.* Seville: Rafael Tarascó y Lassa, 1873.

Aviñon, Juan de. *Sevillana medicina: que trata el modo conservativo y curativo de los que habitan en la muy insigne ciudad de Sevilla, la cual sirve y aprovecha para cualquier otro lugar de estos reinos.* 1545. Seville: Enrique Rasco, 1885.

Azpilcueta Navarro, Martín de. *Manual de confesores, y penitentes, que clara y brevemente contiene la universal, y particular decisio de quasi todas las dudas, que en las confesiones suelen ocurrir de los pecados absoluciones, restituciones, censuras, irregularidades.* Toledo: Juan Ferrer, 1554.

Canons and Decrees of the Council of Trent. Translated H. J. Schroeder, O.P. St. Louis and London: Herder Books, 1941.

Carbon, Damian. *Libro del arte de las comadres o madrinas y del regimiento de las preñadas y paridas y de los niños.* Majorca?: n.p., 1541.

Cardenas, Juan de. *Breve relación de la muerte, vida, y virtudes del venerable caballero Don Miguel Mañara Vicentelo de Leca, Caballero del Orden de Calatrava, Hermano Mayor de la Santa Caridad.* 1679. Seville: E. Rasco, 1903.

Caro Mallén de Soto, Ana. *El Conde de Partinuplés.* 1653. In *Biblioteca de Autores Españoles,* 49: 125–38. Madrid: M. Rivadeneyra, 1859.

Cerda, Juan de la. *Vida política de todos los estados de mugeres: en el qual se dan muy provechosos y Christianos documentos y avisos, para criarse y conservarse devidamente las mugeres en sus estados.* Alcalá de Henares: Juan Gracian, 1599.

Enríquez de Guzmán, Feliciana. "Censura de las antiguas comedias españolas," in *Biblioteca de Autores Españoles,* 42: 545. Madrid: M. Rivadeneyra, 1855.

———. *Tragicomedia: Los jardines y campos sabeos.* Lisboa: Gerardo de la Vinlea, 1624.

Espinosa, Juan de. *Diálogo en laude de las mujeres.* 1580. Edited by Angela González Simón. Madrid: Consejo Superior de Investigaciones Científicas, 1946.

Farfan, Francisco. *Regimiento de castos: Y remedio de torpes. Donde se ponen XXVIII remedios contra el peccado de la torpeza: Y por otras tantas vías se exhorta el christiano al amor de la castidad.* Salamanca: Cornelio Bonardo, 1590.

———. *Tres libros contra el peccado de la simple fornicación: donde se averigua, que la torpeza entre solteros es peccado mortal, según ley divina, natural, y humana; y se responde a los engaños de los que dizen que no es peccado.* Salamanca: Herederos de Matthias Gast, 1585.

González Dávila, Gil. *Teatro eclesiástico de las iglesias metropolitanas, y catedrales de los reynos de los dos Castillas.* 2 vols. Madrid: Pedro de Hornay Villanueva, 1647.

Gregoria Francisca (de Santa Teresa) de la Parra Queinoge. *Poesías de la Venerable*

Madre Gregoria Francisca de Santa Teresa Carmelita Descalza en el convento de Sevilla. Paris: Librería de Garnier Hermanos, 1865.

Heywood, Thomas. *Exemplary Lives and Memorable Acts of Nine the Most Worthy Women of the World: Three Jewes, Three Gentiles, Three Christian*. London: Richard Royston, 1640.

Juan de Mariana, "Tratado contra los juegos publicos." In his *Obras*, vol. 30 in *Biblioteca de Autores Españoles*, pp. 413–62. Madrid: M. Rivadeneyra, 1855.

Las Siete Partidas. Edited by Samuel Parsons Scott. Chicago, New York, and Washington: Commerce Clearing House, 1931.

López, Gregorio. *Tesoro de medicinas para diversas enfermedades*. Madrid: Imprenta de Música, 1708.

Luis de León, fray. *La perfecta casada*. 1583. In *Biblioteca de Autores Españoles*, 37: 211–46. Madrid: M. Rivadeneyra, 1855.

Magdalena de San Jerónimo, madre. *Razón, y forma de la galera y casa Real, que el Rey nuestro señor manda hazer en estos Reynos, para castigo de las mugeres vagrantes, ladronas, alcahuetas y otras semejantes*. Valladolid: Francisco Fernández de Córdova, 1608.

Martín de Córdoba, fray. *Jardín de nobles donzellas*. Edited by Harriet Goldberg. University of North Carolina (Chapel Hill Campus) Studies in the Romance Languages and Literatures, no. 137. Chapel Hill: University of North Carolina Department of Romance Languages, 1974.

Martínez de Mata, Francisco. *Memoriales y discursos de Francisco Martínez de Mata*. Edited by Gonzalo Anes Alvarez. Madrid: Moneda y Crédito, 1971.

Mercado, Thomas de. *Summa de tratos y contratos*. Seville: Hernando Diaz, 1571.

Mexía, fray Vicente. *Saludable instrucción del estado de matrimonio*. Córdoba: Juan Baptista Escudero, 1566.

Morgado, Alonso. *Historia de Sevilla*. Seville: Andrea Pescioni y Juan de León, 1587.

Navagero, Andres. *Viaje a España*. Translated by José María Alonso Gamo. Valencia: Editorial Castalia, 1951.

Ortiz de Zuñiga, Diego. *Anales eclesiásticos y seculares de la muy noble y muy leal ciudad de Sevilla*. 1677. 5 vols. Madrid: Imprenta Real, 1796.

Osuna, Francisco de. *Tercer abecedario espiritual*. 1527. In *Nueva Biblioteca de Autores Españoles*, 16: 319–587. *Escritores místicos españoles*. Madrid: Librería Editorial de Bailly, 1911.

Pacheco, Francisco. *Arte de la pintura*. Seville: Simon Faxardo, 1649.

———. *Libro de descripción de verdaderos retratos, de ilustres y memorables varones*. Seville: Ayuntamiento, 1599.

Padilla, Luisa de. "Elogios de la verdad e invectiva contra la mentira." 1640. In *Biblioteca de Autores Españoles*, 270: 107–13. Madrid: Atlas, 1975.

Pedro de León. *Compendio de algunas experiencias en los ministerios de que vsa la Comp^a de IESVS con q practicamente se muestra con algunos acaecimientos y documentos el buen acierto en ellos*. Granada: n.p., 1619.

Pérez de Herrera, Cristóbal. *Amparo de pobres*. 1598. Madrid: Espasa-Calpe, 1975.

———. *Discurso de la reclusión y castigo de las mugeres vagabundas y delinquentes destos reynos*. Madrid: Luis Sánchez, 1608.

Pérez de Valdivia, Diego. *Aviso de gente recogida.* 1585. Madrid: Universidad Pontífica de Salamanca y Fundación Universitaria Española, 1977.

Quevedo Villegas, Francisco de. *Historia de la vida del Buscón.* Zaragoza, 1626. Reprinted in *Novela picaresca: Textos escogidos.* Madrid: Taurus, 1962. Translated by Michael Alpert as *The Swindler,* in *Two Spanish Picaresque Novels.* Harmondsworth, Middlesex: Penguin, 1981.

Sabuco de Nantes Barrera, Oliva. "Coloquio del conocimiento de sí mismo." 1587. In *Biblioteca de Autores Españoles,* 65: 332–72. Madrid: Librería de los Sucesores de Hernando, 1922.

Salazar, Pedro de. *Crónica y historia de la fundación y progreso de la provincia de Castilla, de la Orden del diaventurado padre San Francisco.* Madrid: Imprenta Real, 1612.

Sigüenza, José de. *Historia de la órden de San Jerónimo.* 1464. Madrid: Bailly, Bailliére é Hijos, 1907.

Sorapan de Rieros, Dr. Juan. *Medicina española contenida en proverbios vulgares de nuestra lengua.* Vol. 16 of *Biblioteca clásica de la medicina española.* Madrid: Real Academia Nacional de Medicina, 1949.

Soto, Juan de. *Obligaciones de todos los estados, y oficios, con los remedios, y consejos mas eficaces para la salud espiritual, y general reformación de las costumbres.* Alcalá: Andres Sánchez de Ezpleta, 1619.

Teresa of Jesus. *The Complete Works of Saint Teresa of Jesus.* 3 vols. Translated by E. A. Peers. London and New York: Sheed and Ward, 1957.

———. *The Letters of Saint Teresa.* Translated and edited by E. Allison Peers. London: Burns, Oates and Washbourne, 1951.

———. *The Life of St. Teresa of Avila, Including the Relations of Her Spiritual State.* Translated by David Lewis. Westminster, Md.: Newman Press, 1962.

Vives, Juan Luis. *Del socorro de los pobres, o de las necesidades humanes.* 1526. Madrid: Sucesores de Hernando, 1922.

———. *Libro llamado instrucción de la mujer cristiana.* 1524. Translated by Juan Justiniano. Madrid: Signo, 1936.

———. *A Very Frvtfvl and pleasant boke called the Instruction of a christen woman, made fyrst in latyne, by the right famous clerk mayster, Lewes Vives, and tourned out of latyne into Englishe by Richard Hyrde.* London: Thomas Berthe, 1547.

Zayas y Sotomayor, María de. *Desengaños amorosos.* Edited by Alicia Yllera. Madrid: Ediciones Cátedra, 1983.

———. *Novelas amorosas y exemplares* Zaragoza: Hospital Real de Nuestra Señora de Gracia, 1637.

———. *Parte segunda del Sarao y entretenimiento honesto.* Zaragoza: Hospital Real y General de Nuestra Señora de Gracia, 1647.

BOOKS

Alvarez Miranda, Vicente. *Glorias de Sevilla: En armas, letras, ciencias, artes, tradiciones, monumentos, edificios, carácteres, costumbres, estilos, fiestas y espectáculos.* Seville: Carlos Santigosa, 1849.

Alvarez Santaló, León Carlos. *Marginación social y mentalidad en Andalucía occiden-*

tal: Expósitos en Sevilla (1613–1910). Seville: Consejería de Cultura de la Junta de Andalucía, 1980.

Anderson, Perry. *Lineages of the Absolutist State*. New York: Schocken, 1979.

Andrés Martín, Melquiades. *Los recogidos: Nueva visión de la mística española (1500–1700)*. Madrid: Fundación Universitaria Española, 1975.

Arana de Varflora, Fermin. *Hijos de Sevilla ilustres en santidad, letras, armas, artes, o dignidad*. Seville: Vázquez é Hidalgo, 1791.

Ariés, Philippe, and André Béjin, eds. *Western Sexuality: Practice and Precept in Past and Present Times*. Translated by Anthony Forster. Oxford and New York: Basil Blackwell, 1985.

Ashe, Geoffrey. *The Virgin*. London: Routledge and Kegan Paul, 1976.

Astrain, Antonio. *Historia de la Compañía de Jesús en la asistencia de España*. Madrid: Administración de Razón y Fe, 1912.

Baker, Derek, ed. *Schism, Heresy, and Religious Protest*. Vol. 9 of *Studies in Church History*. Cambridge: Cambridge University Press, 1972.

Ballesteros, Antonio. *Sevilla en el siglo XIII*. Madrid: Juan Pérez Torres, 1913.

Bataillon, Marcel. *Erasmo y España: Estudios sobre la historia espiritual del siglo XVI*. 2 vols. Mexico and Buenos Aires: Fondo de Cultura Economica, 1950.

Becker, Howard S. *Outsiders: Studies in the Sociology of Deviance*. New York and London: The Free Press, 1963.

Bell, Rudolph M. *Holy Anorexia*. Chicago and London: University of Chicago Press, 1985.

Bennassar, Bartolomé, et al. *L'Inquisition espagnole XVe–XIXe siècle*. Paris: Hachette, 1979.

Bermejo y Carballo, José. *Glorias religiosas de Sevilla o noticia histórico-descriptiva de todas las cofradías de penitencia, sangre y luz fundadas en esta ciudad*. Seville: Salvador, 1882.

Bernstein, Marcelle. *Nuns*. London: Collins, 1976.

Bilinkoff, Jodi. *The Avila of Saint Teresa: Religious Reform in a Sixteenth-Century City*. Ithaca: Cornell University Press, 1989.

Blanco Freijeiro, Antonio. *La ciudad antigua de la prehistoria a los visigodos*. Vol. 1 of *Historia de Sevilla*. Seville: Universidad de Sevilla, 1979.

Boccaccio, Giovanni. *Concerning Famous Women*. London: George Allen and Unwin, 1964.

Bossy, John, ed. *Disputes and Settlements: Law and Human Relations in the West*. Cambridge and New York: Cambridge University Press, 1983.

Bravo-Villasante, Carmen. *La mujer vestida de hombre en el teatro español (siglos XVI–XVII)*. Madrid: Sociedad General Española de Librería, 1976.

Bridenthal, Renate, and Claudia Koonz, eds. *Becoming Visible: Women in European History*. Boston: Houghton-Mifflin, 1977.

Brown, Jonathan. *Images and Ideas in Seventeenth-Century Spanish Painting*. Princeton: Princeton University Press, 1978.

Caffarena, Angel. *Apuntes para la historia de las mancebías de Málaga*. Málaga: Juan Such, 1968.

Callahan, William J. *La Santa y Real Hermandad del Refugio y Piedad de Madrid, 1618–1832*. Madrid: Consejo Superior de Investigaciones Científicas, 1980.

Cano Navas, María Luisa. *El Convento de San José del Carmen de Sevilla. Las Teresas. Estudio histórico-artístico.* Seville: Universidad de Sevilla, 1984.

Carboneres, Manuel. *Picaronas y alcahuetes, o la mancebía de Valencia.* Valencia: El Mercantil, 1876.

Carmona García, Juan Ignacio. *El sistema de hospitalidad pública en la Sevilla del Antiguo Régimen.* Seville: Diputación Provincial de Sevilla, 1979.

Caro Baroja, Julio. *Las formas complejas de la vida religiosa: Religión, sociedad y carácter en la España de los siglos XVI y XVII.* Madrid: Akal, 1978.

Castresana, Luis de. *Catalina de Erauso: La monja alférez.* Madrid: Afrodisio Aguado, 1968.

Christ, Carol. *Diving Deep and Surfacing: Women Writers on Spiritual Quest.* Boston: Beacon, 1980.

Christian, William A., Jr. *Apparitions in Late Medieval and Renaissance Spain.* Princeton: Princeton University Press, 1981.

———. *Local Religion in Sixteenth-Century Spain.* Princeton: Princeton University Press, 1981.

Cobos de Villalobos, Amantina. *Mujeres célebres sevillanas.* Seville: F. Díaz, 1917.

Cohn, Norman. *The Pursuit of the Millennium: Revolutionary Messianism in Medieval and Reformation Europe and Its Bearing on Modern Totalitarian Movements.* New York: Harper Torchbooks, 1961.

Collantes de Teran, Francisco. *Los establecimientos de caridad de Sevilla, que se consideran como particulares: Apuntes y memorias para su historia.* Seville: El Orden, 1886.

Colon y Colom, Juan. *Sevilla artística.* Seville: Francisco Alvarez y Compañía, 1841.

Contreras, Jaime. *El Santo Oficio de la Inquisición de Galicia: Poder, sociedad y cultura.* Madrid: Akal, 1982.

Davis, Natalie Zemon. *Fiction in the Archives: Pardon Tales and Their Tellers in Sixteenth-Century France.* Stanford: Stanford University Press, 1987.

———. *The Return of Martin Guerre.* Cambridge, Mass. and London: Harvard University Press, 1983.

———. *Society and Culture in Early Modern France.* Stanford: Stanford University Press, 1977.

Deleito y Piñuela, José. *La vida religiosa española bajo el quarto Felipe: Santos y pecadores.* Madrid: Espasa-Calpe, 1952.

Dickens, A. G. *The Counter-Reformation.* London: Thames and Hudson, 1968.

Domínguez Guzmán, Aurora. *El libro sevillano durante la primera mitad del siglo XVI.* Seville: Diputación Provincial de Sevilla, 1975.

Domínguez Ortiz, Antonio. *El Barroco y la Ilustración.* Vol. 4 of *Historia de Sevilla.* Seville: Diputación Provincial de Sevilla, 1976.

———. *The Golden Age of Spain 1516–1659.* Translated by James Casey. London: Weidenfeld and Nicolson, 1971.

———. *Orto y ocaso de Sevilla: Estudio sobre la prosperidad y decadencia de la ciudad durante los siglos XVI y XVII.* Seville: Diputación Provincial de Sevilla, 1946.

———. *El estamento eclesiástico.* Vol. 2 of *La sociedad española en el siglo XVII.* Madrid: Consejo Superior de Investigaciones Científicas, 1970.

———. *Sociedad y mentalidad en la Sevilla del Antiguo Régimen*. Seville: Ayuntamiento, 1979.

Donahue, Darcy, ed. *Social Bodies, Spiritual Selves: Women and Religion in Early Modern Spain*. Forthcoming.

Douglas, Mary. *Natural Symbols: Explorations in Cosmology*. London: Cresset Press, 1970.

———. *Purity and Danger: An Analysis of Concepts of Pollution and Taboo*. New York and Washington: Frederick A. Praeger, 1966.

Durán, María Angeles, ed. *La mujer en la historia de España (siglos XVI–XX)*. Actas de las Segundas Jornadas de Investigación Interdisciplinaria. Madrid: Universidad Autónoma, 1984.

———. *Las mujeres medievales y su ámbito jurídico*. Actas de las Segundas Jornadas de Investigación Interdisciplinaria. Madrid: Universidad Autónoma, 1983.

———. *Nuevas perspectivas sobre la mujer*. Actas de las Primeras Jornadas de Investigación Interdisciplinaria. 2 vols. Madrid: Universidad Autónoma, 1982.

Eckenstein, Lina. *Women under Monasticism: Chapters on Saint-lore and Convent Life between A.D. 500 and A.D. 1500*. New York: Russell and Russell, 1963.

Erikson, Kai T. *Wayward Puritans: A Study of the Sociology of Deviance*. New York: John Wiley & Sons, 1966.

Fairchilds, Cissie. *Domestic Enemies: Servants and Their Masters in Old Regime France*. Baltimore: Johns Hopkins University Press, 1984.

Febvre, Lucien. *A New Kind of History and Other Essays*. Edited by Peter Burke. Translated by K. Folca. New York: Harper & Row, 1973.

Ferrer, Joaquin María de. *Historia de la monja alférez, doña Catalina de Erauso, escrita por ella misma*. 1625. Paris: Julio Didot, 1829.

Fisher, Sheila, and Janet E. Halley, eds. *Seeking the Woman in Late Medieval and Renaissance Writings: Essays in Feminist Contextual Criticism*. Knoxville: University of Tennessee Press, 1989.

Flandrin, Jean-Louis. *Families in Former Times: Kinship, Household and Sexuality*. Translated by Richard Southern. Cambridge: Cambridge University Press, 1985.

Flors, Juan, ed. *Corrientes espirituales de la España del siglo XVI*. Barcelona: Universidad Pontificia de Salamanca, 1963.

Forcione, Alban. *Cervantes and the Humanist Vision: A Study of Four Exemplary Novels*. Princeton: Princeton University Press, 1982.

Foucault, Michel. *Discipline and Punish: The Birth of the Prison*. Translated by Alan Sheridan. New York: Pantheon, 1977.

———. *The History of Sexuality: An Introduction*. Vol. 1 of *The History of Sexuality*. Translated by Robert Hurley. New York: Pantheon, 1978.

———. *Language, Counter-Memory, Practice*. Edited by Donald F. Bouchard. Ithaca: Cornell University Press, 1980.

———. *The Use of Pleasure*. Vol. 2 of *The History of Sexuality*. Translated by Robert Hurley. New York: Pantheon, 1985.

Gallichan, Walter M. *The Story of Seville*. London: J. M. Dent, 1903.

García Ballester, Luis. *Los moriscos y la medicina: Un capítulo de la medicina y la ciencia marginadas en la España del siglo XVI*. Barcelona: Editorial Labor, 1984.

García-Baquero López, Gregorio. *Estudio demográfico de la parroquia de San Martín de Sevilla (1551–1749)*. Seville: Diputación Provincial de Sevilla, 1982.

García Cárcel, Ricardo. *Herejía y sociedad en el siglo XVI: La inquisición en Valencia 1530–1609*. Barcelona: Ediciones Península, 1980.

———. *Orígines de la inquisición española: El tribunal de Valencia, 1478–1500*. Barcelona: Ediciones Peninsulas, 1976.

García-Nieto París, María Carmen, ed. *Ordenamiento jurídico y realidad social de las mujeres*. Actas de las Cuartas Jornadas de Investigación Interdisciplinaria. Madrid: Universidad Autónoma, 1986.

García Olloqui, María Victoria. *La Roldana: Escultora de Cámara*. Seville: Diputación Provincial de Sevilla, 1977.

Garfinkel, Harold. *Studies in Ethnomethodology*. Englewood Cliffs, N.J.: Prentice-Hall, 1967.

Geertz, Clifford. *The Interpretation of Cultures*. New York: Basic Books, 1973.

Gestoso y Pérez, José. *Sevilla monumental y artística: Historia y descripción de todos los edificios notables, religiosos y civiles, que existen actualmente en esta ciudad y noticia de las preciosidades artísticas y arqueológicas que en ella se conservan*. 3 vols. Seville: La Andalucía Moderna, 1889–1892.

Ginzburg, Carlo. *The Cheese and the Worms: The Cosmos of a Sixteenth-Century Miller*. Translated by John and Anne Tedeschi. New York: Penguin, 1980.

———. *Nightbattles: Witchcraft and Agrarian Cults in the Sixteenth and Seventeenth Centuries*. Translated by John and Anne Tedeschi. New York: Penguin, 1985.

Goffman, Erving. *Interaction Ritual: Essays on Face-to-Face Behavior*. Garden City, N.Y.: Doubleday, 1967.

González, Tomás, ed. *Censo de población de las provincias y partidos de la corona de Castilla en el siglo XVI, con varios apéndices para completar la del resto de la peninsula en el mismo siglo, y formar juicio comparativo con la del anterior y siguiente, según resulta de los libros y registros que se custodian en el Real Archivo de Simancas*. Madrid: Imprenta Real, 1829.

Gove, Walter R., ed. *The Labelling of Deviance: Evaluating a Perspective*. Beverly Hills: Sage, 1980.

Gramsci, Antonio. *Selections from the Prison Notebooks of Antonio Gramsci*. Translated by and edited by Quentin Hoare and Geoffrey Nowell Smith. New York: International Publishers, 1972.

Granero, P. Jesús María. *Don Miguel Mañara*. Seville: Artes Gráficas Salesianas, 1963.

Granjel, Luis S. *La medicina española del siglo XVII*. Salamanca: Ediciones Universidad de Salamanca, 1978.

———. *La medicina española renacentista*. Salamanca: Ediciones Universidad de Salamanca, 1980.

Grice-Hutchinson, Marjorie. *Early Economic Thought in Spain, 1177–1740*. London: Allen and Unwin, 1978.

Griffin, Susan. *Pornography and Silence*. New York: Harper and Row, 1981.

Guichot y Parody, Joaquin. *Historia del Exmo. Ayuntamiento de la muy noble, muy leal, muy heróica é invicta ciudad de Sevilla*. Vols. 1 and 2. Seville: Tipografía de la Región, 1896.

Gutiérrez, Ioannis. *Praxis criminalis civilis et canonica in librum octanum nouae Recopilationis Regiae*. Lyons: Sumptibus Lavrentii Anisson, 1660.

Haliczer, Stephen, ed. *Inquisition and Society in Early Modern Europe*. London: Croom Helm, 1986.

Harris, Barbara J., and JoAnn K. McNamara, eds. *Women and the Structure of Society: Selected Research from the Fifth Berkshire Conference on the History of Women*. Durham, N.C.: Duke University Press, 1984.

Henningsen, Gustav. *The Witches' Advocate: Basque Witchcraft and the Spanish Inquisition*. Reno: University of Nevada Press, 1980.

Henningsen, Gustav, and John Tedeschi, eds. *The Inquisition in Early Modern Europe: Studies in Sources and Methods*. DeKalb: Northern Illinois University Press, 1984.

Hepworth, Mike, and Bryan S. Turner. *Confession: Studies of Deviance and Religion*. London: Routledge & Kegan Paul, 1982.

Herrera Puga, Pedro. *Sociedad y delincuencia en el Siglo de Oro*. Madrid: Biblioteca de Autores Cristianos, 1974.

Himmelfarb, Gertrude. *The Idea of Poverty: England in the Early Industrial Age*. New York: Alfred A. Knopf, 1984.

Huerga, Alvaro. *Predicadores, alumbrados e inquisición*. Madrid: Fundación Universitaria Española, 1973.

Hufton, Olwen. *The Poor of Eighteenth-Century France, 1750–1789*. Oxford: Oxford University Press, 1974.

Imirizaldu, Jesús. *Monjas y beatas embaucadoras*. Madrid: Editorial Nacional, 1977.

James, Jennifer, et al. *The Politics of Prostitution*. Seattle: Social Research Associates, 1977.

Janes, Clara, ed. *Las primeras poetisas en lengua castellana*. Madrid: Editorial Ayuso, 1986.

Justiniano y Martínez, Manuel. *El Hospital de las Cinco Llagas (Central) de Sevilla*. Seville: Crónica Oficial de la Provincia, 1963.

Kamen, Henry. *Inquisition and Society in Spain*. Bloomington: Indiana University Press, 1985.

Kaplan, Steve, ed. *Understanding Popular Culture: Europe from the Middle Ages to the Nineteenth Century*. New York and Berlin: Mouton, 1984.

Kubler, George, and Martin Soria. *Art and Architecture in Spain and Portugal and Their American Dominions 1500–1800*. Harmondsworth, Middlesex: Penguin, 1959.

Kuhn, Annette. *Women's Pictures: Feminism and Cinema*. Boston: Routledge and Kegan Paul, 1982.

Labalme, Patricia H., ed. *Beyond Their Sex: Learned Women of the European Past*. New York and London: New York University Press, 1980.

Lea, Henry Charles. *Chapters from the Religious History of Spain Connected with the Inquisition*. Philadelphia: Lea Brothers & Co., 1890.

———. *A History of the Inquisition of Spain*. 4 vols. New York and London: Macmillan, 1922.

Leistikow, Dankwart. *Ten Centuries of European Hospital Architecture*. Ingelheim am Rhein: C. H. Boehringer Sohn, 1967.

Lemert, Edwin M. *Human Deviance, Social Problems and Social Control.* Englewood Cliffs, N.J.: Prentice-Hall, 1967.

Lerner, Gerda. *The Creation of Patriarchy.* New York: Oxford University Press, 1986.

Licata, Salvatore J., and Robert P. Petersen, eds. *Historical Perspectives on Homosexuality.* Vol. 2 of monograph series, *Research on Homosexuality.* New York: Haworth Press; Stein and Day, 1981.

Lisón Tolosana, Carmelo. *Invitación a la antropología cultural de España.* Madrid: Editorial Adara, 1977.

———, ed. *Temas de antropología española.* Madrid: Akal, 1976.

Llamas Martínez, Enrique. *Santa Teresa de Jesús y la Inquisición española.* Madrid: Consejo Superior de Investigaciones Científicas, 1972.

Lleó Cañal, Vicente. *Nueva Roma: Mitología y humanismo en el renacimiento sevillano.* Seville: Diputación Provincial de Sevilla, 1979.

Llorden, P. Andrés, O.S.A. *Apuntes históricos de los conventos sevillanos de religiosas agustinas.* Escorial: Imprenta del Monasterio, 1944.

Llorente, Juan Antonio. *A Critical History of the Inquisition of Spain.* Williamstown, Mass.: John Lilburne Co., 1967.

López Martínez, Celestino. *Mudéjares y moriscos sevillanos.* Seville: Tipografía Rodriguez, Giménez y Compañía, 1935.

———. *Teatros y comediantes sevillanos del siglo XVI.* Seville: Diputación Provincial de Sevilla, 1940.

McDonnell, Ernest W. *The Beguines and Beghards in Medieval Culture.* New Brunswick, N.J.: Rutgers University Press, 1954.

Macfarlane, Alan. *Witchcraft in Tudor and Stuart England.* New York: Harper and Row, 1970.

McKendrick, Melveena. *Woman and Society in the Spanish Drama of the Golden Age: A Study of the Mujer Varonil.* London: Cambridge University Press, 1974.

Maravall, José Antonio. *Estudios de historia del pensamiento español.* 3 vols. Madrid: Cultura Hispánica, 1983.

Márquez, Antonio. *Los Alumbrados, orígines y filosofía, 1525–1559.* Madrid: Taurus, 1972.

Martín Hernández, Francisco. *Miguel Mañara.* Seville: Universidad de Sevilla, 1981.

Martz, Linda. *Poverty and Welfare in Habsburg Spain: The Example of Toledo.* Cambridge: Cambridge University Press, 1983.

Mata Carriazo, Juan de. *Protohistoria de Sevilla en el vértice de Tartesos.* Seville: Guadalquivir Ediciones, 1980.

Matilla, María Jesús, and Margarita Ortega, eds. *El trabajo de las mujeres: Siglos XVI–XX.* Actas de las Sextas Jornadas de Investigación Interdisciplinaria sobre la Mujer. Madrid: Universidad Autónoma, 1987.

Matute y Gaviria, Justino. *Hijos de Sevilla.* 2 vols. Seville: El Orden, 1886–1889.

Mauss, Marcel. *The Gift: Forms and Functions of Exchange in Archaic Societies.* Translated by I. Cunnison. London: Cohen and West, 1966.

Menéndez y Pelayo, Marcelino. *Historia de los heterodoxos españoles.* 2 vols. Madrid: Biblioteca de Autores Cristianos, 1956.

Merchant, Carolyn. *The Death of Nature: Women, Ecology and the Scientific Revolution*. San Francisco: Harper and Row, 1980.

Merton, Robert, and Robert Nisbet, eds. *Contemporary Social Problems*. New York: Harcourt Brace, 1961.

Miguel Serrera, Juan, and Enrique Valdivieso González. *La época de Murillo: Antecedentes y consecuentes de su pintura*. Seville: Diputaciones, 1982.

Miller, Beth, ed. *Women in Hispanic Literature*. Berkeley and Los Angeles: University of California Press, 1983.

Monter, E. W. *Frontiers of Heresy: The Spanish Inquisition from the Basque Lands to Sicily*. Cambridge and New York: Cambridge University Press, 1990.

Morales, Juan Luis. *El niño en la cultura española*. Madrid: Talleres Penitenciarios de Alcalá de Henares, 1960.

Morell Peguero, Blanca. *Contribución etnográfica del Archivo de Protocolos*. Seville: Universidad de Sevilla, 1981.

——. *Mercaderes y artesanos en la Sevilla del descubrimiento*. Seville: Diputación Provincial de Sevilla, 1986.

Murphy, Yolanda, and Robert F. Murphy. *Women of the Forest*. New York: Columbia University Press, 1974.

Ortner, Sherry B., and Harriet Whitehead, eds. *Sexual Meanings: The Cultural Construction of Gender and Sexuality*. Cambridge: Cambridge University Press, 1981.

Ozment, Steven. *The Age of Reform, 1250–1550: An Intellectual and Religious History of Late Medieval and Reformation Europe*. New Haven: Yale University Press, 1980.

Parker, Alexander A. *The Philosophy of Love in Spanish Literature, 1480–1680*. Edited by Terence O'Reilly. Edinburgh: Edinburgh University Press, 1985.

Parker, Jack H. *Juan Pérez de Montalván*. Boston: Twayne, 1975.

Payne, Stanley. *Spanish Catholicism: An Historical Overview*. Madison: University of Wisconsin Press, 1984.

Pérez Baltasar, María Dolores. *Mujeres marginadas: Las casas de recogidas en Madrid*. Madrid: Gráficas Lormo, 1984.

Pérez Villanueva, Joaquin, ed. *La inquisición española: Nueva visión, nuevos horizontes*. Madrid: Siglo Veintiuno de España, 1980.

Perry, Mary Elizabeth. *Crime and Society in Early Modern Seville*. Hanover and London: University Press of New England, 1980.

Perry, Mary Elizabeth, and Anne J. Cruz, eds. *Cultural Encounters: The Impact of the Inquisition in Spain and the New World*. Berkeley and Los Angeles: University Press of California, 1991.

Petroff, Elizabeth A. *Medieval Women's Visionary Literature*. New York and Oxford: Oxford University Press, 1986.

Phillips, Dayton. *Beguines in Medieval Strasburg: A Study of the Social Aspect of Beguine Life*. Stanford: Stanford University Press, 1941.

Pike, Ruth. *Aristocrats and Traders: Sevillian Society in the Sixteenth Century*. Ithaca: Cornell University Press, 1972.

Pilar Onate, María del. *El feminismo en la literatura española*. Madrid: Espasa-Calpe, 1938.

Pinero Ramírez, Pedro M. *La Sevilla imposible de Santa Teresa.* Seville: Ayuntamiento de Sevilla, 1982.

Pitt-Rivers, Julian. *The Fate of Shechem, or the Politics of Sex: Essays in the Anthropology of the Mediterranean.* Cambridge: Cambridge University Press, 1977.

———. *The People of the Sierra.* Chicago: University of Chicago Press, 1971.

Pullen, Brian. *Rich and Poor in Renaissance Venice: The Social Institutions of a Catholic State, to 1620.* Cambridge: Harvard University Press, 1971.

Rahner, Hugo, S.J. *Saint Ignatius Loyola Letters to Women.* Edinburgh and London: Nelson, 1960.

Redondo, Augustin, ed. *Amours légitimes, amours illégitimes en Espagne (XVIe–XVIIe siècles).* Paris: Publications de la Sorbonne, 1985.

Rico-Avello, Carlos. *Vida y milagros de un pícaro médico del siglo XVI: Biografia del bachiller Juan Méndez Nieto.* Madrid: Cultura Hispánica, 1974.

Rodríguez Solís, Enrique. *Historia de la prostitución en España y América.* Madrid: Biblioteca Nueva, 1921.

Rosaldo, Michelle Zimbalist, and Louise Lamphere, eds. *Woman, Culture and Society.* Stanford: Stanford University Press, 1974.

Rose, Mary Beth, ed. *Women in the Middle Ages and the Renaissance: Literary and Historical Perspectives.* Syracuse: Syracuse University Press, 1986.

Ruether, Rosemary, and Eleanor McLaughlin, eds. *Women of Spirit: Female Leadership in the Jewish and Christian Traditions.* New York: Simon and Schuster, 1979.

Russell, Jeffrey B. *Dissent and Reform in the Early Middle Ages.* Berkeley and Los Angeles: University of California Press, 1965.

Scudder, Vida Dutton. *The Franciscan Adventure: A Study in the First Hundred Years of the Order of St. Francis of Assisi.* London, Toronto, and New York: J. M. Dent and Sons, 1931.

Segura Graiño, Cristina, ed. *Las mujeres en las ciudades medievales.* Actas de las Terceras Jornadas de Investigación Interdisciplinaria. Madrid: Universidad Autónoma de Madrid, 1984.

Selke, Angela. *El Santo Oficio de la Inquisición: Proceso de fr. Francisco Ortiz (1529–1532).* Madrid: Ediciones Guadarrama, 1968.

Serrano y Sanz, Manuel. *Apuntes para una biblioteca de escritoras españolas desde el año 1401 al 1833.* Vols. 268, 269, 270, 271 of *Biblioteca de Autores Españoles.* Madrid: Atlas, 1975.

Shepherd, Simon. *Amazons and Warrior Women: Varieties of Feminism in Seventeenth-Century Drama.* Brighton: Harvester, 1981.

Showalter, Elaine, ed. *The New Feminist Criticism: Women, Literature and Theory.* New York: Pantheon, 1985.

Southern, R. W. *Western Society and the Church in the Middle Ages.* Harmondsworth, Middlesex: Penguin, 1970.

Spierenburg, Pieter, ed. *The Emergence of Carceral Institutions: Prisons, Galleys and Lunatic Asylums, 1550–1900.* Rotterdam: Erasmus University, 1984.

Stone, Lawrence. *The Family, Sex and Marriage in England 1500–1800.* New York: Harper, 1979.

Sylvania, Lena E. V. *Doña María de Zayas y Sotomayor: A Contribution to the Study of Her Works.* New York: Columbia University Press, 1922.

Tilly, Charles, ed. *The Formation of National States in Western Europe.* Princeton: Princeton University Press, 1975.

Torres Villaroel, Diego. *Vida exemplar, virtudes heróicas, y singulares recibos de la V. Madre Gregoria Francisca de Santa Theresa.* Salamanca: Antonio Villarroel y Torres, ca. 1738.

Trens, Manuel. *María: Iconografía de la virgen en el arte español.* Madrid: Editorial Plus Ultra, 1946.

Tubino, Francisco M. *Pedro de Castilla: La leyenda de doña María Coronel y la muerte de d. Fadrique.* Madrid: Principales Librerías, 1887.

Turner, Victor. *From Ritual to Theatre: The Human Seriousness of Play.* New York: Performing Arts Journal Publications, 1982.

——. *The Ritual Process. Structure and Anti-Structure.* Ithaca: Cornell University Press, 1969.

Ullersperger, J. B. *La historia de la psicología y de la psiquiatría en España: Desde los más remotos tiempos hasta la actualidad.* Madrid: Editorial Alhambra, 1954.

Valdevieso, E., and J. M. Serrera. *El Hospital de la Caridad de Sevilla.* Seville: Editorial Sever-Cuesta, 1980.

Velázquez y Sánchez, José. *Anales epidémicos: Reseña histórica de las enfermedades contagiosas en Sevilla desde la reconquista cristiana hasta de presente.* Seville: José María Geofin, 1866.

Vigil, Mariló. *La vida de las mujeres en los siglos XVI y XVII.* Madrid: Siglo XXI, 1986.

Viñas Mey, Carmelo. *El problema de la tierra en la España de los siglos XVI y XVII.* Madrid: Consejo Superior de Investigaciones Científicas, 1941.

Warner, Marina. *Alone of all Her Sex: The Myth and the Cult of the Virgin Mary.* New York: Vintage, 1983.

Weber, Max. *Sociology of Religion.* Translated by Ephraim Fischoff. Boston: Beacon, 1963.

Wilkinson, Catherine. *The Hospital of Cardinal Tavera in Toledo: A Documentary and Stylistic Study of Spanish Architecture in the Mid-Sixteenth Century.* New York: Garland Publishing, 1977.

ARTICLES AND ESSAYS

Abad, Camilo Mª, S.I. "Gil González Dávila, S.I., Sus Pláticas sobre las reglas de la Compañía de Jesús." In Flors, *Corrientes espirituales,* pp. 363–91.

Alvarez Santaló, León Carlos. "La Casa de Expósitos de Sevilla en el Siglo XVII." *Cuadernos de Historia* 7 (1977): 491–532.

Arenal, Electa. "The Convent as Catalyst for Autonomy: Two Hispanic Nuns of the Seventeenth Century." In Miller, *Women in Hispanic Literature,* pp. 147–83.

Ariés, Philippe. "The Indissoluble Marriage." In Ariés and Béjin, *Western Sexuality,* pp. 140–57.

Bilinkoff, Jodi. "Charisma and Controversy: The Case of María de Santo Domingo." Paper delivered to the Society for Spanish and Historical Studies, Vanderbilt University, 1988.

Bilinkoff, Jodi. "The Holy Woman and the Urban Community in Sixteenth-Century Avila." In Harris and McNamara, *Women and the Structure of Society*, pp. 74–80.

Borrero Fernández, Mercedes. "El trabajo de la mujer en el mundo rural sevillano durante la baja edad media." In Durán, *Las mujeres medievales*, pp. 191–99.

Bossy, John. "The Counter-Reformation and the People of Catholic Europe." *Past and Present* 47 (1970): 51–70.

Bravo Lozano, Jesús. "Fuentes para el estudio del trabajo femenino en la edad moderna: El caso de Madrid a fines del siglo XVII." In Matilla and Ortega, *El trabajo de las mujeres*, pp. 21–32.

Caro Petit, Carlos. "La Cárcel Real de Sevilla." *Archivo Hispalense*, ser. 2, 11 (1945): 317–48; 12 (1945): 39–85.

Casey, James. "Household Disputes and the Law in Early Modern Andalusia." In Bossy, *Disputes and Settlements*, pp. 189–217.

Chill, Emanuel. "Religion and Mendicity in Seventeenth-Century France." *International Review of Social History* 7 (1962): 400–425.

Christian, William A., Jr. "De los Santos a María: Panorama de las devociones a santuarios españoles desde el principio de la Edad Media hasta nuestros días." In Lisón Tolosana, *Temas de antropología española*, pp. 49–106.

Collantes de Teran, Francisco. "Testamento de la muy ilustre señora doña Catalina de Ribera, fundadora del Hospital de Las Cinco Llagas, vulgo de la Sangre, de Sevilla." *Archivo Hispalense* 3 (1887): 51–66.

Crompton, Louis. "The Myth of Lesbian Impunity: Capital Laws from 1270 to 1791." In Licata and Petersen, *Historical Perspectives*, pp. 11–25.

Cruz, Anne J. "Sexual Enclosure, Textual Escape: The Pícara as Prostitute in the Spanish Picaresque Novel." In Fisher and Halley, *Seeking the Woman*, pp. 135–59.

Davis, Kingsley. "The Sociology of Prostitution." *American Sociological Review* 2 (1937): 744–55.

Davis, Natalie Zemon. "Beyond the Market: Books as Gifts in Sixteenth-Century France." *Transactions of the Royal Historical Society*, 5th ser., 33 (1983): 69–88.

———. "Women's History in Transition: The European Case." *Feminist Studies* 3, nos. 3–4 (1976): 83–103.

Dedieu, Jean-Pierre. "Le modèle sexuel: La défense du mariage chrétien." In Bennassar et al., *L'Inquisition espagnole*, pp. 313–38.

"Documentos relativos a la mancebía." *Archivo Hispalense*, 1st ser., 3 (1887): 16–18.

Domínguez Ortiz, Antonio. "La Congregación de la Granada y la Inquisición de Sevilla (un episodio de la lucha contra los alumbrados)." In Pérez Villanueva, *La inquisición española*, pp. 636–46.

———. "La mujer en el tránsito de la edad media a la moderna." In Segura Graiño, *Las mujeres*, pp. 171–78.

———. "Vida y obras del Padre Pedro de León." *Archivo Hispalense*, ser. 2, 26–27 (1957): 157–96.

Dufresne, Nicole. " 'I Wish I Were a Man': The Gender Role Transgressions of Lorca's Tragic Heroines." Paper presented to Themes in Drama Conference, North America Session, University of California at Riverside, February 1986.

Durán, María Angeles. "Lectura económica de fray Luis de León." In Durán, *Nuevas perspectivas*, 2: 257–73.

Erikson, Kai T. "Notes on the Sociology of Deviance." *Social Problems* 9 (Spring 1962): 303–14.

Escamilla, Michèle. "A propos d'un dossier inquisitorial des environs de 1590: Les étranges amours d'un hermaphrodite." In Redondo, *Amours légitimes*, pp. 167–82.

Escobar Camacho, José Manuel, Manuel Nieto Cumplido, and Jesús Padilla González. "La mujer cordobesa en el trabajo a fines del siglo XV." In Segura Graiño, *Las mujeres*, pp. 153–60.

Espejo, Cristóbal. "La carestía de la vida en el siglo XVI y medios de abaratarla." *Revista de Archivos, Bibliotecas y Museos*, ser. 3, 41 (1920): 159–204 and 329–354; and 42 (1921): 1–18 and 199–225.

Fairchilds, Cissie. "Masters and Servants in Eighteenth-Century Toulouse." *Journal of Social History* 12 (Spring 1979): 368–93.

Fernández Vargas, Valentina, and María Victoria López-Cordón Cortezo. "Mujer y régimen jurídico en el antiguo régimen: Una realidad disociada." In García-Nieto París, *Ordenamiento jurídico*, pp. 13–40.

Flandrin, Jean-Louis. "Sex in Married Life in the Early Middle Ages: The Church's Teaching and Behavioural Reality." In Ariés and Béjin, *Western Sexuality*, pp. 114–29.

Foucault, Michel. "The Battle for Chastity." In Ariés and Béjin, *Western Sexuality*, pp. 14–25.

Galán Sánchez, Angel, and María Teresa López Beltrán. "El 'status' teórico de las prostitutas del reino de Granada en la primera mitad del siglo XVI (las ordenanzas de 1538)." In Segura Graiño, *Las mujeres*, pp. 161–69.

García Cárcel, Ricardo. "El fracaso matrimonial en la Cataluña del Antiguo Régimen." In Redondo, *Amours légitimes*, pp. 121–32.

Garfinkel, Harold. "Conditions of Successful Degradation Ceremonies." *American Journal of Sociology* 61 (March 1956): 420–24.

Garrison, Fielding H. "An Epitome of the History of Spanish Medicine." *Bulletin of the New York Academy of Medicine*, 2d ser., 7, no. 8 (1928): 589–634.

Gil Ambrona, Antonio. "Entre la oración y el trabajo: Las ocupaciones de las otras esposas. Siglos XVI–XVII." In Matilla and Ortega, *El trabajo de las mujeres*, pp. 57–67.

Graullera, Vicente. "Mujer, amor y moralidad en la Valencia de los siglos XVI y XVII." In Redondo, *Amours légitimes*, pp. 109–19.

Guilhem, Claire. "L'Inquisition et la dévaluation des discours féminins." In Bennassar et al., *L'Inquisition espagnole*, pp. 197–240.

Helms, Lorraine. "The Martial Art of Captain Moll: From Elizabethan Cross-Dressing to Jacobean Androgyny." Unpublished MS, 1986.

Henningsen, Gustav. "El 'banco de datos' del Santo Oficio: Las relaciones de causas de la Inquisición española (1550–1700)." *Boletín de la Real Academia de la Historia* 174 (1977): 547–70.

Hufton, Olwen. "Women in Revolution, 1789–1796." *Past and Present* 53 (1971): 90–107.

Jutte, Robert. "Poor Relief and Social Discipline in Sixteenth-Century Europe." *European Studies Review* 11 (1981): 25–52.

Kagan, Richard. "Eleno/Elena: Annals of Androgyny in Sixteenth-Century New Castile." Paper presented to the Society for Spanish and Portuguese Historical Studies, University of Minnesota, April 1986.

———. "Prophecy and the Inquisition in Late Sixteenth-Century Spain." In Perry and Cruz, *Cultural Encounters.*

Kelly-Gadol, Joan. "Did Women Have a Renaissance?" In Bridenthal and Koonz, *Becoming Visible*, pp. 137–64.

King, Margaret L. "Book-Lined Cells: Women and Humanism in the Early Italian Renaissance." In Labalme, *Beyond Their Sex*, pp. 66–90.

Kitsuse, J. I. "Societal Reaction to Deviant Behavior: Problems of Theory and Method." *Social Problems* 9 (Winter 1962): 247–57.

Labalme, Patricia. "Sodomy and Venetian Justice in the Renaissance." *The Legal History Review* 52 (1984): 217–54.

Lamb, Mary Ellen. "The Countess of Pembroke and the Art of Dying." In Rose, *Women in the Middle Ages*, pp. 207–26.

Larquié, Claude. "Amours légitimes et amours illégitimes à Madrid au xviiᵉ siècle." In Redondo, *Amours légitimes*, pp. 69–91.

Liebowitz, Ruth P. "Virgins in the Service of Christ: The Dispute Over an Active Apostolate for Women During the Counter-Reformation." In Ruether and McLaughlin, *Women of Spirit*, pp. 131–52.

Lingo, Alison Klairmont. "Empirics and Charlatans in Early Modern France: The Genesis of the Classification of the 'Other' in Medical Practice." *Journal of Social History* 19, no. 4 (1986): 583–603.

Littleton, Christine A. "Debating the Legal Meaning of Sexual Equality." Paper presented to the UCLA Faculty Seminar on Women, Culture, and Theory, November 1986.

Llorca, Bernardino. "Documentos inéditos interesantes sobre los alumbrados de Sevilla de 1623–1628." *Estudios Ecclesiásticos* 11 (1932): 268–84, 401–18.

Luna, Lola. "Sor Valentina Pinelo, intérprete de las sagradas escrituras." *Cuadernos Hispanoamericanos*, no. 464 (February 1989): 91–103.

McKendrick, Geraldine, and Angus MacKay. "Visionaries and Affective Spirituality during the First Half of the Sixteenth Century." In Perry and Cruz, *Cultural Encounters*. pp. 50–72.

McLaughlin, Eleanor. "Women, Power and the Pursuit of Holiness in Medieval Christianity." In Ruether and McLaughlin, *Women of Spirit*, pp. 99–130.

Mayberry, Nancy. "The Controversy over the Immaculate Conception in Fifteenth-Century Art, Literature and Society." Unpublished manuscript. 1989.

———. "Dramatic Representations of the Immaculate Conception in Tirso's Time." *Estudios* 156–57 (1987): 79–86.

Monter, E. W. "Women and the Italian Inquisitions." In Rose, *Women in the Middle Ages and the Renaissance*, pp. 78–87.

Nash, Mary. "Desde la invisibilidad a la presencia de la mujer en la historia: Corrientes historiográficas y marcos conceptuales de la nueva historia de la mujer." In Durán, *Nuevas perspectivas*, 1: 18–37.

Olsen, Frances E. "From False Paternalism to False Equality." Paper presented to the National Women's Studies Association, at the University of Illinois School of Law, Champaign-Urbana, Illinois, June 1986.

———. "The Sex of Law." Paper presented to the UCLA Faculty Seminar on Women, Culture, and Theory, March 1985.

O'Neil, Mary R. "Sacerdote ovvero Strione: Ecclesiastical and Superstitious Remedies in Sixteenth Century Italy." In Kaplan, *Understanding Popular Culture*, pp. 53–84.

Orcutt, James. "Societal Reaction and the Response to Deviation in Small Groups." *Social Forces* 52 (December 1973): 259–67.

Ordóñez, Elizabeth J. "Woman and Her Text in the Works of María de Zayas and Ana Caro." *Revista de Estudios Históricos* 19, no. 1 (January 1985): 3–15.

Ortner, Sherry. "Is Female to Male as Nature Is to Culture?" In Rosaldo and Lamphere, *Woman, Culture and Society*, pp. 67–87.

Palacios Alcalde, María. "Hechicería e Inquisición en Andalucía." *Codice* 2 (1987): 43–65.

Pérez, Joseph. "La femme et l'amour dans l'Espagne du xvie siècle." In Redondo, *Amours légitimes*, pp. 19–29.

Perry, Mary Elizabeth. "Beatas and the Inquisition in Early Modern Seville." In Haliczer, *Inquisition and Society in Early Modern Europe*, pp. 147–68.

———. "Deviant Insiders: Legalized Prostitutes and a Consciousness of Women in Early Modern Seville." *Comparative Studies in Society and History* 27, no. 1 (1985): 138–58.

———. "Male Discourse and Female Offenders in the Spanish Inquisition." In Donahue, *Social Bodies, Spiritual Selves*.

———. "Las mujeres y su trabajo curativo en Sevilla, siglos xvi y xvii." In Matilla and Ortega, *El trabajo de las mujeres*, pp. 40–50.

Pike, Ruth. "Sevillian Society in the Sixteenth Century: Slaves and Freedmen." *Hispanic American Historical Review* 47 (1967): 344–51.

Puig, Angelina, and Nuria Tuset. "La prostitución en Mallorca (s. xvi): El estado un alcahuete?" In García-Nieto París, *Ordenamiento jurídico*, pp. 71–82.

Pullen, Brian. "Catholics and the Poor in Early Modern Europe." *Transactions of the Royal Historical Society*, 5th ser., 26 (1976): 15–34.

Remón Pérez, María Luisa. "Trabajo doméstico e ideología patriarcal: Una constante histórica." In Durán, *Nuevas perspectivas*, 2: 201–12.

Rose, Mary Beth. "Gender, Genre, and History: Seventeenth-Century English Women and the Art of Autobiography." In Rose, *Women in the Middle Ages and the Renaissance*, pp. 245–78.

Rossiaud, Jacques. "Prostitution, jeunesse et société dans les villes du sud-est au xve siècle." *Annales, E.S.C.* 31, no. 2 (1976): 289–325.

Rothe Vallbona, Rima-Gretchen. "Historic Reality and Fiction in *Vida y sucesos de la monja alférez*." Ph.D. diss. Middlebury College, 1981.

Sánchez Ortega, María Helena. "La beata de Villar del Aguila." *Historia 16* 74 (1986): 23–34.

———. "Flagelantes licenciosos y beatas consentidores," *Historia 16* 14 (1981): 37–54.

Sánchez Ortega, María Helena. "La mujer, el amor y la religión en el antiguo régimen." In Durán, *La mujer en la historia de España*, pp. 35–58.

———. "La mujer en el antiguo régimen: Tipos históricos y arquetipos literarios." In Durán, *Nuevas perspectivas*, 1: 107–26.

Scott, Joan. "Gender: A Useful Category of Historical Analysis." *American Historical Review* 91, no. 5 (December 1986): 1053–75.

Segura Graiño, Cristina. "Las mujeres andaluzas en la baja edad media." In Segura Graiño, *Las mujeres*, pp. 143–52.

———. "Las mujeres en el medievo hispano." *Cuadernos de Investigación Medieval: Guía crítica de temas históricos* 1, no. 2 (1984): 7–56.

Simón Palmer, María del Carmen. "La higiene y la medicina de la mujer española a través de los libros (s. XVI a XIX)." In Durán, *La mujer en la historia de España*, pp. 71–84.

Stuard, Susan Mosher. "The *Annales* School and Feminist History: Opening Dialogue with the American Stepchild." *Signs*, 7, no. 1 (1981): 135–43.

Thomas, Keith. "The Double Standard." *Journal of the History of Ideas* 20 (1959): 195–216.

———. "Women and the Civil War Sects." *Past and Present* 13 (1958): 42–62.

Thompson, E. P. "The Moral Economy of the English Crowd in the Eighteenth Century." *Past and Present* 50 (1971): 76–136.

Velasco, B. "Fundación del convento de terciarias franciscanas de Santa Isabel en Cuellar." *Archivo Ibero-Americano*, ser. 2, 31 (1971): 477–81.

Weeks, Jeffrey. "Inverts, Perverts, and Mary-Annes: Male Prostitution and the Regulation of Homosexuality in England in the Nineteenth and Early Twentieth Centuries." In Licata and Petersen, *Historical Perspectives*, pp. 115–17.

INDEX